fragile
Paradise

DEVELOPMENT OF WESTERN RESOURCES

The Development of Western Resources is an interdisciplinary series

focusing on the use and misuse of resources in the American West.

Written for a broad readership of humanists, social scientists, and resource

specialists, the books in this series emphasize both historical and

contemporary perspectives as they explore the interplay between resource

exploitation and economic, social, and political experiences.

John G. Clark, University of Kansas, Founding Editor

Hal K. Rothman, University of Nevada, Las Vegas, Series Editor

fragile Paradise

THE IMPACT OF TOURISM ON MAUI

1959–2000

MANSEL G. BLACKFORD

UNIVERSITY PRESS OF KANSAS

© 2001 by the University Press of Kansas

Published by the University Press of Kansas (Lawrence, Kansas 66049), which was organized by the Kansas Board of Regents and is operated and funded by Emporia State University, Fort Hays State University, Kansas State University, Pittsburg State University, the University of Kansas, and Wichita State University

Library of Congress Cataloging-in-Publication Data

Blackford, Mansel G., 1944–
    Fragile paradise : the impact of tourism on Maui, 1959–2000 / Mansel G. Blackford.
       p. cm. — (Development of western resources)
      Includes bibliographical references and index.
      ISBN 0-7006-1086-3 (alk. paper)
       1. Tourism—Environmental aspects—Hawaii—Maui. 2. Maui (Hawaii)—Economic conditions. I. Title. II. Series.
    TD195.T68 B53 2001
    363.7'02'099692—dc21   00-012009

British Library Cataloguing-in-Publication Data is available.

Printed in the United States of America

10 9 8 7 6 5 4 3 2 1

The paper used in this publication meets the minimum requirements of the American National Standard for Permanence of Paper for Printed Library Materials Z39.48-1984.

For the people of Maui,

with my great thanks

CONTENTS

MAPS AND ILLUSTRATIONS

Maps

Illustrations

PREFACE

This history grew out of my personal experiences and professional interests. I have long had the privilege of spending time on Maui. My parents retired to the island in the 1970s, and my family and I visited them on numerous occasions. More recently, with the passing of my parents, my sister and I decided to keep their condominium on Maui, and our families have been able to use it on a regular basis. I have also had the pleasure in the 1990s to teach on Maui for the University of Hawai'i, Manoa. Perhaps inevitably, living and working on Maui, and getting to know a variety of people on the island, piqued my interest in developmental and environmental issues shaping Maui County, leading me to explore Maui's past.

I owe a lot, especially, to my students on Maui. Several incidents stand out in my mind. Once a student was late to class because he had been gored in the foot by a wild boar he had been trying to trap as a ranger in the West Maui watershed. From him I began to learn about some of the relationships between water use and plant life, which wild pigs destroyed, on Maui. Conversation with another student led to a discussion about the largest Hawaiian religious altar *(heiau)* on the island, for her family was its stewards. Most of my students were nontraditional students working full time (classes met at night) and were involved, one way or the other, in Maui's visitor industry. For many of them that employment was a love/hate relationship; it was a necessary, and sometimes profitable and enjoyable, way to earn a living, but a type of employment, many of them thought, that placed limits on how much they could achieve. Many of the students attended my classes as part of their efforts to earn a bachelor's degree, which, they hoped, would enable them to find better positions.

My exploration of Maui's recent past has also permitted me to pursue my major interests as a professional historian — interests in business and economic history, the history of the American West, environmental history, and the history of the Pacific Rim (or Pacific Basin). The more closely I looked at the histories of Maui and the other Hawaiian Islands, the more convinced I became that their pasts speak to issues and people beyond their boundaries. I hope that you agree and that you find this excursion worthwhile.

ACKNOWLEDGMENTS

I would like to thank the librarians at the Kahului and Wailuku public libraries on Maui for their friendly assistance. Lani Scott of the Kahului library was especially helpful. The librarians at Maui Community College were also most kind. Diane Wakamatsu, the deputy county clerk for Maui, deserves my thanks for helping me locate county documents. I owe thanks to William Childs, Randy Roth, and David Stebenne of the Ohio State University, Donald Pisani of the University of Oklahoma, and David Sicilia of the University of Maryland for commenting on parts of earlier drafts of this book. James Kraft of the University of Hawai'i, Manoa, and Gail Ainsworth (formerly Gail Bartholomew) of Maui Community College provided very helpful critiques of an earlier version of this study. Suggestions by the two readers for the University Press of Kansas — Hal Rothman of the University of Nevada, Las Vegas, and James Juvic of the University of Hawai'i, Manoa — also greatly improved this work for publication. I remain, of course, solely responsible for any errors of fact or interpretation that my history may still contain.

I would like to thank, as well, the many people who allowed me to interview them as part of my research: James "Kimo" Apana, William Bonnet, David Craddick, Elmer Cravalho, Madelyn D'Enbeau, David DeLeon, Lucienne de Naie, Everett Dowling, Harry Eagar, Robbie Ann A. Kane Guard, Dana Naone Hall, Isaac Hall, Robert Johnson, Celeste King, Alice Lee, Neil Luna, Michael Lyons II, Donald Malcolm, Dick Mayer, Earl "Mo" Moler, Dorothy Pyle, Sally Raisbeck, Antonio Ramil, Mark Sheehan, Jeanne Skog, Steven Sutrov, Terryl Vencl, Mary Lou Whitman, and Marsha Wienert.

Finally, two universities deserve my thanks. I taught on Maui for the University of Hawai'i, Manoa, on three occasions during the 1990s, and that work both enhanced my knowledge of Hawaiian history and helped support my research into Maui's past. I would also like to thank the Ohio State University for a sabbatical for the academic year of 1999–2000, during which time I engaged in research and writing about Maui, and for a grant-in-aid to fund the preparation of maps and illustrations for this study.

INTRODUCTION: APPROACHING MAUI

With its bright greens and blues — greens for the sugar cane, blues for the ocean, always the ocean — Maui has the power to entrance residents and visitors alike.[1] "Sun-kissed," residents of Maui like to call their island, "Magic Maui," a paradise, indeed. Characteristically, "*Maui no ka ʻoi*," which means "Maui is the best," is the official governmental motto for Maui County. However, divisions have always rent the seeming paradise: splits between chiefs in precontact times, sometimes resulting in bloody battles; divisions between labor and management on sugar cane and pineapple plantations, which led to acrimonious strife; and ethnic divisions, which for decades kept workers from forming unions. This book is, however, about a different set of cleavages, those separating Maui's inhabitants on developmental and environmental matters since the late 1950s. This study also examines how Maui's residents have tried to bridge those splits to arrive at workable compromises.

In the late twentieth century economic development and environmental concerns increasingly divided the people of Maui. How best to handle land and water issues, how to deal with transportation matters (especially whether or not to expand their island's leading airport at Kahului), and how to provide their island with electric power were among the most controversial aspects of these general concerns. Complex, interrelated opinions, with many shadings, arose. Environmental organizations, labor unions, business associations, and Native Hawaiian groups held varying views on these matters, as did a number of outspoken individuals, and there existed differences of opinion within each of the groups.

At the heart of the debates lay the explosive growth of tourism. The rapid development of a visitor industry transformed the Hawaiian Islands, including Maui, after World War II. From scant beginnings in the prewar years, tourism became by far the most important segment of Maui's economy from the 1970s on. Many on Maui saw the development of a visitor industry as a panacea, a solution to all of their economic problems. Tourism proved, however, to be a double-edged sword. While bringing prosperity to some, prosperity not available from other endeavors, tourism also placed demands, many of which were unexpected, on Maui's residents. Tourism strained the island's transportation infrastructure, its sewer and water systems, and its electrical

Even used car lots, like this one near the Kahului airport, proclaimed that Maui was the best.

supplies, making costly additions essential. Tourism greatly affected lifestyles and ways of thinking, and it altered Maui's natural environment. Above all, the growth of the visitor industry forced Maui's residents to make difficult choices about the future development of their island.

In an important work on the American West, the historian Hal K. Rothman has recently labeled tourism "a devil's bargain."[2] More than most earlier scholars, Rothman has emphasized the many trade-offs involved in the development of tourism: trade-offs in types of economic growth, which locals rarely controlled beyond the initial stages, and, above all, trade-offs in the quality of life for people in areas affected by tourism. Tourism was certainly a mixed blessing on Maui. Tourism often promised more than it delivered; it required wrenching changes in the lifestyles of those embracing it, and even of those shunning it. People came to harbor strong emotions about tourism and its many impacts, as revealed in a bumper sticker seen on an automobile in Maui's main town during the summer of 1999: "If it's tourist season, why can't we shoot them?"[3]

From the 1960s on, Maui's residents, like other inhabitants of Hawai'i, were caught up in a crisis, as their economy shifted away from the plantation crops of sugar cane and pineapple to tourism. Nor was that all. Hit hard during the late 1980s and 1990s by economic recessions in California and Asia, the sources of many visitors to Maui, the tourist industry faced rough times. Nonetheless, tourism remained at the center of what many proponents of development believed Maui's economy should be; only an expansion of tourism could, they thought, promote general economic growth on their island. Others, however, deeply mistrusted placing their island's fate in the hands of tourism. Critics charged that boosting tourism was a self-defeating strategy, because doing so would damage Maui's environment and economy. Only by constructing a more diversified economy, one not dependent on tourism or any other single industry, they believed, could Maui flourish. Economic issues merged with social and cultural ones. As Maui's residents were caught up in economic crises, they coped with them in ways that led them to think anew about what they wanted their island and their lives to be. Some tried to capitalize on the situation in which tourism reigned supreme, if only to cover their bets and make up for losses in other parts of their economy. Others sought to preserve their culture and heritage. Land, water, transportation, and electric power controversies became wrapped up in environmental issues and in topics concerned with protecting the rights of Native Hawaiians.

A detailed investigation of what occurred on Maui allows a close look at how groups of people viewed relationships between economic and environmental developments and how they sought to shape those developments, topics of great interest to scholars of the American experience.[4] Exactly how were environmental, economic, and cultural issues perceived by Maui's residents? How did different groups see the trade-offs between possible economic development and likely environmental changes? How did they work to try to accomplish their goals? An examination of events on Maui helps clarify, especially, the nature of environmentalism and its importance in the evolution of public policy making. Historians of the United States have recently been revisiting basic questions about environmentalism, and a look at Maui contributes to that discussion. Was environmentalism a top-down phenomenon directed by experts or a grassroots movement with broad public participation? What people and groups were involved? How did they interact with each other? What were the results?[5]

The imitation church at a major resort in Wailea served as a wedding chapel.

An exploration of events on Maui offers a valuable way to investigate the development of public policies for growth, and it shows, like many recent studies, the significance of government decision making for economic and environmental issues. Particularly noticeable in the case of Maui was the importance of citizen mobilization to influence political decisions, along with the use of new tools, such as court challenges to environmental impact statements, made possible by the passage of environmental legislation by the U.S. Congress in the late 1960s and early 1970s.[6]

All of this is not to say that the only way to view Hawaiian history is through the lens of American history.[7] Hawai'i, of course, had a long sovereign exis-

tence, a shorter period as a kingdom, followed by a five-year period as a republic, before being annexed by the United States in 1898, and that history
has profoundly shaped the development of Hawai'i, including Maui, to the
present day.[8] Maui's past has played important roles in the development of
recent events, as can be seen in how Native Hawaiian rights issues have affected the outcomes of many events. Still, as we shall see, Hawaiian developments, especially in the economic and environmental spheres, shared
important elements with developments in the United States, especially with
many of those taking place in the Trans-Mississippi West.

An examination of the topics dealt with in this book also illuminates questions about global economic growth — issues concerning relationships between center and peripheral regions in the world, as discussed by some world
systems scholars. One way to think of the economic development of parts of
the United States, such as the South and the Trans-Mississippi West, is to
consider it, especially before World War II, in terms of center-peripheral
relations. The South and West were largely subservient to midwestern and
eastern centers before the 1940s. In light of this approach, it is worth asking
what types of economic futures different groups of Maui's residents wanted
for their island — ones based on a single industry, tourism, or ones that were
more diversified. How did these different possibilities relate to worldwide
developments? Why did certain paths seem to prevail over others?[9]

The experiences of Maui's citizens with tourism, economic development,
and environmentalism have relevance for people beyond the United States.
Beginning in the mid-1970s scholars have examined the development of tourism as a business worldwide and have sought to document its varied impacts
on different regions. Sociologists and anthropologists have taken the lead in
these investigations, often seeing in their works on tourism ways to present
"an introduction to the structural analysis of modern society."[10] Political scientists and faculty in business schools have also investigated tourism. The
largest single industry in the world by the 1980s, if not earlier, tourism has
attracted the attentions of these scholars in terms of its impacts on economic
development, on the creations of "winners and losers" in host nations, and
on the roles states can play in these developments.[11] Perhaps because tourism as a major industry has had only a short life, historians have generally
been less concerned than scholars in other fields have about examining its
development.[12]

The Pacific Basin has recently attracted the attention of scholars dealing with tourism, as they have looked at the roles tourism might play in economic growth — including close examinations of the results of state actions to encourage tourism, how tourism has changed the lives of members of various ethnic groups (and relations among those groups), and the impacts of tourism on the natural environment.[13] Maui's engagement with tourism transcends national boundaries to inform ongoing debates in the Pacific. Residents in the Pacific Basin are wrestling with issues similar to those with which people on Maui have grappled for several decades: how to create or preserve various sorts of socioeconomic systems, how best to provide infrastructures for those systems, how to ensure a desirable quality of life, how to foresee how different groups will be affected by the development of tourism, and how to use the powers of government to influence what happens. A look at what has occurred on Maui is of importance for what it says about developments well beyond the island's boundaries.

The first two chapters of my study analyze the economic development of the Hawaiian Islands and Maui. The recent debates and decisions on Maui can be fully understood only in light of that history. Chapter 1 describes how a capitalistic economy based on the staple crops of sugar cane and pineapple developed in the nineteenth and early twentieth centuries, how that economy was transformed by the growth of tourism after World War II, especially after Hawai'i achieved statehood in 1959, and how some people on Maui have tried to diversify their island's economy in recent years. Chapter 2 looks closely at the organizations, groups, and people involved in economic and environmental developments and begins to probe how they have interacted and what the results have been.

Four chapters examine discrete, but closely related, topics with which Maui's residents have had to deal as a result of the expansion of tourism. Chapter 3 examines the history of land use on Maui, especially efforts to channel visitor industry developments, preserve agricultural land, and address Native Hawaiian land claims. Chapter 4 analyzes water rights issues, subjects at the heart of developmental controversies on Maui. This chapter looks at how a changing legal framework for water matters in the Hawaiian Islands — a volatile mix of riparian rights, prior appropriation, and Native Hawaiian doctrines — affected developments. How to supply electric power to Maui's growing resident and transient population is the topic of Chapter 5. As tourism greatly increased the demand for electricity, people on Maui had to grapple with questions about what types of power sources would be developed and where new power plants would be located. Chapter 6 investigates matters swirling around the question of how to expand Maui's major airport at Kahului and looks at what economic and environmental changes might result from its expansion.

Common themes run though each of these issues. Each topic involved trade-offs between economic and environmental concerns. As might be expected, many of the same individuals and associations were engaged in working out how those concerns were resolved, often through compromises. And, above all, the individual topics all involved quality-of-life issues. At stake, as most of those engaged in the issues clearly realized, were questions that went well beyond immediate economic and environmental matters. These issues, Maui's residents recognized, went to the heart of concerns about how they viewed changes occurring in their lifestyles.

Chapter 7 examines how land, water, transportation, and electric power issues affected the development of two different regions on Maui: South Maui, a resort area, and Upcountry Maui, a more bucolic, agricultural area. In these regions environmental and economic issues mixed in sometimes unexpected ways. Choices made by citizen groups in these areas offer glimpses into decision-making processes and their results.

The conclusion to this work relates the specific issues of each chapter to choices Maui's residents have recently made and are continuing to make about the future of their island. The choices have become increasingly difficult, not simply with respect to individual issues, but also with regard to Maui's overall future. Whether or not to commit Maui primarily to tourism, and what that commitment might entail in terms of economic and environmental developments, has run through all of the discussions of discrete topics. Nor, the conclusion shows, are events on Maui unique. This study closes by comparing developments on Maui to those in the other Hawaiian Islands and throughout the American West, the Pacific Basin, and some other parts of the world.

A sentence or two is necessary about Maui at the outset.[14] Maui is one of four major islands composing Maui County — the others being Lāna'i, Moloka'i, and Kaho'olawe — which, in turn, is one of four counties in the State of Hawai'i. Forty-eight miles long and twenty-six miles wide, Maui has

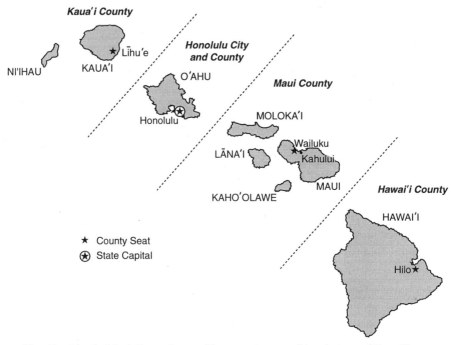

Hawaiian Islands. Maui County is one of four counties comprising the state of Hawai'i.

126 miles of coastline and covers 728 square miles, making it the second-largest of the Hawaiian Islands, after the Big Island of Hawai'i. Composed of two volcanic mountains with a connecting isthmus, Maui rises to an elevation of 10,023 feet at the summit of Haleakalā and to 5,788 feet at the crest of the West Maui mountains. In 1996, 117,000 people lived in Maui County, 91 percent of them on the island of Maui. The populations of Hawai'i's other three counties were 872,000 for Honolulu, 138,000 for Hawai'i, and 56,000 for Kaua'i. State and county governments share responsibility for the governance of Maui County (there are no city governments in the county), and within the county government a mayor and county council, both elected at large, work together. This situation is, as we shall see, rife with the possibility for disagreements, especially as state and county officials jockey for position.

Finally, let me address my use of the Hawaiian language. Some words, names, and place names in the Hawaiian language call for the use of diacritic marks. Hawaiian words not in common use in the English language are italicized. In providing the diacritic marks I have generally followed Mary Kawena

Pukui and Samuel H. Elbert, *New Pocket Hawaiian Dictionary,* 2d ed. (Honolulu: University of Hawai'i Press, 1992) for words and Sonia P. Juvic and James O. Juvic, eds., *Atlas of Hawai'i,* 3d ed. (Honolulu: University of Hawai'i Press, 1998) for names. I have, of course, neither placed diacritic marks nor italicized any Hawaiian words in direct quotations in my work, unless such marks or italicizing were present in the original.

1

Maui's Economic Development

"When you are talking of economics, you are speaking about the opportunities for the younger generation to stay at home, so they can have career paths and jobs here," observed James "Kimo" Apana, Maui County's mayor, in the summer of 1999. "In my father's age, when they finished high school, they almost all went into the military, because there was nothing here," he noted. "Not everyone wanted to work in the agriculture industry, basically as field hands." While favoring economic growth that accompanied the development of Maui's visitor industry, Apana understood well that embracing it involved trade-offs. "We have to ask," he continued, "is it for someone else or for us here. . . . In the long run, did we gain? I think the jury's still out." Looking back at his boyhood on Maui, Apana wistfully remembered pleasures no longer easily found: "I miss camping on the beach; I miss going fishing and actually catching fish from a rock. . . . The question," he concluded, "is what shall we leave our children beyond the dollar?"[1]

Apana addressed basic questions about economic growth in modern-day Maui, ones that ran through the development of the Hawaiian Islands and many other parts of the world: What kinds of jobs did growth, especially that coming from tourism, create? Who benefited? What should the government do, if anything, to try to channel development? How did choices about economic development affect people's the lives and thoughts? The questions Apana and others on Maui raised were grounded in their county's history.

Maui's development took place largely in terms of monocultures. Single industries dominated the county's evolution in different time periods, with little economic diversity resulting. This type of development characterized much of global economic activity from the sixteenth century into the twen-

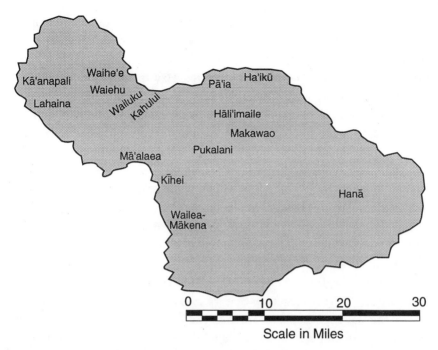

The island of Maui. Subregions and towns marked the landscape.

tieth century, as European nations and businesses established hegemony over large parts of the world. As ties of global trade and colonization spread, outer areas saw their diversified, often subsistence, economies give way to commercial economies based on a handful of staple crops or mineral resources. Thus, the Hawaiian economy became one based on plantation agriculture and, after World War II, tourism.

Capitalistic Economic Development in the Hawaiian Islands

Capitalistic economic development began in the Hawaiian Islands shortly after contact with the West. Such development was taking place around the globe, especially during the first half of the nineteenth century. For several decades beginning in the 1790s westerners looking for trade goods with which to pay for tea imported from China found one in sandalwood, which grew in Hawaiian forests. Hawaiian chiefs *(ali'i)* soon took part in the trade, forcing commoners to harvest the sandalwood trees but keeping most of the profit for themselves. Largely denuded of sandalwood, the islands emerged in the 1830s as an important supply point for whaling fleets plying the Pacific, a distinction maintained into the early 1870s. Hawaiians grew potatoes and onions for the whalers and were once more drawn into a growing global commercial economy. The port of Lahaina on Maui emerged as the center for this trade, with 429 ships arriving there in 1846 alone. In that year Lahaina had a population of 3,000 people living in fifty-nine wooden houses and 882 grass huts. Urged on by their chiefs, Hawaiians came to focus on commercial crops. Some 20,000 barrels of white potatoes grown in upcountry Kula on Maui reached the whaling ships each year. The discovery of gold in California and the consequent demand for food by miners further boosted the growing of onions and potatoes in Kula, which became known as "Nu Kaleponi," meaning "New California."[2]

Sugar cane replaced the whaling trade as Hawai'i's major commercial enterprise in the late nineteenth century, and the development of sugar cane pulled the Hawaiian Islands more closely into an American orbit. After considerable stumbling and some outright failures during the 1840s and 1850s, sugar plantations began over the next two decades to assume the shapes they would hold well into the twentieth century. By 1880 sixty-three sugar cane plantations covered 20,000 acres in the islands. Major plantation centers emerged, including ones at Wailuku, Lahaina, and Makawao on Maui. On these plantations, one scholar has observed, took place "an invasion of agricultural practices, technologies, and population that supplanted native production systems and repeopled the land with foreigners and Hawaiians from other islands."[3] Central to the growth of a plantation economy were changes in landholding.

The concept of private land ownership had little place in Hawaiian thought.[4] Rather, land was held and worked in common. Hawaiians lived in extended family groups, called 'ohana, and worked cooperatively on land parcels called ahupua'a. Most ahupua'a consisted of a stretch of land running from the mountaintop down to the sea as a sort of wedge. Thus, each 'ohana shared in all of the fruits of its island and the surrounding ocean — from trees growing on the mountain slopes (which could be used in making canoes and dwellings and whose bark could be made into tapa cloth for clothing) to vegetables (taro, yams, sugar cane, breadfruit, and bananas) grown in the lowlands, to fish taken from inshore waters or raised in ponds. Each *'ohana* was mainly self-sufficient, with only a modest amount of bartering taking place across *ahupua'a* boundaries. Chiefs and subchiefs exercised considerable power over land in the Hawaiian Islands but did not have absolute ownership over it. Rather, they held the land — in theory, at least — in trust for the commoners who actually worked it and who could move from place to place.

Unified by King Kamehameha I in the late 1700s and early 1800s, the Kingdom of Hawai'i moved away from this communal way of life and landholding to develop a more commercialized economy after contact with the West in 1778. In the early 1800s the king nominally "owned" all of Hawai'i, but in practice much of the effective control was delegated to his chiefs. Ownership was also tempered by a sense of stewardship, a sense that the king should act in the best interests of all Hawaiians. Pressured especially by westerners who wanted to own land in the islands, King Kamehameha III altered this setup in 1848. By the terms of the Great Mahele (Grand Division) of that year, all the lands of Hawai'i — roughly 4.1 million acres — were divided between the king and his major chiefs. The king retained 2.5 million acres, 60 percent of the total, which he then divided into two categories, 1.5 million acres that he set aside as Government Lands for the chiefs and people of the Hawaiian Kingdom, and about one million acres called the King's Lands, which he kept for his own use. In 1865 the Hawaiian legislature designated the King's Lands as Crown Lands and declared them inalienable; that is, the king could not sell them. Nearly all the rest of the land of the Hawaiian Islands, 1.5 million acres (about 40 percent of the total), went to 245 chiefs.[5]

Importantly, while the Great Mahele firmly established the principle of private land ownership — as desired by westerners — it did not extinguish the idea of communal rights to land. A sense of stewardship remained associated with the Government and Crown Lands. Even after those lands became part of the Territory of Hawai'i in 1898 and the State of Hawai'i in 1959, Native Hawaiians would seek benefits from them, arguing that they were being held in trust for their common good. Land issues would loom large in a rebirth or "renaissance" of Native Hawaiian rights from the 1960s.

Other laws elaborated on the Great Mahele. A land law of 1850 gave commoners the right to own *kuleana* lands, lands that they had traditionally worked. However, it proved difficult for most commoners to patent such

lands; legal obstacles and a general unfamiliarity with the concept of private
land ownership hindered such efforts. Only 28,600 acres had been claimed
as *kuleana* lands by 1855, the deadline for doing so. The 1850 law also gave
foreigners the right to own land. By 1886 foreigners held two-thirds of the
arable land of the islands, and by the 1890s, four-fifths of it. Only about 5,000
of the 90,000 Native Hawaiians owned any land as the nineteenth century
came to a close.[6]

Political developments spurred the growth of plantation agriculture. In
1876 Congress approved a treaty with the Hawaiian Kingdom that removed
all duties on the importation of Hawaiian products, most notably raw sugar,
into America. By 1890 Hawai'i was exporting ten times as much sugar to the
United States as it had in 1875. Sugar had become so important to the Hawaiian economy that much of the motivation for the revolution of 1893 — in
which white planters, originally mainly from the United States, seized political control of the islands — came from fears about the McKinley Tariff of
1891. That tariff undercut the duty-free treaty of 1876 by giving subsidies to
American sugar growers. Only by becoming part of the United States, many
Hawaiian planters reasoned, could they receive those bounties and thus compete, as they saw matters, on an equal playing field with growers in Louisiana
and other American states.[7]

With the aid of American military forces in the area, the revolutionaries
overthrew the Kingdom of Hawai'i and set up the Republic of Hawai'i, in
which Native Hawaiians found their political rights severely limited. Offered
the islands by the revolutionaries, President Grover Cleveland, who was generally opposed to imperialism and who viewed American military support of
the Hawaiian revolution as illegal, refused to allow the United States to acquire them. President Cleveland's reservations about American imperialism
prevented annexation in 1893, a move that had to wait until America's expansion with the Spanish-American War of 1898. More open to imperialistic
expansion and more concerned about the aims of other powerful nations,
President William McKinley accepted the islands, and they became an American territory.

Sugar dominated the economy of the Territory of Hawai'i, with pineapple
developing as a secondary crop, accelerating the erosion of the islands' diversified economy. In 1935 sugar and pineapple made up $90 million of the
$95 million in exports from the islands, with all but $1.3 million worth of those

Narrow-gauge railroads like this one at Lahaina, now a tourist attraction called the Sugar Cane Railroad, once carried sugar cane to the mills on Maui.

exports going to the American mainland. In return, manufactured goods and a growing amount of food flowed to Hawai'i.[8] With the spread of sugar and pineapple plantations, land ownership became more concentrated, until by the early 1940s about half of the land in the islands was owned by only eighty estates, corporations, or individuals. Most of the rest lay in the hands of the government, which leased the desirable tracts to planters at low rates. This concentration continued well into the years after World War II, in Maui County as elsewhere.[9]

Like many other peripheral regions of the world — places away from major urban and industrial centers — Hawai'i became a land dominated by the growth of just a few staple products: sandalwood, supplies for whalers, sugar cane, and pineapple. With profits high in these fields, little thought was given to the need to create a diversified economic base on the islands. To the contrary, even foodstuffs were imported for workers in the cane fields and the sugar mills.

The Hawaiian Islands were far from alone in exhibiting this type of economic development. Examples of monocultural, single-industry, economic developments and the damage they caused to their natural environments in the Trans-Mississippi West of the United States are well known.[10] Gold mining, especially hydraulic mining, which involved washing down entire hillsides, left scars on the landscape that can still be seen today. In California dirt and gravel silted up rivers, which, in turn, flooded and hurt nascent agriculture. On the Great Plains unrestricted grazing on the public domain destroyed the prairie grass; that destruction, combined with severe winters, led to the "big die-off" of the mid-1880s, in which perhaps three-quarters of the cattle perished. In the 1870s and 1880s pioneer farmers pushed too far west onto arid lands. The result, all too often, was abortive farming efforts resulting in the erosion of topsoil and the creation of dust bowls. Similarly, little thought was given to the future by lumbermen and fishermen. Only when signs that fish and timber were not inexhaustible became unmistakably clear did they institute conservation measures, sometimes under pressure from others. The typical western impulse was to put resources to use, not to preserve or conserve them.[11]

The story was similar over much of the Caribbean and the Pacific, both of which regions developed as peripheral areas in the emerging global economy. The spread of American influence in the Caribbean after the Spanish-American War hastened the development of sugar cane growing and milling as an industrial crop. To be sure, sugar cane growing had existed much earlier, and there were considerable differences in its importance to various islands, but sugar cane's significance grew in the early twentieth century. As one scholar studying Cuba, Puerto Rico, and the Dominican Republic has recently observed, "The social and economic structure of the three islands during the high period of sugar monoculture dominated by U.S. capital during the first three and a half decades of the twentieth century" was transformed. Land ownership became more concentrated, mills grew larger, and possibilities for independent work became more limited. In Micronesia — the Mariana, Caroline, and Marshall Islands — growing copra long dominated the commercial sectors of many island economies, and the mining of phosphate destroyed the physical environment of Angaur in the Palau group. Despite concerted efforts, it proved difficult to establish viable, diversified economies for the islands even after World War II. In many other Pacific islands diversified, subsistence economies gave way over time to plantation economies, much as happened in the Hawaiian Islands.[12]

Much of Hawai'i's economy came to be controlled by the so-called Big Five companies: Alexander and Baldwin, Castle and Cooke, C. Brewer, American Factors (Amfac), and Theo Davies. All had been factors supplying goods and financial services for sugar planters, and several had even earlier been involved in supplying the whaling industry. Over the decades they came to own many of the plantations and sugar refining mills. The Big Five also controlled most of the banking, electrical systems, and transportation systems on the islands, and they jointly set up the Matson Line to handle their ocean shipping needs. Only one outsider — Claus Spreckels, the California sugar king — offered effective competition to the Big Five. Through buying land, especially on Maui, he came for a time to control a vertically integrated empire of plantations, mills, and ships — along with some towns, including Spreckelsville, which would later figure in the contest over the Kahului Airport.[13]

Postwar Economic Problems

Challenges to Hawai'i's plantation agriculture stiffened after World War II. Increasing competition to its cane sugar came from sugar refined from sugar beets, which were grown in many western states, and from sugar cane grown in the Caribbean and the Philippines. The results were a glut of sugar on American and world markets and correspondingly low prices. The development of high-fructose corn syrup as a sweetener also bit into the sugar market from the 1970s. Likewise, Hawaiian pineapple faced competition from pineapple grown in Taiwan and the Caribbean. At the same time, costs of production rose, especially after Hawai'i's plantation and mill workers unionized in 1946. The average daily wage for field workers leapt upward from just under $6 in 1945 to about $104 in 1986, an eighteenfold increase during a time when the Honolulu Consumer Price Index rose only sixfold. Even so, the workers did not live high on the hog. Given the high cost of living in Hawai'i, they were often hard-pressed to afford life in the islands.[14]

Plantation workers were varied in background. In 1872 Hawaiians or part-Hawaiians composed 83 percent of the plantation workforce in the islands, with laborers from China making up an additional 12 percent. However, Hawaiians succumbed to diseases unintentionally brought in from the West to which they had no natural immunities. As their numbers declined by at least 40 percent between 1823 and 1900, Hawaiians became a smaller segment of the plantation workforce. By 1882 Chinese constituted 49 percent of the plantation labor force, and Hawaiians only 25 percent. Immigrants from Japan also became important. By 1892 Japanese laborers made up 63 percent of the plantation workforce and ten years later composed 73 percent of it. Filipino laborers became significant as plantation workers in the twentieth century, making up 10 percent of the workforce in 1912 and 29 percent by 1920. The Hawaiian Islands thus developed a multiethnic society. This was certainly true of Maui. Of the 100,000 people living on Maui in 1990, 22,000 were Caucasian, 17,000 were Japanese American, 16,000 were Filipino American, 1,000 were Chinese American, and 2,000 were Native Hawaiian. Another 24,000 residents were part Native Hawaiian, with yet an additional 17,000 of other mixed ancestries.[15]

Despite tremendous increases in productivity, Hawai'i's sugar cane and pineapple companies found it increasingly difficult to compete with lower-cost overseas producers, and plantation agriculture declined. Between 1970 and 1986 the land planted in sugar cane dropped from 238,000 acres to just 184,000 acres. An investigation of the sugar industry undertaken for the State of Hawai'i concluded in 1989 that while "the sugar industry is still important to Hawai'i," it "is no longer an economic mainstay of the State." By 1995 only 121,000 acres remained planted in sugar cane, and the value of Hawai'i's sugar cane crop had dropped to $127 million. The story was similar for pineapple. By 1985 Hawai'i produced only 17 percent of the world's pineapple, down from a peak of 73 percent in 1950. The value of Hawai'i's crop fell from $108 million in 1991 to $87 million four years later.

Maui fared better than some other Hawaiian islands in retaining plantation crops, but even on Maui there was little growth. Land devoted to pineapple in Maui County dropped from 16,000 acres in 1991 to only 9,500 acres in 1995, and the value of Maui's pineapple crop fell from $46 million to just $25 million. The land planted in sugar cane in Maui County held steady at about 42,000 acres in the early and mid-1990s, and the value of the county's annual sugar cane crop stayed at about $58 million. All was not well, however. In 1999 Pioneer Mill in West Maui, one of the few remaining sugar cane plantations on the island, closed. By the late 1990s, too, the two companies still growing sugar cane were trying to develop a strain that could be harvested without burning, because tourists complained that smoke from the fields cast a brown pall over Maui's clear blue sky.[16]

Toward a Tourist Economy

From a state whose economy was based on agriculture, Hawai'i became one in which tourism played the leading role. The coming of statehood in 1959 combined with the arrival of jet airplanes that same year greatly boosted tourism. So did the increased incomes and leisure time most Americans enjoyed for several decades after World War II. Between 1958 and 1973 the number of tourists visiting the Hawaiian Islands rose an average 20 percent per year, increasing from 171,000 to 2,631,000! Tourism continued to expand in the 1970s, with close to four million visitors coming to the Hawaiian Islands in 1979. The switch from agriculture to tourism occurred at different times on different islands. It took place first on O'ahu, home of Honolulu, in the 1950s and 1960s. The other islands, so-called outer or neighbor islands, changed later.[17]

Maui's residents began fostering tourism during the 1950s and 1960s. With sugar cane and pineapple slipping, job opportunities seemed limited. In 1953, 37 percent of Maui's workers labored in agriculture, mainly on sugar cane and pineapple plantations. Another 17 percent worked in sugar mills, and an additional 12 percent found employment in pineapple canneries. Only 1 percent worked in hotels, and just 2 percent labored in construction. Looking for better jobs, people left the county. Maui's population fell from 42,400 in 1944 to 40,100 in 1950 and to just 37,600 in 1956, the nadir. It still stood at only 42,576 in 1960. Two-thirds of those who graduated from Maui's high schools in 1952 were living outside of the county four years later. Elmer Cravalho, who as Maui's mayor during the 1970s would lead the county into a period of unprecedented economic growth, later recalled the dismal situation: "Maui County was at the bottom of the economic spectrum. I saw and lived through the process of Front Street in Lahaina being boarded up, the closing of the canneries, the reduction of sugar cane, population diminishing."[18]

Alarmed, Maui's business and political leaders acted. Hawaiian Commercial and Sugar, Maui Land and Pineapple, and the Maui Electric Company financed a study of economic possibilities in 1955. A major recommendation was that the county should promote tourism. Maui's business leaders thereupon set up the Maui Economic Development Association (MEDA) to encourage new business ventures, especially in the visitor industry. MEDA had as its goal "the stimulation of the development of facilities for tourists both along the lines of increased accommodations and also entertainment and amusement." Government encouragement was also important. In 1957 the Hawaiian Territorial Legislature passed an act calling for "a planned, coordinated program of developing the economic potential of the territory." Observing that tourism offered "the greatest potential for expanding the economy of the Territory," the legislature established a Territorial Planning Office to prepare a general plan for the territory. Each county was to draft a plan to be subsumed in the territorial one. Maui did so in 1959. Stating that "Maui's future lies in the developments of the tourist industry," the county's plan called for improvements to street, sewer, and water systems, along with the creation of parks and civic centers, to aid visitor industry developments. "Halting and reversing the flow of population away from Maui" was the major goal.[19]

With business and government help, tourism blossomed. In 1956 only 29,000 tourists visited Maui. As economists at the University of Hawai'i observed, "the visitor industry on Maui, from its infancy till 1960, was characterized by a slow but steady growth in tourist expenditures, and hotel employment." Even in 1960 Maui possessed just 247 hotel rooms, while the Big Island of Hawai'i had 581 and Kaua'i had 237. O'ahu led the way with more than 8,000.[20] The year 1961 was a turning point for Maui: Visitor travel to the outer islands overall dropped 8 percent, but travel to Maui rose 16 percent. It jumped still more over the next three years. In 1964, 131,000 tourists visited Maui — more than the 126,000 who went to Hawai'i, and nearly as many as the 134,000 who ventured to Kaua'i. Maui was coming into its own as a center for tourism. While a far cry from what would develop later, Maui had 885 hotel rooms, more than Kaua'i's 709 rooms or Hawai'i's 831 units. O'ahu was still by far the most important center of tourism in the Hawaiian Islands, but Maui's share of the tourist expenditures in the state had risen to 5 percent, up from just 1 percent in 1952.[21]

The Big Five firms turned to tourism as one way to escape declining agriculture, and this was certainly the case on Maui. The leaders in resort development in Maui County were Castle and Cooke on Lāna'i and Amfac and Alexander and Baldwin on Maui. Particularly important were developments in West Maui. With the construction of a resort complex at Kā'anapali, Amfac demonstrated that comprehensive resort developments — the creation of resort destinations, not simply individual hotels — could succeed economically. A development at nearby Kapalua by Maui Land and Pineapple drove home that lesson.

Amfac led the way. In 1960 the firm's holdings at what would become its Kā'anapali resort consisted of two hundred acres in sugar cane and four hundred acres in grazing land. Close cooperation among federal, state, and county governments paved the way for development in this area, just as was envisioned by Maui's business and political leaders. Major road improvements increased the accessibility of West Maui, and the construction of a 69,000-volt transmission line from Kahului across the West Maui Mountains by Maui Electric Company provided a necessary boost in electricity. However, it was the vision of Amfac's owners that they could build the first comprehensive resort complex in the Hawaiian Islands that made the Kā'anapali development a reality. In 1962 the first units in Amfac's Kā'anapali Beach Resort, twenty cottages of the Royal Lahaina Beach Hotel, opened. A year later the Sheraton Maui opened its doors, and the Royal Lahaina increased its facilities to more than two hundred rooms. More hotels, condominiums, prize-winning golf courses, and shopping areas followed in later years, making Kā'anapali one of the premier destination resorts in the world. By 1980 the resort covered 2,000 acres, employed more than 2,000 workers, and consisted of 3,764 hotel rooms and 773 condominium units.[22]

The Kapalua resort developed by Maui Land and Pineapple — headed by Colin Cameron, a fifth-generation *haole* (Caucasian) on Maui — soon followed. Eager to move his company in new profitable directions, Cameron wanted to create a resort on six hundred acres of pineapple lands. Described by one of his friends as "a sensitive man with a rare combination of esthetic ideals and entrepreneurship," Cameron envisioned Kapalua as including "an 'Aspen' like conference center."[23] In 1966 Maui Land and Pineapple commissioned a study of the feasibility of turning some of its West Maui lands into a resort destination. More investigations followed, most notably a series of workshops held in 1970. Despite careful planning, however, problems occurred. Difficulties initially arose in raising financing as a result of a nationwide recession in the early 1970s, and plans for the resort's first hotel were scrapped when Cameron decided that its design was inappropriate. Arrangements also had to be worked out with the county. Maui Land and Pineapple gave the D. T. Fleming Beach Park at Honokahua to the county in return for aid in building the infrastructure for its resort. By 1979 Maui Land and Pineapple had overcome its teething problems to build a hotel, condominiums, beach club, and tennis club, with numerous additions following over the next two decades.[24] Nor was the idea of a conference center forgotten. Beginning in 1981 Kapalua hosted numerous conferences dealing with Maui's development and, indeed, with that of the Pacific Rim. Then, too, Cameron started the Kapalua Music Festival. He was also active, with others, in restoring nearby Lahaina, Maui's old whaling port, and that town became a bustling center for tourism in its own right.[25]

These comprehensive resort developments stimulated further growth in Maui's visitor industry. In 1968 the magazine *Hawaii Business and Industry* reported, "While the whole economy on Maui is prospering, it is widely recognized that tourism has been the catalyst for the situation." Maui hosted 400,000 visitors in 1970, and three years later the *Maui News* observed that the visitor industry on Maui was responsible for "hundreds of projects, ranging from extravagant shopping center complexes to single-family dwellings." Some 1.1 million visitors came to Maui in 1976, and 1.4 million did so in 1980. The number of hotel and condominium rooms on Maui rose to 2,743 in 1970 and to 9,701 in 1980. Prospective buyers eagerly bid for new units. In early July 1978, 1,500 people came from as far away as London, Hong Kong, and Australia to participate in an auction of 134 luxury condominium units at the Ridge in Kapalua! By 1980 hotel jobs accounted for 14 percent of employment on Maui, a proportion greater than the 11 percent in agriculture. Nor was Maui alone in its growth. By 1990 the neighbor islands possessed 46 percent of the state of Hawai'i's hotel rooms, up from just 15 percent in 1960.[26]

If Amfac and Maui Land and Pineapple were most important in West Maui's development, Alexander and Baldwin dominated resort construction in South Maui. A foretaste of Alexander and Baldwin's resort work can be glimpsed in that company's additions to the town of Kahului after World War II.

That Kahului would become Maui's major city was not apparent in the prewar years. In precontact times the Kahului area had been home to Hawaiians who fished in the nearby ocean. In the mid-1750s a leading chief constructed two fish ponds there, Kanahā and Mauoni, in which mullet were raised. With the growing of sugar cane on Maui, Kahului emerged as a shipping and service center in the nineteenth and twentieth centuries. Still, the town was small and the pace of life relatively slow, with its residents able to walk wherever they needed to go.[27]

Modern Kahului is mainly a postwar creation of Alexander and Baldwin. The major grower of sugar cane on Maui, Alexander and Baldwin centralized its operations after World War II. As part of that reorganization, the company switched from railroad to truck transportation and sought to relocate its workers from field camps to a single site, an enlarged Kahului. In 1930 Alexander and Baldwin had operated twenty-six camps housing more than 7,000 employees. The manager of the Hawaiian Commercial and Sugar Company, a subsidiary of Alexander and Baldwin, announced plans for the expansion of Kahului as a "Dream City" in 1948. The plan called for the construction of 700 homes over five years, covering three square miles. Maui's Board of Supervisors (now the Maui County Council) quickly endorsed the plan, and the first new home was completed less than a year later. Kahului was a thoroughly planned development, complete with parks, schools, and a shaded shopping center. Between 1950 and 1963 houses and lots were sold to workers in six phases at prices ranging from $6,600 to $9,200. By 1985 Alexander and Baldwin had disposed of more than 3,000 lots in fourteen housing developments, with two-thirds of the lots purchased by its current or former employees.[28]

In the 1970s and 1980s Alexander and Baldwin developed Wailea in South Maui as a planned resort community, as we shall see in Chapter 7. The company's work in Kahului served as a prelude to its later resort development efforts. Influenced by its efforts in Kahului, Amfac's success at Kā'anapali, and Maui Land and Pine's work at Kapalua, Alexander and Baldwin developed Wailea as a comprehensive destination resort, in sharp contrast to the many other uncoordinated developments in South Maui.

Discussions of Economic Diversification

Even as many of Maui's residents embraced tourism, some questioned its role in economic development. They were unwilling to trade dependence on one sort of economic monoculture, plantation agriculture, for another, tourism. An economic recession that hurt much of the world in the early 1980s, the worst downturn since the Great Depression of the 1930s, spurred questioning. Tourism in the Hawaiian Islands fell off, as a stagnant American economy with high unemployment coupled to high interest rates, a combination called "stagflation," bit into travel. Although it suffered less than the other Hawaiian Islands, Maui was hurt. The number of visitors to Maui fell 3 percent in 1980 and another 3 percent during the first nine months of 1981. Maui's hotel occupancy rate dropped to just 62 percent in 1981, down from 69 percent in the previous year.[29]

If the recession of the early 1980s acted as a catalyst for intense discussions about tourism, questioning had begun earlier. As early as 1968 Maui County chairman Elmer Cravalho stressed the need for balance in economic growth. "Tourism is a good thing," he noted, "but the problem is to keep it in reasonable bounds. We aren't going to let tourism spoil the charm and beauty of Maui." In his annual report for 1976–77, Cravalho, by then Maui's mayor (the office of mayor for the county was created in 1969, and Cravalho was elected as Maui's first mayor in that year) reiterated that theme. Maui, he observed, was like "a tightrope walker." The county required, he thought, continuing development and jobs, but it needed to avoid becoming all "concrete and asphalt." Quality-of-life concerns ran through Cravalho's thinking. "Values, respect, help for one another, opportunities for young people," Cravalho later explained, needed to be at the center of matters so that "we do not become a Los Angeles, a Chicago, a New York, an O'ahu."[30]

Others echoed Cravalho. Cummins Speakman Jr., who had recently retired as president of Mauna Olu College, Maui's only four-year institution of higher learning, warned that "the two foremost dangers Maui would have to face in the future would be . . . a depression or other 'disaster' [cutting] off the tourist trade, or . . . the tourist 'invasion' plus lack of control by the people of Maui and their government [ruining] the environment."[31] Similarly, in 1979 the president of the Maui County Council urged fellow council members to work for "the establishment of a balance between our economic needs and our accepted lifestyle" and called on them to help business leaders find "pragmatic economic opportunities" in fields beyond plantation agriculture and tourism.[32]

Questioning influenced planning. In the late 1970s county authorities drew up a plan for Maui's development as part of a ten-year planning cycle in the state of Hawai'i. Intended to guide Maui into the 1990s, the county plan called for balance in development. It had as its goals "the growth of resident and visitor populations so as to avoid social, economic and environmental disruptions," and "to limit growth by in-migration to correspond with the County's economic needs." A major objective was "to perpetuate the unique lifestyles of our people." To accomplish these goals the plan called for the "diversification of the County's economic base" through "the development of ecologically clean industries." Diversified agriculture and aquaculture won special praise. These goals represented a real change from those laid out in the 1959 plan, which had sought economic and population growth above all else. With resort developments approaching maturity in West Maui and under way in South Maui, their county was, many of Maui's residents realized, rapidly changing in ways they had not fully foreseen. A final section in the 1980 plan asked that county officials take steps "to ensure that visitor industry facilities shall not disrupt agricultural and social pursuits and will not be allowed to deplete the County's natural resources."[33] Quality-of-life issues were coming to the fore.

Responding to such thoughts, Maui's newly elected Mayor Hannibal Tavares sponsored a three-day Maui Mayor's Conference in late 1981 to examine the economic challenges facing Maui. "One of the first things I did when I was elected mayor in 1979," Tavares explained, "was think about the direction Maui should be following." He further observed, "I saw that tourism was strong throughout the county and state, but I was concerned that our economy was too dependent on the visitor industry and I wanted to look at economic alternatives to sugar, pineapple, tourism, and so forth." As Tavares concluded, "I got the idea of forming an economic development committee as an advisory group to the mayor." Tavares asked Colin Cameron "to sit down with me and discuss some of these ideas" and subsequently asked him to head the committee. Funding came from the county council, prodded by Tavares, and from Cameron, who contributed $100,000.[34]

Convened by Cameron and held at his Kapalua Bay Resort, the conference was attended by business and political leaders from Maui and from well beyond the county — representatives came from Japan and mainland America. The conference concluded, as Cameron put it, that "a means of providing continuous, vigorous attention and action toward the goal of a diversified economy is required." Maui's economy, the conferees agreed, showed "limits on growth in all our current major activities — tourism, sugar and pineapple." Conference members hoped, therefore, that Maui's residents would "start a process which will lead to community-accepted new economic directions." High-technology "clean" industries and diversified agriculture received special notice as being most likely to lead Maui's economy into a viable future.[35]

A Mayor's Advisory Committee, chaired by Cameron, sponsored the conference and continued work for several months after it. The advisory committee recommended that the county set up and help finance a Maui Economic Development Board, which, in turn, would try to attract new, desirable businesses to Maui. Committee members envisioned that a high-technology park would be established. In support of these actions, the advisory committee urged, the county should also work to improve education on Maui, especially higher education. At the same time, the county should try to help established businesses, especially those in diversified agriculture and aquaculture.[36]

High-Technology Efforts: The Maui Research and Technology Park

The most immediate result of the mayor's conference was the formation of the Maui Economic Development Board (MEDB) in 1982 to assist "Maui County Community by serving as a catalyst in creating a strong and diversified economy." More specifically, the MEDB was to nurture high-technology ventures through the creation of a high-tech park. The quest for high-tech business was statewide, not limited to Maui. In 1981 the state adopted a Hawaii High Technology Development Plan, which, in the words of Gov. George Ariyoshi, aimed at a "major diversification of our economy." High-technology initiatives were favored because their products had a high value for their weight — an important consideration given Hawai'i's location far from most markets — because they required the use of few indigenous natural resources, and because their fabrication was nonpolluting. Ocean mining, spaceports, and computer centers were among the ventures that attracted attention. A few high-tech enterprises already existed on Maui, but those forming the MEDB believed that much more could be accomplished: that high-technology businesses could become a "third leg" of Maui's economy, along with agriculture and tourism.[37]

Beyond Mayor Tavares, two others were especially important in establishing the MEDB. Tavares had asked Cameron to chair his advisory committee and oversee the Kapalua conference, and Cameron went on to serve as the first chairman of the MEDB until his death in 1992. Cameron, in turn, brought in Donald Malcolm, who accepted the presidency of the MEDB.

Malcolm had a varied background, having served in public and private organizations. He grew up in Indiana, where he graduated from Purdue in

1940 as a "public service engineer." After college, Malcolm went to work for General Motors in Indianapolis, where the automaker was building aviation engines for World War II. From there he went into the navy. Stationed in the Pacific, he visited Hawai'i for the first time as a radioman on a carrier-based torpedo-bomber. After the war Malcolm taught engineering, first at Purdue and then at the University of California, Berkeley, becoming very interested in statistical analysis as a way of controlling production processes. Malcolm's interests and his growing national prominence led him into military defense work. With the Cold War heating up, these were, Malcolm later recalled, "heady times" for engineers. From a career as an educator, Malcolm went into consulting, first with Booz-Allen and Hamilton and the RAND Corporation, and later on his own. Returning to academic life, Malcolm became dean of the School of Business at California State University, Los Angeles. When living in California, Malcolm served as the chair of the Santa Monica Planning Commission, an experience that helped him in his efforts to establish a high-technology park on Maui.[38]

Malcolm met Cameron on a visit to Maui in 1973 and was very favorably impressed by his plans for Kapalua. In the mid-1970s Malcolm and his wife vacationed on Maui and, intending to retire on the island at some point, purchased land near Kapalua. Cameron persuaded Malcolm to serve on the Mayor's Advisory Committee, and Malcolm played a leading role in organizing the Kapalua conference. It was a logical step for him to become president of the MEDB. For the next decade Cameron and Malcolm worked closely together to make what became known as the Maui Research and Technology Park (MRTP) a reality.[39]

Those hoping to create a high-technology park on Maui had, first of all, to establish an organizational structure. They set up the MEDB as a nonprofit "public-private partnership" composed of a who's who of Maui's business and political leaders. In addition to Tavares, Cameron, and Malcolm, members included representatives of the First Hawaiian Bank, the Bank of Hawai'i, Maui Electric, Alexander and Baldwin, C. Brewer, and the Maui Chamber of Commerce. Others on the board were Masaru "Pundy" Yokouchi (an important developer on Maui) and a member of the county council. The initial plan was for the MEDB to find a mainland developer who had the capital and resources needed to construct the MRTP and then step into the background.

Donald Malcolm spearheaded the development of the Maui Research and Technology Park. (Courtesy of Donald Malcolm)

The MEDB would, its members envisioned, act as "a catalyst in helping the developer and would ultimately turn its efforts to other pursuits in assisting Maui's diversifications."[40]

Site selection was the first task. After considering a number of possibilities, including three in Upcountry Maui, the MEDB chose a site in Kīhei in 1983. Here the Haleakalā Ranch provided 415 acres of scrubland. Prodded by Tavares, the county gave permission for the research park to be developed as a special project district, which put the site on a fast track for development. Then problems surfaced. In 1984 the MEDB chose Joel Smolen, a California developer who had built a research and development park in Santa Clara County, to put up the MRTP. With the California economy faltering, the savings and loan that had been financing Smolen's Santa Clara work failed, and Smolen's business empire collapsed. Smolen withdrew from the Maui project in 1986. The MEDB then picked a development company from Phoenix, Arizona, but within a year that firm had withdrawn. When questions about groundwater and sewage delayed the project, the developer "got cold feet" and decamped.[41]

With these turns of events, it became apparent that Maui's leaders would have to take a very active role — that they could not depend on mainland developers, if a research park were to become more than simply a vision. In 1989 Maui's business leaders formed the Maui R and T Partners to develop the park — with the MEDB acting as the managing partner for the development, a major enhancement of the board's role. Malcolm's work was essential in effecting this change. Just one day after the Arizona developer pulled out, Malcolm came up with the plan of shifting work to local people. As Malcolm later recalled, he "sat down with Colin" to decide what to do. Cameron, Malcolm remembered, agreed "to bootstrap a little bit." It was, thought Malcolm, "a matter of pride for Colin" that the research park be built. At any rate, "Colin went to his friend Pundy, and they agreed to come up with a million dollars" to jump-start the MRTP.[42]

Maui's leaders also sought state and federal government funding. Malcolm traveled to Honolulu, where, with the strong support of State Sen. Mamoru Yamasaki, he persuaded the state government to finance the first major building, called the Maui Research and Technology Center, to serve as an incubator for newly formed high-technology companies. The state's agreement to participate in the MRTP broke the impasse. Private firms constructed a second building named Premier Place, a state-of-the-art commercial office complex. Next came the Maui High Performance Computing Center — complete with a supercomputer, which was very important for the success of the MRTP — made possible by funding from the federal government secured by Hawai'i's U.S. senator Daniel Inouye. Other installations followed in the mid- and late 1990s.[43]

As the managing partner, the MEDB oversaw these developments, entering into a series of agreements with the State of Hawai'i, the University of Hawai'i, Maui County, and the federal government. The MEDB also sponsored important conferences on Maui's economic future. In 1988 the board worked with county and state officers to hold a conference about land use and transportation challenges facing Maui and the other Hawaiian Islands. Five years later the board sponsored a conference to look at the future of high-

technology developments on Maui. The 1993 meeting was especially important in convincing Maui County mayor Linda Lingle to look more favorably
on the research park; she had earlier been lukewarm. After the conference
Lingle backed the expenditure of $200,000 in county funds on the MRTP.[44]

Still, even with the active involvement of Maui's leaders, it was difficult at
first to attract tenants. Infrastructure improvements helped, and the MRTP
quickly provided satellite uplinks and downlinks, microwave and fiberoptic
communications, and access to the Internet. A business information center and
research library were also attractions, as was the supercomputer. Nonetheless,
the MEDB had to undergo a learning process before it succeeded in helping
high-technology firms develop. The first incubator firms accepted for the research park were, recalled the president of the MEDB in 1999, "quite fledgling
and their chances of success were probably quite slim." However, she observed,
the situation improved with experience, with later years' incubator companies
becoming "very much stronger and very much more viable."[45]

A major challenge lay in a dearth of scientists and technicians. MEDB
members took steps to address it, initiating programs in Hawaiian elementary
schools to create excitement about science, so that Maui could eventually
produce its own high-technology workers. In the late 1990s the educational
efforts extended beyond elementary schools. A group called the South Maui
Learning 'Ohana was formed to push for the building of a new high school
with a science-based curriculum on land next to the research park. Proposed
as the state of Hawai'i's first charter high school, it would be a public school
built by both public and private money and operated independently of the
state's department of education. In early 2000 the Hawaiian state government
funded planning grants for twenty-one charter schools, including the one at
Kīhei. There were by this time 1,700 charter schools in thirty-one states across
America.[46]

Even so, there remained a long way to go in improving public elementary
and secondary education in the Hawaiian Islands. Historically very centralized,
the Hawaiian educational system depended on appropriations from the state
legislature, not local property taxes, for its funding, and these were often inadequate. As late as 1986 Hawai'i ranked dead last among states in its spending
per pupil; its graduation rate was only thirty-third among the states.[47]

Maui's business and civic leaders also worked to improve higher education
on Maui. Unlike many other high-technology regions — California's Silicon

Valley and Route 128 around Boston, for example — Maui had no university from which it could draw for expertise. For nearly a century the Mauna Olu College came closest to offering higher education to residents of Maui. Started as a female seminary by missionaries in 1861, the school became a private, coeducational community college in 1950. In 1964 it enrolled some 200 students at its campus on Baldwin Avenue between Pā'ia and Makawao. However, the college faced hard times, when the State of Hawai'i opened Maui Community College in Kahului in 1966. Not even the adoption of a four-year curriculum leading to a bachelor of arts degree could save the institution, which was sold to the United States International University in 1971. Headquartered in San Diego, this university soon found itself in financial trouble resulting from rapid expansion and sold its Maui campus to the county in 1975. Failing in efforts to operate the campus as an agricultural training facility and unable to reach agreements for its use by other institutions, the county used the campus as a dormitory for off-island students attending Maui Community College. Finally, in 1986 the former campus was taken over as a training center by the United States Job Corps.[48]

A continued desire for higher education on Maui did bear some fruit. In 1994 a task force set up by Mayor Lingle reported that there existed "an increasing demand for higher education alternatives in Maui County." Four years later the University of Phoenix began offering classes in a limited number of fields in Wailuku.[49] All in all, however, Maui was ill served by institutions of higher learning. Private colleges could not fully compensate for the lack of a four-year state university on Maui. Maui Community College offered only two-year courses of instruction. Residents of Maui who wanted a four-year state university education were expected to travel to the University of Hawai'i in Honolulu. The University of Hawai'i took steps to improve the situation by creating an Outreach Program through which its faculty members and visiting faculty members from other colleges and universities taught on Maui. Then, too, a University Center at Maui Community College, established in the mid-1990s, offered a growing variety of classes and degree programs. Maui County contributed $200,000 annually to the operation of the center.[50]

By the late 1990s the MRTP was beginning to fulfill its promise. The Maui Research and Technology Center housed "high technology oriented start-up companies" and sought to "nurture them to health." These incubator companies ranged from computer software firms such as DiagSoft and Dancing Bear Enterprises to multimedia companies such as Chameleon Multimedia. The center was also home to "phase-in companies (established high-tech businesses)," like SandA International, a high-technology security firm, and the Pacific Disaster Center. "Anchor tenants" such as the University of Hawai'i completed the list of those occupying the center. By the winter of 1998 the twenty-some companies and organizations in the center's building employed about one hundred people. Premier Place and the High Performance Computing Center, for which Congress approved an additional $10 million in the fall of 1998, housed additional high-technology businesses. Altogether, about 350 people worked at the MRTP.[51]

High-technology companies did not yet, however, comprise a third leg of Maui's economy. It was too soon for that to have occurred. Getting a research park up and running is a long-term undertaking, and because of the difficulties with mainland developers, the first buildings at the MRTP did not open until 1991–92. Moreover, that Maui would have trouble developing high-technology businesses was hardly surprising. Many regions in the United States and abroad have tried to emulate the development of California's Silicon Valley, but few have succeeded. Honolulu had not emerged as a high-technology center, despite considerable government investment. A detailed report on high-technology developments in the Hawaiian Islands published in 1994 observed that for all its efforts, the state government had accomplished little. The Hawaiian Islands lacked, the report stated, many of the factors needed to attract and nurture high-technology businesses: factors ranging from the lack of a first-class university to favorable government policies toward business (high tax rates hurt business development, for example). It would require at least another twenty-five to thirty years, the report concluded, to develop a significant high-technology sector in Hawai'i. Similarly, in 1999 *Forbes* magazine ranked Honolulu 160th out of 162 regions in the United States as a desirable place in which to conduct high-technology businesses, ahead of only Spokane, Washington, and Johnson City, Texas.[52]

Silicon Valley entrepreneurs got ahead by creating over several decades a large informal and very flexible network of linked, but independent, companies. These companies worked very closely with suppliers of components, with venture capitalists, and with specialized legal and marketing consultants. Highly educated workers moving from job to job and company to company transferred information across firm boundaries. By the close of the 1970s a dense network of some 3,000 high-technology firms, mostly small businesses, populated Silicon Valley. Stanford University and the Stanford Research Institute lent some cohesion to developments, especially during the 1950s and early 1960s.[53]

Would the MRTP eventually emerge as a new Silicon Valley? Could a large cluster of high-technology firms be nurtured to maturity on Maui? Those associated with Maui's high-technology efforts remained convinced of success as the 1990s closed. Malcolm stressed the need to adopt a long time horizon and pointed out that the MRTP could already count considerable accomplishments: It had spurred improvements in education on Maui, provided the first good Internet service for people on the island, attracted conferences to Maui, and, in general, boosted computer literacy. Michael Lyons II, the senior vice-president and district manager of the Bank of Hawai'i on Maui, agreed with Malcolm. A charter member of the MEDB, Lyons served as its chair after Cameron died in 1992. When asked if he saw high-technology ventures playing a significant role in Maui's economic future, Lyons replied that he did; he also ruefully observed that "I've been seeing it that way for quite a long time and it hasn't happened."[54]

Whatever the eventual success of the MRTP might be, it was clear that it would not come cheaply. Already by early 1993 about $47.5 million had been spent on high-technology ventures on Maui. Of that funding, $22.2 million had come from the federal government, $12.2 million from the state government, and $12.2 million from the private sector. Only $225,000 had come from the county, with the University of Hawai'i contributing another $275,000.[55]

Specialized Agriculture

While some of Maui's residents sought diversification through high-technology businesses, others turned to specialized agriculture. In 1899 the Nahiku Rubber Company had begun the first rubber plantation on American soil, with plantings on Maui's windward side. Technically successful — rubber trees may still be seen in the area — the effort failed commercially in 1916, unable to compete with less expensive latex from Malaysia.[56] Far from limited to Maui, the effort to diversify agriculture was statewide. With Hawai'i's sugar cane and pineapple facing increasing challenges after World War II, the search for alternative crops assumed a new urgency. A report prepared by the state on Maui's economy in 1965 observed that with markets for sugar and pineapple becoming more competitive, "now seems the time to take a good look at the diversified farming sector"; and the same Mayor's Advisory Committee that called for a high-technology park also recommended diversified agriculture as a way to spur economic development.[57]

Aquaculture also seemed promising. In precontact days chiefs had raised fish in ponds on Maui and the other islands. Maui's residents made concerted efforts to reenter aquaculture in the 1970s. Starting in 1971 aquafarmers led by Carter Pyle sought to raise Malaysian prawns in part of Keālia Pond near Kīhei. At the time, local residents were upset by dust blowing south from Keālia when the tidal pond dried up each summer. Pyle saw aquaculture as a way both to earn money and to solve a community problem by stabilizing the water level of the pond. In a second project government officials worked with officers of the Pacific Tuna Development Foundation to try to develop a bait fish industry during the late 1970s and early 1980s. Designed to raise minnows as bait for the tuna fishing industry, the fishery was also to be located in a section of Keālia Pond. Altogether, the number of aquaculture operations on Maui rose from five in 1983 to eighteen by 1994; by the latter year the value of the county's aquaculture production amounted to $328,000. However, these operations did not take place in Keālia Pond, which had become a federal wildlife sanctuary.[58]

Agricultural specialization took numerous forms. Some had long existed on Maui — the growing of potatoes and onions in Kula, for example. Many crops were tried. In the mid-1970s Emil Tedeschi, who had grown up in California's Napa Valley, opened a vineyard and winery on the sunny south slopes of Haleakalā. Processing grapes and pineapple, the Tedeschi Winery sold 100,000 bottles of wine annually by 1984. Wailuku Sugar diversified into macadamia nut growing, setting out seedlings on 484 acres near Wailuku in 1979. The goal, its manager stated, was to help even out "the roller coaster ride of sugar prices." By 1993 the company had 1,300 acres in macadamia nuts. Eddie Wendt began raising taro commercially on the Ke'anae Peninsula in 1985, building a poi factory in which his crop was processed. Soon some growers sought to boost their profits by raising golden apple snails imported from South America in the waterlogged taro patches as a food for humans and live-

Agricultural diversification on Maui included making wine.

stock. This plan backfired, however, when the snails unexpectedly damaged the taro plants. The farmers found themselves having to import snail-eating ducks to fight the snail menace.[59]

Government aid helped agricultural development. As early as 1969 members of the Maui County Council recognized that farmers faced many obstacles "in the areas of adequate suitable lands, water resources, facilities for shipment of produce, competing with the thriving hotel business to pay comparable wages for farmhands, roads, and taxes."[60] Nine years later they again lamented the problems specialized growers faced, many of which continued through the 1990s. Competition from crops grown on the mainland, especially California; the high costs of seeds, fertilizers, and machinery; and the inefficiency of small-scale operations hindered developments on Maui.[61]

To help growers become established, Maui County officials worked with their state and federal counterparts to create the Kula Agricultural Park on the lower slopes of Haleakalā in the early 1980s. Administered by Maui County, Kula Park leased land to farmers at low rates, with the state providing technical assistance. One of nine such agricultural parks created in the Hawaiian Islands at that time, the Kula Agricultural Park covered 450 acres. Perhaps even more important than Kula Park, however, was federal funding for other agricultural projects. In 1998 alone the federal government appropriated $1.6 million for research on aquaculture on the islands of Moloka'i and Hawai'i. It set aside, as well, nearly $1 million for sugar cane and diversified crop research, $296,000 for research on papaya growing, $250,000 for work on floriculture, and $131,000 for research on other forms of diversified agriculture in the Hawaiian Islands. In 1999 Moloka'i was designated a federal Rural Enterprise Community, whereupon the federal government made $250,000 available to community planners to bring 400 acres of taro into cultivation, with the promise of additional funds over the next decade.[62]

Even so, the growth of specialized agriculture did not compensate fully for decline in plantation crops. In 1963 the value of the diversified crops grown in Maui County came to $1.2 million, while the value of Maui's sugar cane crop stood at $37 million and that of pineapple at $38 million. By 1995 the gap had lessened but still remained large. Growers in Maui County sold about $15 million worth of vegetables and fruit (other than pineapple) and another $8 million worth of flowers and nursery products. These figures compared with $59 million worth of unprocessed sugar cane and $25 million worth of pineapple. Specialty fruit and vegetables were still in their adolescence, accounting for just over 1 percent of the value of Maui County's economic output in 1996. Nor did rapid growth seem imminent. The value, harvested acreage, and production weight of vegetables and melons on Maui fell between 1991 and 1995; the same years saw declines in the county's floriculture and nursery products.[63]

Many problems dogged efforts to develop specialized agriculture. As an officer of the Bank of Hawai'i observed in 1981, "The question here in Hawaii is not whether we can grow something, but first, can it be produced economically and, second, can we market it profitably." Production costs were high. Labor, water, and land cost more than they did in competing agricultural regions of the world, whether in California, the Caribbean, or Asia. Moreover, imported inputs of gasoline, fertilizer, and pesticides usually cost more. Then, too, markets remained far away. Both Caribbean growers of tropical fruit and California growers of temperate-zone fruit and vegetables were much closer to the big mainland American market. Hawaiian markets, even that of Honolulu, remained small, limiting the possibility of scale economies in production.[64] There was a saying on Maui that "if you can grow it in the San Joaquin Valley, you cannot grow it on Maui."[65]

Like high-technology businesses, then, specialized agriculture seemed unlikely to provide a full solution to Maui's economic challenges. In 1963 vegetables and melons grown in the Hawaiian Islands supplied 38 percent of those consumed in Honolulu, by far the largest market in the state, with most of the rest coming from the mainland. Over next three decades market demands grew more quickly than home-grown supplies, so that in 1991 the Hawaiian Islands produced only about 30 percent of the fresh fruit and vegetables consumed in Honolulu.[66] Specialized agriculture remained, noted the head of Maui County's Office of Economic Development, "a difficult industry to be in." Unable to meet competition with larger concerns, the Haleakalā Dairy, the last milk producer on Maui, shut its milking sheds in early 1999; as the year 2000 began, Wailuku Agribusiness decided to close its macadamia nut orchard.[67]

New Directions in Tourism on Maui?

Even as Maui's leaders sought to spur the development of diversified agriculture and high-technology businesses, they looked for ways to bolster their county's visitor industry. As the United States recovered from the recession of the early 1980s, tourism boomed. The number of visitors to Maui County climbed from 1.4 million in 1980 to a peak of 2.5 million in 1990. The number of hotel and condominium rooms in the county rose to 18,169 in 1993, up from 9,701 thirteen years earlier. By 1989 hotels and tourism accounted for 54 percent of Maui County's gross county product, trailed by finance at 15 percent; construction, much of which was related directly to tourism, at 9 percent; government at 9 percent; agriculture at 8 percent; and manufacturing at just 5 percent.[68]

Japanese investments stood out in the development of tourism on Maui. By the late 1970s Japanese companies had invested about $1.8 billion in Hawai'i, with one-third of that sum going directly into tourism (total foreign investment in Hawai'i came to $3 billion in 1978). About 17 percent of the hotel rooms in the islands were owned by Japanese firms. There was little concern about this investment at first. A public forum sponsored by the Maui Chamber of Commerce in 1977 to discuss Japanese investment in Maui attracted only twenty participants. The Japanese presence increased during the 1980s, especially during the latter part of the decade, and concerns mounted. With their economy booming, Japanese sought investment opportunities overseas. The Hawaiian Islands, where many Japanese vacationed and where land prices were relatively low (at least when compared to those in many parts of Japan), were magnets for Japanese capital. Between 1986 and 1990 Japanese investments in the Hawaiian Islands came to $11 billion. By the early 1990s Japanese firms owned 65 percent of the hotel rooms in the islands, more than half of the private golf courses, and half of the office space in downtown Honolulu. Constructed by the Seibu Company in the 1980s, the Maui Prince Hotel in South Maui was the best-known example of Japanese investments on the island of Maui. However, with the bursting of their "bubble" economy in the 1990s, the Japanese sold many of their resort holdings, including the Maui Prince. Japanese purchases of Hawaiian real estate fell from $2.9 billion in 1990 to just $328 million two years later.[69]

The burst of growth in tourism sputtered to a standstill during the 1990s. Japan's economic woes hit the Hawaiian Islands especially hard. With the onset of a worldwide recession in 1990, tourism fell off in Maui, just as it had during the recession of the early 1980s. While Maui again suffered less than many of the other Hawaiian Islands, it saw a decline in visitors. The number of visitors to Maui fell to a low point of 2.26 million in 1993, before recovering a bit to 2.32 million three years later. The number of hotel and condominium rooms in Maui County rose only slightly, increasing from 18,169 in 1990 to 19,024 four years later. As hotels found themselves in financial trouble, some changed hands in the late 1990s — the Kea Lani and Grand Wailea in Wailea, the Westin Maui and Maui Marriott Resort in Kā'anapali, and the Hana Ranch Hotel in Hanā.[70]

Faced with repeated ups and downs in tourism, those involved in Maui's visitor industry sought to widen the net for visitors. Most tourists had long come from the Pacific Coast of the United States, especially California. By the mid-1990s the Pacific Coast market was, the head of the Maui Visitors Bureau (MVB) believed, "pretty well saturated," and the bureau was conducting programs to attract more visitors from the Midwest and the East Coast.[71] Those in Maui's tourist industry also sought to broaden the range of visitors to their county. While not abandoning the luxury market in which Maui excelled, they hoped to diversify the appeal of Maui.

As they sought to attract tourists with varied interests, Maui's visitor industry representatives realized, somewhat belatedly perhaps, that they needed to create attractions. Especially as new resort destinations sprang up around the world — including many resorts closer to mainland America, such as resorts in the Caribbean — people had to be given a reason to travel to Maui. This competition for the tourist dollar was nothing new. As early as 1965 economists at the University of Hawai'i observed that "Maui faces stiff international and national competition" from "established resorts such as the Caribbean, the Bahamas, and many century-hewn attractions of Europe and of the Far East." Still, if not brand-new, competition seemed to increase during the 1990s.[72]

Sports events seemed promising. Maui hosted a college basketball tournament, the Maui Invitational, every November, and golf and windsurfing events at other times of the year. The biggest attraction was getting football's Hula Bowl to move from O'ahu to Maui for five years beginning in 1998.[73] Beyond sports events, those in Maui's visitor industry pursued other avenues. Working with their counterparts at the MRTP, they tried to attract high-technology conferences to Maui, with considerable success by the late 1990s. They also encouraged the building of new tourist attractions on the island. Opened in 1984, the Maui Tropical Plantation showcased tropical crops to visitors in a comfortable setting. Museums and restored buildings, including a whaling museum at Kā'anapali and a sugar museum near Kahului, grew in popularity. An aquarium opened at Mā'alaea in 1998.[74] Still other possibilities were in their infancy or planning stages — various forms of ecotourism, wellness centers, and vacations linked to education. Along these lines, Maui County officials looked into the possibility of building a multipurpose center in Lahaina as a site for sports events and conventions.[75]

Efforts on Maui were similar to attempts to broaden tourism throughout the Hawaiian Islands. "Leisure travel," a report commissioned by the state observed in 1999, "has been increasing worldwide." However, the report lamented, "Hawai'i has not participated in this growth, with overall visitor arrivals continuing to approximate 1990 levels." The report discussed many reasons for Hawai'i's decline relative to other areas. However, the main difficulty, the report stated, was that Hawai'i faced more competition from other places (and cruise ships) for the tourist dollar than had earlier been the case. To try to reinvigorate Hawai'i's visitor industry, the state government established the Hawai'i Tourism Authority in the summer of 1998. This body issued recommendations a year later, ideas running the

Resort destination hotels, sometimes making use of Polynesian themes, were built in South Maui during the 1980s.

gamut from improving airports (including lengthening the major runway at Maui's Kahului Airport) to placing more emphasis on the development of "niche" tourism.[76]

The place of Hawaiian culture and history in any reconfiguration of Maui's visitor industry was unclear. "Cultural tourism is based on the history of the place," observed a Maui resident in the summer of 1999. "Maui becomes a unique adventure for tourists when they visit an ancient site, walk through an historic town or hike a historic path." Moreover, she thought, cultural tourism could bring visitors and residents together. "Cultural tourism is an alternative way of teaching," she concluded. "It shows pride and integrity toward our culture, which is losing itself to development."[77] Officials in Maui's visitor industry realized that many tourists wanted to learn about Native Hawaiians and recognized that there was a danger of treating Hawaiian culture simply as a commodity in their promotion efforts. The head of the Mayor's Office of Economic Development thought that business and civic leaders needed to make Hawaiian culture "more real . . . so that it's part of the people's lifestyle versus a commodity." Maui County helped fund the construction of a Hawaiian canoe for educational purposes, and the head of the MVB suggested that Hawaiian "crafts, dance, and language" be encouraged and promoted. Another possibility might be, she thought, a display that would "talk about how important the ocean has been to Native culture."[78]

Still, questions remained. A case in point lay in indecision about what to do about petroglyphs at Olowalu. Several hundred years old, these drawings carved by Hawaiians on a cliff not far from Lahaina were inadequately protected. Located on land owned by Amfac, the petroglyphs suffered from vandalism. As early as 1973 the Maui County Council had explored steps to save the drawings but did little — a situation that persisted five years later despite a request from Charles Kauluwehi Maxwell, a Hawaiian rights activist, that something be done.[79] By the 1990s the matter had become more complex. While some of Maui's residents wanted the Olowalu site cleaned up and preserved, not all did. Some feared that any attempted restoration would change the site and wanted it left alone. Meanwhile, petroglyphs were commodified by some in the tourist trade, with T-shirts and cocktail glass coasters bearing the likenesses of the drawings on sale in stores throughout Maui.[80]

Actions taken by a team of developers — the realtor Peter Martin, the builder Jim Riley, and the physician Jim Bendon — in late 1998 promised a possible change in the situation. Purchasing 734 acres at Olawalu from Amfac, they said that they envisioned the creation of a Hawaiian Culture Preserve running from the ocean up through the land around the petroglyphs. A low-density development, the projected complex at Olawalu would include "a living presentation of traditional water use and farming practices — people planting kalo [taro] and pounding poi." Such an attraction would, they hoped, bring more people to West Maui. "People want to see culture," observed one of the developers. "I know that's why people come to this island instead of Waikiki."[81]

Into a New Millennium

In a massive, four-volume report on Maui's economy prepared in 1965, economists at the University of Hawai'i observed that "while balanced economic growth is desirable," Hawai'i, "by its location in the mid-Pacific, with limited resource potentials and the narrow market of an island economy," had not developed that way. Instead, the Hawaiian Islands grew sugar cane and pineapple. The economists praised the nascent development of tourism but warned about continued economic imbalances. "There is yet another over-all problem — that of stable growth," they noted, writing specifically about Maui. "Overemphasis on the development of tourism" might, they feared, "subject the economy to undue external influences." Stressing tourism too much would, they were afraid, "detract from stable growth and from maximum socio-intellectual advancement."[82] Those were prescient words, at a time when the hotel industry accounted for only 6 percent of Maui's employment.

The question of how to achieve stable and balanced economic growth continued to plague Maui's residents through the 1990s. In 1991 they adopted an updated plan for their county's development. Observing that since 1980 Maui had developed "a larger dependency on the visitor industry," which placed "greater demands upon infrastructure systems" and created "significant new demands for affordable housing," the 1991 plan called for "the diversification of the County's economic base." Diversified agriculture and aquaculture were singled out for praise once again. Reflecting a growth in environmentalism, the plan had as one of its leading objectives "to control the development of visitor facilities so that it does not infringe upon the traditional social, economic and environmental values of our community." Moreover, the plan called on county officials to "encourage a sustainable rate of economic development which is linked to the carrying capacity of the infrastructure systems and the fiscal ability of the County to maintain those systems." These were strong words, very different from what had been heard in planning sessions a generation before. Economic growth and population increase were no longer the touchstones of public policy that they had once been.[83]

Maui's residents were, however, only partly successful in diversifying their county's economy as the new millennium began. Tourism dominated Maui, and balance in economic development continued to prove elusive. The potentials of high-technology fields and diversified agriculture had not yet been realized, and it remained an open question if they ever would be. Of the 57,150 jobs in Maui County in 1999, 11,000 were in the hotel industry. The county had just 400 jobs in high-technology fields and only about 2,000 in agriculture. Most of the remainder were in fields directly dependent or partly dependent on tourism — wholesaling, retailing, construction, and the like.[84] The centrality of tourism to life on Maui ran through the debates and actions about the issues examined in this study. Tourism's dominance also helped bring to the fore new leaders, organizations, and movements on Maui — the topic of the next chapter — as people on Maui dealt with economic issues and with their quality of life.

2

People, Groups, and Movements

Americans have become increasingly organized into groups that represent their interests since the mid-nineteenth century. As they responded to the growth of a national economy, with its attendant forces of industrialization and urbanization, Americans interacted more through groups than through face-to-face contacts. Professional associations, labor unions, and business associations were some of the bodies that mediated among people. Such was the case in the Trans-Mississippi West, especially after the initial flush stages of development on various frontiers. Hard-rock mine workers formed unions, which battled with associations of mine owners. Cowboys also belonged to unions and sometimes went on strike to try to win concessions from ranchers. Farmers were members of buying and selling cooperatives, which numbered about one thousand by 1907. Social and political organizations were also of great significance, the Patrons of Husbandry (the Grange) for farmers, for example.[1]

Organizations were important in the development of the Hawaiian Islands, including Maui. Labor unions and employers' associations grew in significance after 1945 in the sugar cane, pineapple, and shipping industries. Then, as tourism blossomed and population expanded, new business groups developed in the islands. The rapid expansion of the visitor industry, and with it the coming of more tourists, also led to the formation of environmental organizations devoted to slowing the development of the islands. Some were local chapters of national bodies, but many of the most important were grass-roots, home-grown organizations. Finally, as part of the Native Hawaiian Renaissance, Native Hawaiians formed groups to influence the course of events. It was, then, through the interaction of many organizations that economic and environmental issues were worked out.

Individuals were also of great significance.[2] They were active as leaders of groups. There, was, however, more to the situation. A relatively small island, Maui was a place where people of all sorts ran into each other daily. More than in large, impersonal cities, Maui was a place where face-to-face, personal contact remained important. It was a place where people could disagree strongly on specific issues yet remain friends, or at least acquaintances — a place that encouraged, despite strongly held differences of opinion, a climate of compromise. Ultimately, everyone had to live on the same island, the same speck of land.

Business Organizations

Maui's business groups were varied. Most inclusive was the Maui Chamber of Commerce. Boasting 1,300 members by the late 1990s, the chamber was "dedicated to advancing and promoting the economic well-being of business and to encouraging responsible government, while maintaining Maui's unique attributes." It was in meetings of the chamber's standing committees on agriculture, business technology, commerce, education and training, government action, and marketing that much of the body's work took place. The chamber labored for and against many of the issues dealt with in this book.[3] The chamber was important for Maui's businesspeople in other respects. As Terryl Vencl, who headed the chamber, related, the organization provided "tons of information, tons of phone calls" to people and businesses interested in Maui. Moreover, the chamber's "Business After Hours," an informal, monthly social get-together, provided a forum for networking.[4]

Many of Maui's business organizations were geared to the visitor industry. Two of the most important were the Maui Visitors Bureau (MVB), a section of the Hawai'i Visitors Bureau, and the Maui Hotel Association (MHA), a chapter of the Hawai'i Hotel Association. Here the line between public and private was blurred, with much of the funding coming from governmental sources. Often working with the business organizations on Maui in the 1990s was the Office of Economic Development, a section of the county government in the mayor's office.

The MVB operated, related Marsha Wienert, its executive director, as "the marketing arm for Maui County."[5] The main work of the MVB lay in promoting tourism on Maui, which involved advertising in the media, making presentations to groups on the mainland, and working to attract conferences and other events to Maui. Representatives of the MVB also testified at public hearings on issues that might affect the visitor industry. The MVB grew out of the work of the Hawai'i Visitors Bureau (HVB) and the Maui County Visitors Association (MCVA). Founded in the early twentieth century, the HVB promoted the Hawaiian Islands to mainland America and other parts of the world. It received about 70 percent of its funding from the state government, with the remainder coming from private businesses. Business leaders on Maui formed the MCVA as an independent organization in 1974, "whose sole purpose," one of its founders later recalled, "was the marketing of this county to U.S. mainlanders."[6]

Divisions of opinion hindered efforts by the HVB and the MCVA to secure public funding in the early 1980s. With tourism a new part of Maui's economy, not all residents believed that it should be promoted with tax dollars. Only after heated debate did the Maui County Council support efforts by the HVB to win a larger appropriation from the state legislature in 1980. Some council members noted that "the State derives a great deal of income from the tourist industry" and argued that this fact justified appropriations for the HVB. Others, however, questioned the use of public funding for advertising that would increase private profits for hotel and resort owners. Two years later, as Maui's economy wallowed in a recession, much the same issue arose, when the county council considered helping fund the MCVA. Again, some members opposed using public funds to support advertising. Only by a divided vote did the county council approve the use of the funds by the MCVA. By 1984 the council was contributing $200,000 annually, five times the amount that the MCVA was receiving each year from the HVB.[7]

By the 1990s qualms about public funding for the HVB and the MVB had been allayed. With tourism Maui's lifeblood, the county government worked closely with the MVB. In 1989 the county provided the MVB with $500,000, and by 1998 county funding had risen to $3.3 million. As Wienert explained, in the 1980s there had been some reluctance to use public monies to support the work of the MVB, but those doubts largely vanished in the following decade. "It was perceived to be just for the hotels," she observed, "and people did not have any idea how it affected the rest of the economy. . . . There was a huge learning curve." Maui's residents were, in fact, learning. In 1998, for the fourth year in a row, Linda Lingle, mayor of Maui County, gave the keynote address at the MVB's annual banquet, lauding cooperation between government and business.[8]

Tensions of a different sort remained. Maui's visitor industry leaders had long complained that the outer islands suffered from neglect relative to O'ahu in the promotional efforts of the HVB. By the late 1990s such complaints were being eased. Wienert noted that the HVB "was perceived at one time as being very O'ahu-oriented. . . . We have been very aggressive in getting our voice heard," she continued. "It has gone a long way." She was correct. When a new statewide organization, the Hawai'i Tourism Authority, was established in 1998, the body was more representative of the outer islands than earlier such organizations had been. "The situation has improved somewhat following relentless lobbying," observed the *Maui News*.[9] Terminology reflected thoughts. Once called "outer" islands, the islands beyond O'ahu became known as "neighbor" islands.

Often working closely with the MVB was the MHA. Formed in the mid-1980s, the MHA was "the baby" of Lynn Britton, remembered Vencl, who headed the MHA (as well as the Maui Chamber of Commerce) in 1998. In the mid-1980s Britton had been president of the Maui Chamber of Commerce, and "through her networking at the Chamber she realized there was a need specifically for lobbying for the hotels." When Britton went on to other ventures, Vencl, who had worked at a variety of positions in Maui's tourist industry, took over as executive director of the MHA.[10]

The MHA performed three major tasks. First, it brought hotels and condominium complexes together with the vendors of supplies. Some thirty major properties, including fifteen of the largest hotels on Maui, and roughly 125 suppliers belonged to the MHA by the late 1990s. The MHA created programs, the most prominent of which was a trade fair, by which the managers of the properties and the vendors could get to know each other better. Second, the MHA sponsored community programs of special interest to its members. The MHA underwrote programs in Maui's junior and senior high schools designed "to give exposure to the [visitor] industry and change the image in the minds of young people about the industry." Paid internships were available for interested students. Finally, the MHA engaged in lobbying on tourism-related issues. "Our primary function is to lobby . . . the council, the mayor, the state," observed Vencl, "to educate all of them about the hotel industry, the economy."[11]

Often working with business groups, especially the MVB and the MHA, was the Office of Economic Development (OED) located in the office of the mayor of Maui County. Begun by Mayor Lingle in 1991–92, the OED was headed by Robbie Guard in the mid-1990s. Growing up on O'ahu but attending college in California, Guard considered herself "a Hawai'i girl, born and raised." She moved to Maui to become the deputy director of the OED, recruited for the position. When the director left to help develop the MRTP, Guard became the head of the OED. With a staff of six, she oversaw an annual budget of about $5 million. Much of that budget, about $3.3 million, went through the OED to the MVB; for, as Guard explained, "we contract everything out to them for marketing." The MVB then used the funds to promote tourism on Maui. While primarily engaged in stimulating tourism, the OED was involved in other economic matters. Guard was especially interested in promoting movie making and specialized agriculture on Maui.[12]

Work in 1998–99 on a ten-year plan for tourism on Maui showed how close the ties between the MVB, the MHA, and the OED could be. The initial push for long-term planning for tourism came from Mayor Lingle. For some time she had been asking Wienert to develop a ten-year plan; with Lingle soon to leave as Maui's mayor, Wienert thought the time was ripe to do so. Working with Guard and Vencl, Wienert asked, "What do we want to leave for the next generation?" As the planners envisioned matters, their scheme would encompass four major topics: "culture, environment, physical development, and work force." By the summer of 1998 about sixty people from different walks of life on Maui, including members of environmental organizations and Native Hawaiian groups, worked on task forces involved in the planning effort. The initial results seemed promising. As Wienert explained, "One of the key things that has come out of the process is that we need to establish a carrying capacity" for Maui — that is, to determine how many people Maui's infrastructure and natural resources could support. It was a very "exciting" undertaking, thought Vencl, for "you find out how close we are in what we want for Maui and yet how far away we all are."[13]

Business Leaders

If business organizations were important in Maui's development, so were individual business leaders. They were of all persuasions, ranging from those who sought rapid economic development at any cost to those who sincerely tried to find ways to reconcile economic development, especially for the visitor industry, with environmental concerns. Colin Cameron, who came from a well-established *haole* family on Maui, and whom we have already met in Chapter 1, was for decades one of the acknowledged business heavyweights on Maui.

Born in 1927 at Pā'ia, Cameron dominated business and civic developments on Maui in the postwar years to a greater extent than any other business leader. The son of J. Walter Cameron and Frances Baldwin, Colin traced his lineage on his mother's side back to Charlotte and Dwight Baldwin, who had come to Maui as missionaries in 1836. The Baldwins' son, Henry (Colin's maternal grandfather), had been one of the founders of resort developers Alexander and Baldwin. Colin's father had come to Maui in 1924, married, and started the Maui Pineapple Company. Colin grew up at the family home in Makawao with his sister Mary, nicknamed "Maizie." He was later described as having enjoyed "riding horseback" and "fishing off Kaho'olawe in a sampan" as a child. Colin attended high school at the elite Punahou School in Honolulu and the Deerfield Academy in Massachusetts. After service in the navy during World War II, he earned bachelor's and master's degrees from Harvard University, finishing his academic education in 1953.[14]

Cameron began what would become a decades-long career at the Maui Land and Pineapple Company, the successor to Maui Pineapple, as a spray superintendent. By 1964 he had become the firm's executive vice-president and general manager. After temporarily leaving Maui Land and Pineapple when Baldwin Packers (owned by Alexander and Baldwin) bought the company, Cameron successfully spearheaded his family's efforts to regain control of the firm in 1969. The Camerons purchased Maui Land and Pineapple from Alexander and Baldwin for $16 million. Over the next two decades Cameron fended off unwanted takeover attempts by a corporate raider and led Maui Land and Pineapple into new ventures. In the realm of agriculture, Cameron had the firm sell its pineapple to more than one hundred private-label distributors, a strategy that generally proved more profitable than had selling under its own brand name. Most important, Cameron took Maui Land and Pineapple into resort development at Kapalua. By 1998, six years after Cameron had died of a heart attack, the results of his business moves were clear. The pineapple operations of Maui Land and Pineapple generated $98

million in revenues and $5.5 million in operating profits; the company's re-
sort operations, while accounting for smaller revenues of $42 million, returned
operating profits of $5.2 million.[15] At a time when many Hawaiian pineapple
companies were in trouble, these were good results.

Cameron's position at the head of Maui Land and Pineapple led him into
a broad range of business and cultural activities. Cameron served as a director of other firms important to Maui's development — the Bank of Hawai'i,
Maui Electric, and the Haleakalā Ranch. He was instrumental in establishing
the Maui Economic Development Board (MEDB) and the high-technology
park. Beyond Maui, Cameron was a director and vice-president of the High
Technology Development Corporation of Hawai'i. Cameron was also the
president of Maui Publishing, which owned the *Maui News*. A writer of poetry in some of his scarce spare time, Cameron took an active part in Maui's
cultural development. More than a figurehead, he helped set up the Lahaina
Restoration Foundation, the Maui Community Arts and Cultural Center, the
Kapalua Music Festival, and the Nature Conservancy of Hawai'i. His firm
founded the Kapalua Nature Society and supported partnerships in watershed conservation.

As Maui developed a more diversified economy and as more groups came
to play deciding roles in the island's economic growth, no single business
leader arose to claim Colin Cameron's mantle. The examples of Michael
Lyons II, like Cameron a business leader from a longtime *haole* family, and
Everett Dowling, a newcomer to the island, suggest some of the ways businesspeople have sought economic growth for Maui in recent years.

Although born on O'ahu, Lyons considered himself to be a Maui native.
"I'm from Maui, fifth-generation from Maui," he stressed. His father was a
graduate of the United States Naval Academy and an officer in the navy, and
his family moved back to Maui after the conclusion of World War II. Lyons
attended local schools, then the Kate School in California, a preparatory
school. After graduating from Williams College, Lyons was employed by the
Bank of Hawai'i in 1959. For the next forty years he "worked on all of the islands, almost exclusively as a branch-banker." In 1999 he was the senior vice-
president and district manager for Maui. Through his financial work Lyons
also became "involved in a lot of community activities."[16]

A staunch believer in economic development, Lyons has observed that "if
you don't have economic development, you stagnate; we have to have jobs."

As the head of the Bank of Hawai'i on Maui, Michael
Lyons II was involved in many development plans.
(Courtesy of Michael Lyons II)

He has long favored the development of a diversified economy on Maui —
like Cameron, he was a charter member of the MEDB — but has viewed
tourism as vital to Maui's future. "One of the things I like to say facetiously,"
Lyons has noted, "is that if we can keep the tourists on the beaches everybody will be happy." He has not seen this goal as being at odds with environmentalism on Maui. In fact, his eldest son was the manager of a preserve
for the Nature Conservancy on Maui. What Lyons has seen as "an anti-
business mentality" on the part of state government officials, a perception
shared by many businesspeople in the Hawaiian Islands, has perhaps most
attracted his ire. "What you have," Lyons has observed, is a state government that has created "a lot of regulations, high taxes, all kinds of impedi-
ments for business."

While Cameron and Lyons had extensive family ties to Maui, Everett Dowling did not. Born in 1959, Dowling grew up in Fredericksburg, Virginia, where his family owned real estate and billboard enterprises. Dowling earned his undergraduate degree at nearby Randolph-Macon College, majoring in business. He then worked for several years for David Murdock of Cal Pac Construction and Oceanic Properties on development projects. Dowling went on to earn a master of business administration (MBA) degree at Babson College in 1986, while continuing to work for Murdock into 1989. This labor was a real education, for, as Dowling later recalled, Murdock was involved in all sorts of real estate developments, "everything" from residential to commercial projects, including hotels, golf courses, and resorts. Murdock was engaged mainly in developments in Southern California, but in the mid-1980s he became involved with Castle and Cooke and acquired a one-quarter interest in the firm. Subsequently, Castle and Cooke purchased Tenneco West with developments in the Southwest and West.[17]

It was Murdock's business interests that brought Dowling to the Hawaiian Islands. "I was coming over here frequently," Dowling later explained, and, as time progressed, "I was looking for an opportunity to be on my own and came across some opportunities here." Dowling opened his real estate development firm, the Dowling Company Inc., in March 1989. He chose Maui because "it's a great place, with very warm people, a great climate, a good lifestyle." Dowling recalled that doing business on Maui then "was fun. . . . The boom was still going, so it was an interesting time." Dowling was soon involved in a large project in Central Maui — a 1,000-acre expansion of Kahului called Maui Lani, which he sold out of in 1991 — and then in numerous projects elsewhere on the island.

In reflecting on his work on Maui, Dowling believed that the development process was (and is) about the same as anywhere else, consisting of "basically, just trying to identify demand and then trying to satisfy that demand. . . . What are people looking for? What services do they need? What price range in housing is in demand? Are supplies sufficient?" These were the questions Dowling asked. Not surprisingly, networking was especially important as Dowling got started. As he put it, it was important to "just try and be out there and interact with people as much as possible." When he first came to Maui, Dowling was "involved in a whole lot of organizations, and that created an opportunity to meet people and accelerated my initiation to Maui." Those organizations included the Maui United Way, the Boy Scouts, the Montessori School, and Seabury Hall (a private school). To the extent that doing business on Maui differed from work on the mainland, the difference lay in geography: That is, explained Dowling, everybody seemed to know each other on Maui. This circumstance heightened the need, Dowling believed, to maintain a reputation for high-quality work in tune with community desires. "What goes around comes around really quickly," he observed. "If you do the right things, you have an opportunity to develop a good reputation." On the other hand, he noted, "if you make the wrong decisions, you have a pretty high probability of being blacklisted."

There could be tension between the need for business profits and community desires, Dowling acknowledged. "If community concerns necessitate a design for a project that's not profitable," Dowling stated, "then we just pass on it." Over time, Dowling also came to realize that you cannot please everybody. "You're always going to have a group of constituents for one issue that perhaps you're never going to satisfy," he has noted. "It just goes with the business." He continued, "There's always a certain element that doesn't want any change." Maui, like most communities, Dowling lamented, has a "no-growth" group.

Hailed as a "new breed of developer" by some, Dowling has shown more sensitivity for Native Hawaiian and environmental issues than many developers have. He has served as a member of the Maui/Lāna'i Islands Burial Council, which has been active in protecting Hawaiian burial sites.[18] A strong supporter of education, Dowling was on the board of directors of Babson College and the board of regents of the University of Hawai'i. He hoped that at some point the University of Hawai'i could open a four-year college on Maui. Involved in a number of the issues analyzed in this volume, Dowling was best known for a controversial real estate development in Upcountry Maui called Kulamalu.

Environmentalism and Environmental Groups

While business groups were important in influencing developments on Maui, so were environmental organizations. Concern for the preservation of Maui's environment began in the 1950s and 1960s. Those few conservationists who lived on the island then focused their interest on the Kīpahula Valley, where the commercialization of 'Ohe'o Gulch, called the "Seven Sacred Pools" by

Shown here at the site for Kulamalu, Everett Dowling was
actively involved in land development projects on Maui
during the 1990s. (Courtesy of Everett Dowling and Tony
Novak-Clifford, © 1999)

promoters of tourism, seemed imminent. Preserved through the combined
work of local residents and outside capitalists, mainly Laurence Rockefeller,
this area is now part of Haleakalā National Park.[19] Environmental issues became much more pronounced on Maui in the 1970s and 1980s, paralleling
developments on the mainland.

"Environmentalism," the historian Hal Rothman has written, "is one of
the most important new dimensions to appear in American society in the

post-1945 world. . . . Part social movement, part manifestation of increasing affluence and privilege of American society and different from the conservation movement that preceded it," he has noted, "environmentalism took center stage in the transformation of the values and mores of the second half of the twentieth century." A widespread movement, environmentalism "soon became a middle ground," Rothman has observed, a "universal goal as Americans came to believe in an amorphous right called 'the quality of life.'" The passage of clean air, clean water, wilderness protection, and endangered species acts by Congress in the 1960s and 1970s and the establishment of the Environmental Protection Agency by President Richard Nixon in 1970 signaled that environmentalism had reached a new stage of development.[20]

The publication in 1970 of *Maui: The Last Hawaiian Place,* a book dedicated to the preservation of wild places on Maui, by the Friends of the Earth suggested that environmentalism was growing in significance on Maui. In the 1970s the *Maui Sun* newspaper was especially important in popularizing environmentalism on Maui. Opposing what its editor saw as the overdevelopment of Maui, annual issues called "Condomania" featured maps of all of the developments that had been built in the previous twelve months. This publication "dramatically indicated what the changes were that were taking place," remembered Dick Mayer, an early activist. In 1973 the *Maui News* observed that some on Maui were "afraid that the island is on the verge of over-development"; when the noted biologist and environmental writer Paul Ehrlich came to Maui a year later, the newspaper gave his visit extensive coverage. "The speed with which things are happening here," Ehrlich was quoted as saying, "is frightening." Spurred by such publicity, people on Maui often became interested first in a specific issue, such as preserving a particular beach, and later went on to become deeply involved in more environmental matters.[21]

As environmental issues developed, mainland environmental groups established chapters on the Hawaiian Islands. The Sierra Club set up a Hawaiian chapter, which, in turn, had a Maui group. Beyond sponsoring outdoor activities, the Sierra Club became involved in environmental issues, including many of those dealt with in this book. Through their newsletter, public testimony, legal actions, and, more recently, their Web site, Sierra Club members have influenced the outcome of numerous issues. Active in the 1980s, particularly under the leadership of Mary Evanson, the Sierra Club on Maui became, according to Lucienne de Naie, its conservation chair, "burned out" in the mid-1990s. Within a few more years, however, the Maui group had reorganized and, with about 350 members, was once again engaged in many issues. Similarly, the Audubon Society established a Maui chapter. While involved in a narrower range of activities than their counterparts in the Sierra Club, Audubon Society members played important roles when bird life was threatened, as they thought it was with regard to airport matters.[22]

Two grassroots organizations were most important in stimulating environmentalism on Maui. The first was the Life of the Land, which extended its activities from Oʻahu to Maui in the early 1970s and which, more than any other single organization, started people thinking about threats to the natural environment. The second was Maui Tomorrow. This organization had personnel ties to the Life of the Land and became the leading champion of environmental issues on Maui in the 1990s.

Life of the Land owed its existence to Madelyn "Benni" D'Enbeau and her husband, Anthony "Tony" Hodges. D'Enbeau had come to the Hawaiian Islands with her family right after World War II, when she was three and a half years old. After graduating from the Punahou School, she went to Stanford University, earning a bachelor's degree in history in 1963 and a master's degree in education a year later. In 1963 D'Enbeau married Hodges, who had also graduated from Stanford. After Hodges served a stint in the air force, the couple moved to the Hawaiian Islands, where Hodges flew as a pilot for Hawaiian Airlines for a short time.[23] Living in Honolulu, the couple was dismayed by the polluted conditions of beaches and, along with several friends, sought to improve matters. Around 1968, D'Enbeau later recalled, as "a group of women, mothers, we began to be really concerned about the sewage that at that time was being dumped off Waikīkī. . . . There were five or six of us that got interested in trying to do something about that," she continued. "We passed out literature at Waikīkī; one brochure was entitled 'You Swim in Our Sewage' and had a toilet on the front."[24]

This effort was a grassroots one. As D'Enbeau explained, at the time "no one had even heard the word 'ecology'" in Hawaiʻi. In 1969 Tony ran for the U.S. Senate as a Democrat. "He ran on an environmental platform" in the primary, explained D'Enbeau. "It was a brand-new concept; he rode a bike everywhere." Although he lost to the well-established Daniel Inouye, Tony "created a lot of excitement at the university; a lot of young people came and joined in." By then the Hodgeses had started an art gallery with another couple, and those interested in environmental issues met there to discuss what to do next. "We sat around trying to decide, we wanted to form some type of organization," D'Enbeau recalled. Gavan Daws, who would later become well known for his writing about relationships between politics and land development in the Hawaiian Islands, lived across the street and belonged to this group. "Gavan was the one," D'Enbeau remembered, "who came up with the name 'Life of the Land'" ("Life of the Land" is part of the motto of the State of Hawai'i).[25]

An incisive, if fairly critical, assessment of Life of the Land published in 1974 observed that "while many of its aims appear admirable," the group was "poorly organized." Confrontation through court cases was its preferred method of operation. "Middle class teachers and professionals," the essay continued, "appear most active [among its members] and energy is devoted towards the prevention of special privilege, landscape change, the high cost of land, and the invasion of attractive beach front sites by outsiders."[26]

After receiving newspaper coverage for their beach protests, the Hodgeses moved on to other matters. In the early 1970s Life of the Land unsuccessfully opposed the building of a new runway for the Honolulu airport, on the grounds that the construction would destroy one of the reefs in the city's harbor.[27] O'ahu remained the center of activities for Life of the Land. However, as president of Life of the Land, Hodges found himself traveling to Maui to confer with lawyers willing to handle environmental lawsuits, for there were few such attorneys on O'ahu. D'Enbeau had come to Maui earlier for a vacation after earning a master's in history from the University of Hawai'i. In 1971 she moved to Maui and bought a house in Ha'ikū. Tony began commuting to and from O'ahu, with Life of the Land "going great guns."[28]

Described as very charismatic by many who knew him, Tony Hodges acted as a "guru" for environmentalists. In 1972 he ran for mayor of Maui County, losing, as did several other candidates, to Elmer Cravalho. Still, even in defeat Hodges attracted attention to environmental issues, just as he had in his earlier senatorial campaign.[29] By 1973, in fact, a member of the Maui County Council was complaining that developers were engaged in "a running battle with Life of the Land." Even so, Life of the Land was never firmly established on Maui, for Hodges was not an organization builder.[30] On Maui, however, organization was not everything. Individuals could make a difference; as we shall see, individual members of Life of the Land often took important stands on environmental issues concerning Maui.

Formed in 1989, Maui Tomorrow had no direct organizational ties to Life of the Land, but many of its founders had been involved in the earlier body's work. Many of those starting Maui Tomorrow — Anthony Rankin, Rick Sands, and Mark Sheehan, among others — had been especially active in an effort during the 1980s to have Mākena Beach preserved as a state park. As Sheehan, who served as Maui Tomorrow's president in the late 1990s, recalled, Maui Tomorrow was formed "so that instead of just reacting to developments, we could be more proactive."[31] Maui Tomorrow grew out of a discussion group started by Rankin. For a year the fledgling organization depended on a California physician for its financing, coming into its own with the acquisition of a grant from a foundation in San Francisco.[32] Maui Tomorrow attracted islandwide attention when its leaders publicized a "build-out scenario" for their island. They calculated what the population of Maui would be if all of the developments approved by the county council were actually constructed. They then presented their findings, a much larger population than had been suspected, at a council meeting and at meetings of many of Maui's community associations.[33]

Maui Tomorrow became Maui's largest environmental organization, claiming 700 members in 1994 and more than 1,000 four years later. Many of these were newcomers to Maui, who in Sheehan's words were "people who come here and don't like the progressive urbanization of the island." About 10 percent of the members were mainland residents who visited Maui for vacations. About half of Maui Tomorrow's members lived in Upcountry Maui, and most were well-off financially. Mayer, a longtime member, observed that Maui Tomorrow "has people in there for all kinds of reasons. . . . I think many of them have a New Age aspect" to their lives, he speculated. One commonality, Mayer thought, was that "all would like a less-developed, less-material lifestyle." Even as Maui Tomorrow grew, its organizational culture remained informal. Its members met about once a month, except in the summer, when, as Sheehan explained, "things get a little slack." Sheehan observed tongue in cheek that he had become president "by being out of the room and going to the bathroom" at the meeting during which elections were held.[34]

Educated at the University of California, Berkeley, during the turbulent 1960s, Sheehan earned a doctorate in education from that institution. "Burned out" by activities in which he had engaged at Berkeley, Sheehan taught in a high school at Santa Cruz, which, he soon discovered, was another "intense experience." After engaging in "consciousness training" at the University of California, Santa Cruz, Sheehan visited Maui in 1970 and moved to the island three years later. He taught on Maui for about a decade, during which time he became increasingly involved in environmental matters, especially the effort to preserve Mākena Beach. He entered the real estate profession in the 1980s. His decision to go into real estate resulted from self-questioning. He asked himself: "Where is there opportunity? Where can I make enough money to buy land myself?" Sheehan became president of Landmark Maui Properties and also served as a president of the Makawao Community Association.[35]

Maui Tomorrow had as its mission "to advance the protection of the island of Maui's precious natural areas and prime open space for recreational use and aesthetic value, to promote the concept of ecologically sound development, to preserve the opportunity for a rural lifestyle on Maui." At any given time, Maui Tomorrow members were involved in about twenty issues, which they divided into three groups of priorities. Through testimony at public hearings, court challenges, talks to local community groups, and the maintenance of an elaborate site on the Internet, they publicized environmental causes. Pulling together many different strands of thought, the organization produced a thirty-minute video on Maui's environment in 1998.[36]

Maui Tomorrow members did not want to halt all development on Maui; rather, they desired to make growth "sustainable." Mayer perhaps best explained what that meant. The term "sustainable growth," he observed, "means growth in perpetuity," development that would not increase "the pressure on the physical environment." It meant, above all, "a higher quality of life using fewer physical resources." Sustainable growth "does not mean you will not have any change," he emphasized, but "you don't grow at the expense of future generations." Ideally, Mayer would like to see people on Maui "get back to an environment that over the long term is self-sufficient — what is the carrying capacity of this island without depending on outside resources?"[37]

Environmental Leaders

No single story can capture how some of Maui's residents became engaged in environmental matters, but sketches of how Dick Mayer, Isaac Hall, and Sally Raisbeck became involved illustrate the range of paths that was followed. Well educated and reasonably financially secure, all three moved to Maui from the mainland, bringing with them ideas developed from their earlier experiences. In important respects, their lives typified those of *haole* environmentalists on Maui.

Mayer spent his childhood in the Boston area. His parents came to the United States as Jews fleeing Nazi Germany. "Both left Nazi Germany as refugees," Mayer later recalled. "My father had been in a concentration camp." A former lawyer, Mayer's father entered the United States in 1940 on one of the "last boats to leave Germany." Born in Boston in 1942, Mayer graduated from the Boston Latin School in 1959. He attended Brandeis University in nearby Waltham, earning a bachelor's degree in economics in 1963. Foreshadowing his future work, Mayer became especially interested in institutional as opposed to theoretical economics. As Mayer later explained, he was "interested in the real world of race relations, economic development, and international affairs."[38]

After graduation Mayer entered the Peace Corps, serving in Nepal for two years, which he later called "a really transforming experience." Mayer was involved in community development, which "meant establishing the political structure for the country." He worked in a group responsible for the establishment of village councils in thirty-five communities. His experiences in Nepal emphasized for Mayer the importance of "community development work" and gave him "the confidence that people who are poor can also be very happy." His work in Nepal also, Mayer thought, "molded me to be antidevelopment here on Maui."

From the Peace Corps, Mayer went to graduate school at the University of Washington, where he studied international business and economic geography. Upon the completion of a master's degree, Mayer moved to Maui in 1967. Maui Community College was opening a liberal arts program, and Mayer was soon teaching courses there in world geography and economics. After living for a year in Wailuku and for three years in Makawao, he moved to Kula. Looking out over his land in 1999, he proudly noted that "this was a grassy field when I moved in here; I planted the trees, every one of them."

Mayer became involved in environmental efforts in the early 1970s. Some of his work was at Maui Community College. Mayer taught a course on "social ecology" in 1970, when the first Earth Day took place. For Maui's second Earth Day, Mayer organized a series of seminars for his county's business and political leaders to discuss environmental and developmental matters. At-

Dick Mayer was a leading environmentalist on Maui from the 1970s.

tended by members of the Maui Chamber of Commerce, the county council, and officers of major businesses such as East Maui Irrigation and the Wailea Development Company, as well as by leaders of Life of the Land, the meetings were designed to give everyone present "the chance to learn and appreciate the position of other groups."[39]

Mayer's leadership in Earth Day events led him deeper into environmental concerns. Backed by Mayor Elmer Cravalho, Mayer was appointed to fill a vacant seat on the Maui Planning Commission in 1972. In this position Mayer worked for environmental protection, seeking to do so through cooperation rather than confrontation. He observed at the time, "I don't think you close down the sugar mills just because they're polluting. . . . You work around these things."[40] Still, his work led Mayer "to involvement in protesting against various types of development as being environmentally improper."

Particularly important to Mayer were efforts, partly successful, to alter plans to develop the Māʻalaea region — plans to build a larger harbor, construct an oil refinery, and build a major power plant there. From these beginnings Mayer became involved in a wide range of community development and environmental activities, both on his own accord and as a leading member of Maui Tomorrow.[41]

In his environmental efforts Mayer often found himself working with Isaac Hall. About the same age as Mayer, Hall was born in 1944 and grew up in New Canaan, Connecticut, the son of a corporate attorney practicing law in New York City. Hall went to a private school in Connecticut and then to Princeton, where he studied religion and philosophy, graduating in 1966. Hall next attended the Union Theological Seminary. The seminary was, Hall later explained, "a political hotbed at the time . . . with a lot of organizing in the South and a lot of political, leftish organizing around Vietnam." Hall "got involved in both there."[42]

Work in Harlem was for Hall what the Peace Corps in Nepal was for Mayer. At that time the seminary had an arrangement whereby a student could work outside it and still be connected to it. Hall taught high school dropouts in a Harlem storefront school in 1968. "Things that happened then absolutely shaped everything I've done since then," Hall later reflected. Like many college students in the 1960s, Hall was optimistic about the future and believed strongly that he and others could help shape it, even after he was clubbed by construction workers during a protest march in Lower Manhattan. In New York City Hall was exposed to the Black Power and Black Muslim movements, which he remembered as "hot and heavy." Hall was, he later thought, "getting acculturated." He was also coming to recognize that the ministry and social work were not for him.

Hall believed he saw "a lot of progress" being made through legal actions and decided to go to Columbia Law School. He "wanted to do poverty law," he later recalled. "I wasn't that interested in environmental law at that time." Hall graduated from Columbia Law School in 1971. He received a fellowship to work for a year in Harlem Assertive Rights, a Legal Aid group, and worked on administrative segregation cases in New York City prisons. "We worked on prisoners' rights all over," well beyond Harlem, Hall later explained. It was an "intense" activity, and Hall became temporarily "disillusioned with law," going to work as a carpenter for about a year in New York City's Lower East

Side. By this time Hall had been in New York for seven years and wanted to leave the city.

Hall moved to the Hawaiian Islands in 1973. He visited friends in the islands and, like so many others who first came on vacation, decided to stay, settling on Maui. Hall did not immediately go into the practice of law. Instead, he continued to labor as a carpenter, working on "some of the burgeoning projects in Lahaina." An ongoing effort to have the navy give up Kaho'olawe, an island near Maui, as a bombing range first drew Hall into environmental and Native Hawaiian matters. Around 1975 Hall "ran into" Emmett Aluli and others leading the campaign to save Kaho'olawe. "I was very interested in what they were doing and decided to get involved," Hall later explained; he became one of the protesters who went to Kaho'olawe and was arrested for trespassing. Hall "eventually confessed" that he was a lawyer and helped prepare lawsuits that succeeded in halting the bombing.

Hall's concern for Kaho'olawe led him into other work. In 1976–77 he received two grants from the Hawai'i Committee for the Humanities, which involved him in grassroots community matters. The first award enabled him to set up community panels to discuss land and water issues, among other topics, across Maui. As part of this work, Hall met the *kūpuna* (elders) of Native Hawaiian communities, which was important for him in his later career and life. Hall's second grant permitted him to establish statewide panels to discuss federal and state government responsibilities to Native Hawaiians, especially on land matters. Meanwhile, Hall passed the Hawaiian bar examination. Regaining the enthusiasm he had earlier possessed, he worked for Legal Aid on Maui, which broadened further his Native Hawaiian and environmental contacts. Hall stayed with Legal Aid for eight years, leaving in 1986 to open his own law office in Wailuku. At first Hall was concerned that he would no longer be able to concentrate on environmental and community issues; however, as he later explained, "it turned out that some of the community groups that I had been working for could come up with enough money so that I could make it work." Moreover, businesses and business groups also had environmental problems, Hall discovered, "so I could work on their behalf." Over time Hall became one of the leading environmental lawyers in the Hawaiian Islands.

Sally Raisbeck's movement into environmentalism was different from the routes taken by Hall and Mayer. Raisbeck had no background in community organizing or activism before coming to Maui. She grew up in Illinois, where she attended the University of Chicago. She soon transferred to Stanford University, majoring in mathematics, where, she later recalled, "I was usually the only woman in my classes." A member of Phi Beta Kappa, she graduated in 1950 at the age of twenty. Raisbeck married a graduate student in physics a year before she graduated, and upon graduation she took a position with the Stanford Research Institute (SRI) for seven years while her husband worked on his doctorate. At the SRI Raisbeck analyzed data from nuclear bomb tests, working on "the very first computer Stanford University had, which had 250 words of memory and which was programmed with wires." When her husband received his doctorate, she quit work to raise a family in Palo Alto.[43]

In 1961 Raisbeck moved with her husband to Lexington, Massachusetts, when he took a job in nearby Cambridge. Restless, Raisbeck went back to work when her youngest child started school. Securing a position in 1965 at Lincoln Laboratory, she found herself helping debug the brand-new IBM 360 computer, working on the first model in use in the United States. With that task completed, Raisbeck took three years off to look after her children and then returned to Lincoln Laboratory to engage in additional high-technology work, mainly radar and satellite communications. After a divorce in 1979, she moved to Maui.

Lincoln Laboratory was starting a laser project on Maui, as part of President Ronald Reagan's Strategic Defense Initiative, sometimes called the "Star Wars" project. Raisbeck had a sister living on O'ahu then. "I had visited her," Raisbeck remembered, "and I just hated the winters in Massachusetts. . . . So, I came out to Maui from Lincoln." She worked for Lincoln on Maui for four years, becoming increasingly disillusioned. As Raisbeck later explained, she came to believe that "the PR was more important than the fact. It really bothered me." Raisbeck also had Quaker friends and was impressed by the work of an Australian peace advocate. She took early retirement in 1986, believing that "it was the right thing to do."

Raisbeck became increasingly involved in Maui's environmental issues. She had seen development in the San Francisco Bay Area, which, she later stated, "made me ill, it actually made me ill because it hurt so much." Looking at Maui, when she first came in 1982, she thought, "My God, this is beautiful, but I know it's going to change. I know the beaches are going to be solid con-

Sally Raisbeck typified many of those who sought to obtain environmental protection by entering politics on Maui. (Courtesy of Sally Raisbeck)

crete." Raisbeck felt at first that she should not get involved and told herself, "Don't break your heart over this." However, when she retired and had free time, she "just could not maintain that attitude." Raisbeck thought she could just go to the Maui County Council and tell them they "should not do this bad thing." That is, she urged council members to put the brakes on development. She found that most council members ignored her. Greatly disturbed, Raisbeck concluded, "I thought this isn't the way politics is supposed to work, how come? And so finally I decided I'll run."

Raisbeck ran for county council twice as a Democrat, in 1988 and 1990, and won in the primary once. She ran a third time in 1992 as a representative of Maui's Green Party. In 1998 she ran for the state legislature, losing in the primary. Throughout her political campaigns Raisbeck's main issue

was "Maui, Maui, don't let it be overrun by development." While not winning office, Raisbeck and others like her influenced Maui's political and economic systems. Politics became much more open, with the county council
more likely to consider different opinions on environmental matters. Moreover, through their involvement in politics, Raisbeck and others publicized
environmental issues and forced modifications to development plans.

The Native Hawaiian Renaissance

Business and environmental bodies interacted with Native Hawaiian groups
in setting policies for Maui's development. The issue of Native Hawaiian rights
was (and is) a complex and highly emotional topic. The Native Hawaiian
Renaissance or Native Hawaiian rights movement was never cohesive. Various Native Hawaiian groups sought the return of lost lands, desired national
independence for Hawai'i, and tried to revive aspects of Hawaiian culture. It
is difficult to date precisely the start of the Native Hawaiian Renaissance, but
the early 1970s stand out as something of a watershed. As Dana Naone Hall,
an activist on Maui, has observed, "the early '70s were crucial in changing
the way Hawaiians, particularly younger Hawaiians, saw themselves in rela-
tion to what has been going on in Hawai'i — the rising tide of development
and the destruction of old neighborhoods, old ways of life, the continuing
threat to native land and native species."[44]

Several events acted as midwives in the birth of the Native Hawaiian Renaissance. "The first real movement," Davianna McGregor, a professor of
ethnic studies at the University of Hawai'i and a Hawaiian rights activist, has
written, "grew up around 1969" in the Kalama Valley on O'ahu. Native Hawaiian pig farmers were being evicted from the last slice of agricultural land
that they held on the island's east end to make way for a housing subdivision. Ironically, the land that they were using was owned by the Bishop Estate.
The Bishop Estate had been set up by Princess Bernice Pauahi Bishop, the
granddaughter of King Kamehameha I, and its revenues were supposed to
support educational efforts, especially the Kamehameha Schools, for Native
Hawaiians. In their opposition to removal, the farmers held high banners
reading "Kokua Hawai'i" ("Help Hawai'i"). In a closely related development at about the same time, Native Hawaiian leaders, adopting the words
on the farmers' banners, formed the group Kokua Hawai'i (Join Together

for Hawai'i) to oppose the appointment of a non–Native Hawaiian to the governing board of the Bishop Estate.[45]

From its beginning, then, a concern for land underlay the Native Hawaiian Renaissance, making it, Haunani-Kay Trask, a professor of Hawaiian studies at the University of Hawai'i and a leader in the Native Hawaiian rights movement, has observed, more like the American Indian movement than the black civil rights movement. As described by Trask, Native Hawaiian efforts moved from "an ongoing series of land struggles throughout the decade of the seventies" to "a larger struggle for native Hawaiian autonomy" in the 1980s. The movement also, she noted, "branched out politically to link up with American Indian activists on the mainland, anti-nuclear independence struggles throughout the South Pacific, and international networks in Asia and at the United Nations." Underlying all of these permutations, however, lay an emphasis on the native relationship to land and the "cultural value of *Aloha 'Āina* (love of the land)."[46]

Nowhere was this concern for the real and symbolic value of land more apparent than in a campaign to change land use on the island of Kaho'olawe. This issue served as a catalyst for the Native Hawaiian Renaissance throughout the Hawaiian Islands. Concerns for Kaho'olawe focused on ending the use of the island as a bombing range by the United States Navy, protecting Hawaiian sites on the island, and restoring the island to near its original state of existence. The smallest major island in the Hawaiian archipelago, Kaho'olawe lies seven miles off South Maui. Eleven miles long and seven miles wide, Kaho'olawe covers 28,600 acres, with its highest hill reaching 1,477 feet above sea level.[47]

People lived on Kaho'olawe before World War II. In precontact times it was known for its abundant fishing resources and limited dryland agriculture. The earliest archaeological sites date to A.D. 900–1000, and perhaps 150 people lived on the island in semipermanent settlements as late as the 1770s. Between 1826 and 1843 the Kingdom of Hawai'i used Kaho'olawe as a place of banishment for crimes such as theft and adultery. Leasing Kaho'olawe for ranching began during the 1850s and continued through the 1930s. By the mid-1880s the island was home to 9,000 goats, 12,000 sheep, 200 head of cattle, and 40 horses. Despite occasional efforts to curb the abuse, these animals overgrazed the island, and Kaho'olawe suffered what a government report called "catastrophic environmental degradation," including the destruction of native vegetation. Only one or two people lived on the island by the 1920s and 1930s.[48]

Beginning in World War II the American military used Kaho'olawe as a bombing range, compounding the damage done by ranching. In 1941 the army signed a sublease with the Kaho'olawe Ranch Company, acquiring bombing rights for a dollar per year. After the attack on Pearl Harbor, Kaho'olawe was appropriated for use as a bombing range and training ground. It was on the island's western beaches that troops held dress rehearsals for landings at Tarawa, Okinawa, and Iwo Jima. In 1953 President Dwight Eisenhower signed an executive order reserving Kaho'olawe for use by the navy and placing the island under the navy's jurisdiction. However, this order also stipulated that the navy would at some point return Kaho'olawe in a condition "reasonably safe for human habitation."[49]

Efforts to have Kaho'olawe restored began in the 1960s. In 1969 the discovery of an unexploded 500-pound bomb in a West Maui field, accidentally dropped during a run on Kaho'olawe, led U.S. Rep. Patsy Mink from Hawai'i to call on the navy to halt the bombing. In the same year Maui County Mayor Elmer Cravalho and the Maui County Council called for the "termination of all military activities" on Kaho'olawe, a request repeated throughout the 1970s. Native Hawaiian groups soon led the way in the effort to halt the bombing. Heading the statewide organization Aboriginal Lands of Hawaiian Ancestry (ALOHA), formed to oppose the bombing, Charles Maxwell, a Native Hawaiian activist living on Maui, thanked county officials for their support in 1973 but observed that "our kupunas saw it [the importance of preserving Kaho'olawe] first."[50]

Protests led to actions. On January 4, 1976, nine people — members of both Hui Alaloa, a Native Hawaiian rights group, and the Native Claims group — "invaded" or landed on Kaho'olawe. Maxwell was a principal organizer of the landing. This event was critical in focusing attention on the island and on Native Hawaiians' demands. "With the invasion of Kaho'olawe," one writer has observed, "the issues concerning the importance of land to Hawaiian culture and the military's desecration of this land became linked." Formed two days after the landing, the Protect Kaho'olawe Association, later renamed the Protect Kaho'olawe 'Ohana (PKO), became the leading group in opposing the bombing. The body sponsored additional landings. On March 7, 1977, George Helm and Kimo Mitchell lost their lives at sea when trying to return to Maui after one such landing. The landings, arrests for trespass, and result-ing trials kept attention riveted on Kaho'olawe.[51]

Protests and a lawsuit by the PKO forced the navy to action. When ar-chaeological surveys undertaken at the order of a federal court revealed that Kaho'olawe contained hundreds of Hawaiian sites, the navy agreed in 1980 to a consent decree to begin planning to protect those sites. The decree also mandated that the navy allow members of the PKO regular access to Kaho'olawe for religious, cultural, educational, and restoration activities. A year later the entire island was placed on the National Register of Historic Places.[52] Even so, restricted bombing continued.

Public support for preservation swelled throughout the 1980s, with grow-ing numbers of *haoles* and Native Hawaiians joining the protest against the bombing. These actions brought results. In 1990 President George Bush tem-porarily halted all bombing, and three years later Congress voted to end the use of the island for military purposes and to return it to the State of Hawai'i. Congress also authorized the expenditure of $400 million to clear Kaho'olawe of unexploded ordnance, a task initially expected to be completed by 2004. (The estimated cost was later reduced and the time period lengthened.) The transfer of Kaho'olawe to the State of Hawai'i occurred in 1994, with the island to be held in trust for Native Hawaiians until the formation of "a sov-ereign Hawaiian nation." The state government, in turn, established the Kaho'olawe Island Reserve Commission to replant the island with native vegetation. More than that, the commission staged ceremonies emphasizing the importance of Native Hawaiian culture in the restoration of Kaho'olawe. A community plan prepared in 1995 stressed that the overarching goal was the "restoration, maintenance and protection of Kaho'olawe's environmen-tal and cultural resources through the management of the island as a *wahi pana* (sacred place) and *pu'uhonua* (refuge), exclusive of the military and commercial intrusions."[53]

Even as restoration efforts began, groups of schoolchildren paddled canoes from South Maui to Kaho'olawe for camping trips designed to teach them about Native Hawaiian culture. Still, not all of the actions of the Kaho'olawe Island Reserve Commission won universal acclaim. The 1995 community plan called for the exclusion of commercial fishing within two miles of Kaho'olawe, and in 1998 such a ban went into effect. Beginning that year only subsistence fishing by Native Hawaiians was allowed, an action that drew howls of protest from some commercial fishermen. In the summer of that year a fisherman from Hilo was convicted of breaking the law.[54]

Efforts to end the bombing of Kaho'olawe resonated with similar attempts elsewhere in the Pacific. Between 1946 and 1958 the United States conducted sixty-eight nuclear tests in the Kawajalein Atoll of the Marshall Islands in Micronesia, a United States Trust Territory. The atoll was also used as the target for American missiles launched from thousands of miles away. Hundreds of local inhabitants were displaced. When negotiations with American authorities proved fruitless, local residents left the island of Ebeye, to which they had been moved, in a series of "sail-ins" in 1969, 1977, and 1978 to try to reoccupy their lands, at least those islands not made too radioactive for habitation. When the newly formed Republic of the Marshall Islands signed an agreement permitting the United States to use the atoll as a missile range for an additional fifty years, further demonstrations followed. A compromise was reached in 1983. The United States agreed to shorten its lease on the missile range to thirty years, fund $10 million in improvements for Ebeye, and return six of the islands in the northern part of the Kawajalein Atoll to their original landowners. Even this new agreement met with some continuing protests.[55]

More than any other single issue, the effort to restore Kaho'olawe energized a new generation of Native Hawaiian leaders and won them considerable support from environmentalists in the *haole* community. From their labors to restore Kaho'olawe, Native Hawaiians branched out to deal with many other issues and formed additional organizations to uphold their rights.

Hui Alanui o Makena was organized in the mid-1980s by Dana Naone Hall; her husband, Isaac Hall; and members of Native Hawaiian families with ties to the Mākena area. (In the Hawaiian language *hui* means group, *ala* means way, and *nui* means great or wide; *alanui* means wide path or highway.) Isaac was involved in the effort to end the bombing of Kaho'olawe, and that movement influenced Dana as well. The Halls worked with Hui Alanui o Makena to oppose the closing of the Old Mākena Road on South Maui by Seibu Hawaii, the builders of the Maui Prince Hotel, part of the Japanese Prince chain. The Mākena Road was part of the ancient Alaloa or King's Highway, also called the Pi'ilani Trail, and was valued by Native Hawaiians as part of their culture on Maui. The road would be closed where it passed between the proposed hotel and the beach upon which the hotel would front. The road would be rerouted uphill from the ocean, widened, and paved.

Dana Naone Hall spoke for many concerned about Native Hawaiian rights in a 1984 appearance before the Maui County Council. "What does trail and road mean anyway, this is English," she asked. "In Hawaiian it is 'Ke Alaloa' — the long way, the way to travel from one place to another." The trail, Hall continued, "keeps close to the shoreline and those of us who travel on it today know the refreshment it gives to be only a few steps away from the ocean, wrapped in sea air and the long looked for glimpse, through the gray companion kiawe, of white sand where it meets the breaking wave and the splash of warm blue water." The proposed new road, she observed, "would move us 800 to 1,000 feet farther away from the shore." It would, Hall concluded, "move us off our ancestral trail and away from our long tradition of already established access to the beaches, bays, and rocky places of the coast."[56]

The formation of Hui Alanui o Makena demonstrates well the importance of personal connections on Maui. Those starting the group were friends or were related by family ties, and most owned land in the Mākena area. Several family groups were involved initially. As Dana later explained, the Kapohakimohewas were "a family that used to own land in the Mākena area." Alice Kuloloio was married to Leslie Kuloloio's father, Wally Kuloloio. Helen Peters was related to the Kuloloios. George Ferreira was "also related to Leslie Kuloloio; Helen is his mother," Dana said. Charley Keau had "family land down there." Edward Chang Sr., who was born at the beginning of the century, was "also related." Maipela Wong, now deceased, was George Ferreira's sister. Esther Campbell spent "part of her childhood in the Mākena area." Ned Goodness "comes from an 'Ulupalakua family and was interested in what was happening." Dana remembers that the Kuloloios and Edward Chang Sr. were particularly active in the group.[57]

Dana did not at first know everyone who would become involved in the effort to preserve the Mākena Road. "We all showed up at a County Council meeting on the Kihei-Makena Community Plan around 1984," she later explained, "and testified at one of the first big meetings at the Kīhei School cafeteria." That was, she remembered, the first time people "massed to talk about this issue." After testifying, those opposed to the road closure met again at a horse stable near where the Maui Prince Hotel was going to be built, discussed matters more, and formed Hui Alanui o Makena.[58]

While preserving the trail was most important for those founding Hui Alanui o Makena, a related issue was more pressing for others. Environmentalists wanted to prevent the nearby 1,100-foot-long Mākena Beach (also known as "Big Beach") from being rezoned from agricultural to urban, which would open the way to its private development. As early as 1978 those trying to preserve the Mākena area petitioned the county council with a plea that would be repeated many times over the next decade: "This is one of the last, and certainly the most beautiful, strongholds left on Maui for local people. Will they still be able to enjoy it for swimming and body-surfing when 3,000 people a day are using it? A road through this area will bring in more people than the beach can support and still maintain its relaxed, remote atmosphere."[59] Opponents of development formed an umbrella organization called State Park at Makena (SPAM), which eventually counted about 4,000 members. Many active in SPAM, including members of Life of the Land, were later important in Maui Tomorrow's work.

If Native Hawaiian and environmental groups often cooperated — as they did on Kaho'olawe — the intersection of the Mākena Road and Mākena Beach issues illustrates how they sometimes clashed. Part of the threatened road closure would have resulted from a land exchange between the State of Hawai'i and Seibu to create a state beach park at Mākena. Members of SPAM, Isaac Hall recalled, wanted the land exchange "to work pretty badly." Along with others in Hui Alanui o Makena, the Halls labored to keep the road open and opposed the land exchange, which brought them into some opposition with SPAM. "There was a lot of conflict between SPAM and us," Hall remembered. "We felt SPAM was being insensitive to Native Hawaiian issues."[60]

However, those involved in the Mākena Road dispute were able to reach a compromise in 1987. The judge overseeing lawsuits on the issues brought in Elmer Cravalho, Maui's former mayor, as a mediator, which proved to be a wise move. Respected by most on Maui, Cravalho reconciled the desires of developers, Native Hawaiians, and environmentalists. The Mākena Road was closed to automobile traffic in front of the new Maui Prince Hotel, allowing guests easy access to the beach. The old road was replaced by a twenty-foot-wide, stone-paved walkway maintained by the hotel, with access granted to all. A new modern highway went uphill around the hotel, continuing south. Seibu also constructed several small parks for the general public and agreed to help preserve Hawaiian culture in South Maui. After additional actions, proponents succeeded in having Mākena Beach designated as a state park.[61] The settlement was especially important for the Halls, for the Mākena Road

Now a state park, Mākena Beach in South Maui was the site of intense controversy in the 1980s.

success allowed them to move in new directions. "The magnitude of the things we were getting involved in took a quantum leap" with Mākena, Isaac observed. Their experiences in the Mākena disputes led the Halls and others in Hui Alanui o Makena into a wide range of Native Hawaiian and environmental issues.[62]

Potentially as far-reaching in their impact on Hawai'i's development as work by Native Hawaiians to preserve their lands and regain lost lands were efforts to reestablish political sovereignty. As the executive director of the Native Hawaiian Legal Corporation observed in 1993, there was considerable disagreement among Native Hawaiians on this issue. He thought there existed three major groupings — one that wanted complete separation from the United States as an independent, internationally recognized Hawaiian nation; another that favored nation-within-a-nation status with federal recognition for a new Native Hawaiian nation; and a third that desired maintaining the political status quo while pressing for redress, reparations, and full control of Hawaiian trust assets by Hawaiians. Probably the single most important statewide Native Hawaiian group was Ka Lāhui Hawai'i, organized in 1987.

Headed by Mililani Trask, Haunani-Kay Trask's sister, the body sought a nation-within-a-nation status for Native Hawaiians. Its members called for federal recognition of Hawaiian sovereignty, including recognition of an identifiable land base. The group opposed efforts to settle sovereignty claims with money rather than land.[63]

While disagreements continued through the 1990s, Native Hawaiians won successes. In 1993 President Bill Clinton signed a joint resolution of Congress formally acknowledging that the overthrow of the Kingdom of Hawai'i a century before had been illegal. The Maui County Council had been asking for such an apology for a decade, calling the action "illegal and immoral." In a statewide election held in 1996, 73 percent of eligible Native Hawaiians voted in favor of establishing some sort of political sovereignty for themselves. Exactly what would occur next was unclear, but in 1997 Maui's Native Hawaiian leaders held a series of meetings to try to bring unity to their work. A year later Maxwell and others met with the U.S. Commission on Civil Rights to try to create an independent government for Native Hawaiians, one that they hoped would be "an authentic government that would serve the people."[64]

Spiritual concerns were also important in the Native Hawaiian Renaissance, running, like land and political issues, through many other matters.[65] Some 150 Native Hawaiians celebrated the start of *makahiki,* a traditional Hawaiian season of peace, relaxation, and spiritual rites, atop Maui's highest peak, Haleakalā, in late 1997; groups repeated the ceremonies in succeeding years. As Maxwell, who took part in the ceremonies, observed, "We Hawaiians don't malama [care] for the mountain. Everything is becoming tourist-oriented. It's time now that the Hawaiian people open this thing up and start a spiritual reawakening."[66] In 1998 the sixth annual East Maui Taro Festival showed just how important Native Hawaiian beliefs remained. Held in Hanā, an area of both luxurious tourist hotels and isolated Native Hawaiian living, the three-day-long event was sacred to many. As one Native Hawaiian explained, "It means going back to our roots, back to the earth, back to the aina, that which feeds and nourishes."[67]

Native Hawaiian Leaders

Just as the examination of no single environmental leader can capture the range of personalities involved in Maui's environmental movement, neither can a look at any one Native Hawaiian leader encompass the many nuances of the Native Hawaiian rights movement on Maui. As in the case of environmentalism, it is necessary to look at a number of leaders to begin to understand the complexities involved.

Charles Pili Keau, who became known to many on Maui as simply "Uncle Charley," was (and is) one of the first modern Native Hawaiian leaders on Maui. Born in Wailuku, he left school after the eighth grade. Stationed in Texas during World War II, Keau returned to Maui after the conflict, where he was among those who worked to get the navy to stop bombing Kaho'olawe. Worried that World War II had loosened family and community ties on Maui, Keau began in the early 1970s to work in a state program to restore historical sites on Maui. He learned archaeology and Hawaiian history with the help of Kenneth Emory, one of the leaders in Polynesian archaeology, who was studying sites on Maui. Dorothy Pyle, a historian of Hawai'i and the Pacific, also encouraged Keau. At Mayor Elmer Cravalho's request, Keau worked with Emory and others to restore two famous *heiau* (religious altars) near Wailuku. From these tasks he went on to archaeological work across Maui over the next two decades, assisting, for example, in the preparation of an inventory of sites at Wailea.[68] In an interview in 1977 Keau explained what he thought had changed on Maui over the past generation and what he believed that meant for the preservation of land. "There was a gap," he thought, "between 1920 and 1970 when Hawaiians wouldn't speak up because they feared that people would misinterpret them." For instance, Keau observed, "a local man believes a special place is Kapu or sacred and he tries to tell someone. . . . The listener may think — this man is silly, superstitious, or trying to scare me," Keau concluded, but "what the local man really means to convey are attitudes of respect, carefulness and preservation."[69]

Central to Keau's work was a sense of place. He saw archaeological work and historic preservation, as he explained in the summer of 1999, as a way to help Native Hawaiians "get their *'āina* back." As he put it, "I teach the Hawaiian way . . . stone, stick." Respect for the natural environment was part of his creed. He urged all on Maui to use water "nicely," to drink it, not use it for golf courses. "Nature is here to stay," he said. "We have to live with it." Avoiding confrontation, Keau believed in "negotiating with people." Hawaiians and non-Hawaiians, he thought, needed "to talk story," to "talk from the heart."[70]

Over time, some believed, events overtook Keau's methods. "For a long time Charley was one of the very few people who spoke on behalf of preserving Hawaiian sites," explained Dana Naone Hall. "All roads led to him for a while." Keau was important in bringing home the significance of the Mākena Road to Dana and others. A recognized poet as well as Native Hawaiian activist, Hall wrote in one of her verses, "Uncle Charley took us all to the heiau / mauka of the beach. / From the beginning he said / the road will not be closed."[71] However, times changed, and Hall thought that Keau was overtaken by more advanced thinking on Native Hawaiian issues, especially with regard to "how active one became on behalf of the sites." Speaking was not always enough, Hall believed. "You had to go the next step." Protests and lawsuits sometimes became necessary.[72]

Dana Naone Hall took those steps as the single most important activist for Native Hawaiian issues on Maui from the 1980s. Born on O'ahu, she grew up on the windward side of the island, which she remembered as "very rural." However, Hall had access to a "big, new public library" and later recalled that "many worlds were in that one building." Hall was deeply influenced by her childhood in a country setting. The presence of the Ka'olau Mountains, she observed, provided "a cultural and imaginative landscape." She felt inspired by the "incredible beauty" of Hawai'i's ocean, mountains, sky, and clouds.[73]

Hall attended Kamehameha Schools and then the University of Hawai'i; she was, she felt, "Hawai'i all the way." She graduated in 1974 majoring in liberal studies, with an undergraduate thesis that was a "small collection of poems." After spending nine months on the mainland, she returned to Hawai'i to teach in her state's Poets in the Schools program on O'ahu and Maui for thirteen years. Hall recalled that "it was a nice way to stay in touch with the kids here." Still, the world beyond beckoned, and for about six years she spent every spring in New York City. Hall also spent one summer in France.[74]

Hall moved to Maui in 1976. Even as she continued to teach, she wrote poetry that was evocative of Hawai'i's people and their relationships to the land and ocean.[75] Moving outward from her efforts to preserve the Mākena Road, Hall became an outspoken proponent of Native Hawaiian rights. As we shall see, nearly every subject along those lines caught her attention, and her involvement often had a marked impact on their outcomes. While certainly forthright, Hall sought in all of her efforts to arrive at accommodations, so that all of the people involved could be reasonably content. In this approach she resembled Keau. However, her methods sometimes differed; lawsuits, protests, and demonstrations were among the techniques she employed.[76]

Dana Naone Hall did not become directly engaged in Native Hawaiian sovereignty matters. She feels that "any resolution should involve the return of land" and is quick to add that each island should exercise independent decision-making power over its land base and resources rather than relying on a centralized, O'ahu-based authority. We have a "very complex, modern set of problems," she emphasizes. "We are going to have to face ourselves," she believes, and the choices for Native Hawaiians will be "extremely difficult."[77]

Charles Kauluwehi Maxwell was a third — and perhaps most controversial — Native Hawaiian activist on Maui, described by the *Maui News* as a "tireless Native Hawaiian leader who was on the scene for any meeting or discussion where Hawaiian rights, local culture or the aina was threatened." At age sixty-one in 1999, Maxwell played significant roles from the 1970s through the 1990s. As we have seen, he was among those seeking the restoration of Kaho'olawe. As a member of the Maui/Lāna'i Islands Burial Council, he sought to preserve Hawaiian burial sites. As chairman of the Hawai'i Advisory Committee to the U.S. Commission on Civil Rights, Maxwell worked with state and federal government authorities to have land returned to Native Hawaiians. As with Keau and Hall, a sense of place, of the ocean and the land, ran through Maxwell's work. In the summer of 1999, for example, he advised an aquatics conference meeting in Honolulu that the best way to restore the inshore fisheries of the Hawaiian Islands, which had suffered an 80 percent decline in their catches during the twentieth century, was to return to the Hawaiian *ahupua'a* system of land and ocean management — the method that treated each island section as a complete unit from the mountains to the sea.[78]

Through his many activities, Maxwell came into contact with Kahu David "Kawika" Kaalakea, and the growing personal bond between the two men brought recognition to Maxwell in late 1998. Preparing for death, Kaalakea, one of Maui's leading *kūpuna,* named Maxwell as his successor as the spiritual leader of Native Hawaiians on Maui. A Catholic, Maxwell declined to take over Kaalakea's Pentecostal religious mantle. However, Maxwell did assume his Hawaiian spiritual responsibilities. These, as Maxwell saw things, meant caring for Maui's environment. In 1998 members of the hula school led by his wife were granted special permission to pick rare silversword plants for their costumes, but they decided not to. "We felt, as Native Hawaiians, we have to set an example," noted Maxwell.[79]

Native and Alien Flora and Fauna

In his poem "Native Plants," published in 1985, René Sylva wrote, "The Hawaiian Plants are social plants. / If you go look underneath the Hawaiian tree / There's all kinds of plants that grow under them." On the other hand, he thought that "the non-native plants are antisocial trees / Like kiawe or eucalyptus or the ironwood / Nothing grows under there."[80] A specialist on Native Hawaiian trees and plants, Sylva was at the time engaged in efforts to revegetate Kaho'olawe. As his verse suggests, flora and fauna viewed as native (endemic) to the Hawaiian Islands had a special place in the hearts of many. At the same time that she was working to preserve the Mākena Road, Dana Naone Hall produced an hour-long video titled "Back to the Roots," about taro growing in the Hawaiian Islands.[81] Native Hawaiian leaders were often among those who labored to preserve flora and fauna seen as endemic to the islands from the intrusion of introduced (alien) plants and animals, for to lose their native species would be, many thought, to lose part of their culture. About 95 percent of native Hawaiian flowering plants, insects, and non-migratory birds exist nowhere else in the world — a higher percentage than in any similar area.[82]

Environmentalists also defended native species, as did some farmers and businesspeople, although sometimes for different reasons. Economic factors loomed large, as farmers of specialty fruits and vegetables feared that the accidental introduction of alien insects or other pests might decimate their crops. This was not a new concern. To give just two examples: The first mosquitoes on Maui arrived with the ship *Wellington* in 1826, and in 1971 Moloka'i had a scare when locusts escaped from a load of seed corn being unloaded on the island.[83]

The introduction of plants and animals to the Hawaiian Islands took place in stages. When the first Polynesians sailed to the Hawaiian Islands, the islands contained about 2,700 species of plants, 4,000 species of insects, and seven species of land birds. Only one land mammal (the Hawaiian bat), no reptiles, and no amphibians lived on the islands. As they colonized the islands,

Polynesian groups introduced thirty-two plant species, including taro, sugar cane, bananas, breadfruit, and sweet potatoes. With them also came chickens, dogs, pigs, and rats. As they created plots for taro growing and as their animals and plants competed with native species, Polynesian settlers began to change the biota of the Hawaiian Islands. About sixty species of birds, especially large flightless ones, were driven into extinction. The clearing of forests in the lowlands and more selective cutting in the uplands started transforming the composition of trees and plants on the islands.[84]

The pace of ecological change greatly accelerated after the European discovery of the Hawaiian Islands. Captain James Cook's men planted melons, onions, and pumpkins in 1778. Captain George Vancouver brought oranges, lemons, almonds, and grapes in 1792. Westerners introduced 111 plant species to the Hawaiian Islands by 1840, including 65 fruits and vegetables. By 1980 Westerners had introduced some 5,000 species and varieties of plants. In addition, Europeans and Americans brought animals that multiplied to the point that they became pests very destructive of plant life — goats, pigs, cattle, and sheep. European rats came as well. Vancouver introduced the first goats to Kaho'olawe in 1793. One of the most ill guided efforts at bioengineering by Westerners was the introduction of the mongoose to the Hawaiian Islands in 1883. It was hoped that mongooses would kill rats, but they killed native birds instead. Altogether, "the physical disturbance of the landscape and the introduction of exotic species by humans," one scholar has estimated, had "transformed more than 90 percent of the natural environments of Hawaii" by the close of the 1990s.[85]

Often singled out for special criticism by Maui's residents was the brown tree snake, which, originating in New Guinea, parts of Indonesia, and the Solomon Islands, overran Guam after World War II. Brought to Guam unintentionally by military cargo planes, the brown tree snake reached densities of 20,000 per square mile by the 1990s. Having no natural predators on Guam, the snakes devastated the natural environment there, climbing trees and gobbling up much of the island's bird life. As one observer noted, "There is no birdsong on Guam — the island is silent." The snakes drove nine of Guam's twelve species of birds into extinction. Nor were birds the only prey; small animals of all kinds — chickens, ducks, rabbits, and domestic pets — were at risk. Climbing power poles, the snakes shorted out transformers and caused frequent power outages, resulting in computer downtime and the loss of refrigeration.[86] Some people on Maui feared that brown tree snakes might hitchhike to their island in the wheel wells and cargo holds of airplanes, especially if their island's major airport were enlarged to handle planes arriving directly from Asia. The snakes might then get loose and infest the island.

Hawaiian residents had good reasons to fear the invasion of alien species. While the Hawaiian Islands comprise less than 0.2 percent of the land area of the United States, they accounted for 25 percent of the nation's endangered species and 72 percent of all recorded extinctions of plants and animals by the 1990s. In the late 1990s Hawai'i had 284 plant species and 40 species of birds, mammals, and sea turtles in danger of extinction. "The islands possess," one scholar has noted, "one of the most highly endemic, fragile, and endangered biotas on earth."[87] While the brown tree snake was the most feared alien animal invader, it was not alone. Various alien plants, seaweeds, and even frogs caught the attention of county and state officials, who sought their eradication. In 1997 the Hawaii legislature passed a law designed to prevent "alien aquatic organisms" that might "cause irreparable harm to native Hawaiian marine flora and fauna" from entering their state. Such alien species, they feared, might "adversely impact the state's aquaculture and visitor industries."[88]

Conflict and Cooperation

It was in a hot mix of business, environmental, and Native Hawaiian organizations, along with governmental bodies, that decisions about economic and environmental matters were worked out on Maui. This combination could be explosive, as disagreements boiled over. Yet it was a mixture that often led in the end to meaningful cooperation and the hammering out of workable compromises — as, over time, many residents of Maui came to realize that their seemingly divergent interests actually had a lot in common. Central to other concerns were those about land use, the focus of Chapter 3. In this realm were played out many of the issues that would also run through concerns about water rights, electric power generation, and transportation.

3

Land Use Issues

Among the most important issues residents of Maui debated were those concerning land. More was often involved in the disputes than simply land; as one astute observer writing in 1979 noted, "Land is the basis of power in Hawai'i."[1] Devoted to agriculture and tourism, Maui was a place where land was the very essence of life. Controversies over land in the Hawaiian Islands dated back to the nineteenth century. Land issues changed, however, with a revolution in politics during the 1950s and 1960s and then assumed a heightened urgency as residents contended with a slumping economy from the late 1980s through the 1990s. Questions about how best to balance desired resort developments and the growth of the visitor industry with a rising concern for the environment and a desire to foster diversified economic expansion took center stage. An assertion of Native Hawaiian rights further complicated land matters. As one scholar writing in 1984 observed, "The regulation of land use has become an enormously complex process."[2]

Politics and Land: The Democratic Revolution

Hawai'i's planters used their power in territorial politics to gain access to desired lands. Usually influenced by the Big Five companies, Republicans dominated the territorial legislature, outnumbering Democrats five to one from the turn of the century to World War II. Republican dominance usually permeated local politics as well, including in Maui County. Antonio Ramil, a Filipino American lawyer on Maui who published a searching analysis of his county's politics, accurately observed that "the Republican Party controlled Maui politics until World War II."[3]

Fundamental political changes, alterations that directly affected land use matters, occurred after World War II. In the 1950s and 1960s Democrats replaced Republicans as Hawai'i's ruling political party, a position maintained through the 1990s. This Democratic revolution had its basis in demographic changes. As the children of immigrant plantation workers — who, unlike many of their parents, were American citizens and could vote — came of age, most voted Democratic. The children of Japanese and Chinese immigrants, in particular, formed the backbone of Hawai'i's postwar Democratic Party. Trained in the territory's public schools, the children of immigrants looked to politics as a venue for social advancement and as a way to effect economic changes through politics. In this approach, they resembled how some other immigrant groups — Irish and Italians, for example — had earlier gotten ahead on mainland America.[4]

Jeanne Unemori Skog belonged to one immigrant family that succeeded on Maui. Her paternal grandparents had worked in Maui's pineapple fields. They "eventually did buy some land on their own and started raising pineapples," Skog later recalled, but "then the depression hit," wiping out their gains. One of nine siblings, Skog's father worked in the fields but also managed to finish high school. During World War II several of his brothers served in the highly decorated 442nd regiment, composed of Japanese Americans; three of them took advantage of the GI Bill to go to college after the conflict. They went on to become professionals — engineers, accountants, and so forth. Meanwhile, Skog's father, Jeanne explained, secured enough "money to go buy land in Ha'ikū, which was very much the boondocks at that time." After working at his field job each day, he cultivated his own land each evening. This hard work paid off. As Skog later remembered, "Eventually, he was successful enough to leave Maui Pine and become a pineapple farmer full-time."[5]

Jeanne went to school at St. Joseph's, a parochial school in Makawao, through the eighth grade, and then at St. Anthony's, the Catholic high school in Kahului. Skog "always assumed" that she would obtain higher education and went to the College of St. Catherine's in St. Paul, Minnesota, graduating with a degree in English. After college she worked for four years in state government positions in Minneapolis to put her husband, who was from Minnesota, through school. Skog and her husband moved to Maui in 1977, where she worked in interior design while he operated as an architect. In 1981 the couple moved to Hong Kong, where her husband opened an office for Architects Hawai'i. They returned to Maui several years later, and Skog's husband went on his own as an architect. It was at this time that Skog "saw an ad in the paper" for an executive assistant for the Maui Economic Development Board (MEDB). "The thing that struck me about it was that it said that a college degree was preferred," Skog later recalled, "which — you have to understand Maui — was very unusual at that time." Skog was hired and started work in 1984. Fifteen years later she became the MEDB president.

In several respects, Jeanne Skog's story was typical of how members of immigrant families, especially Asian Americans, got ahead in Hawai'i. They placed a very high value on education. As Skog explained, her family was "a typical immigrant family, in that education was deemed a tremendous value and vehicle." She and her three brothers and sisters all went to college. Then, too, hard work was part of the family ethos. Driven to possess his own plot of land, her father labored long hours on the family holding after already having put in a full day as a field-worker. Running through all of the efforts of the Unemori family was a desire for economic independence and social acceptance, a desire to transcend their plantation roots.

Political changes on Maui mirrored those occurring throughout Hawai'i. The first Chinese American was elected to public office in Maui in 1928, and the first Japanese American four years later. In 1934 the first Democrat in twenty-six years was elected to Maui's Board of Supervisors, the territorial forerunner of the county council. Signaling major alterations to come, Harold Rice, a Republican Party leader on Maui, became a Democrat in 1943 and won election to the Hawaiian Senate a year later. In 1944 Democrats took control of Maui's Board of Supervisors for the first time, a watershed event.[6]

As they grasped the reins of political power, Democrats clamored for land reform. Into the 1960s they hoped to make changes in land ownership, use, and taxation. They attacked on several fronts. Republicans had placed ceilings on the revenues that the counties could collect through real property taxes. Hoping to collect more taxes from the large companies that owned most of Hawai'i's private land, the Democrats abolished those limits. Moreover, under the Democrats land was no longer assessed at simply its current use. It was, instead, assessed at its "highest and best possible use," which meant that plantation owners could not reap all of the windfall profits to which they had become accustomed from the rising value of their agricultural lands near cities. The Democrats also closed loopholes in land tax laws. Moreover, a law passed in 1963 encouraged that land be put to the most intense use possible — that, if possible, buildings be constructed on land — by assessing buildings at much lower tax rates than land.[7]

The State Land Use Commission and Early County Land Planning

The most far-reaching change in Hawai'i's land policies came with the passage of the State Land Use Law of 1961. Based on a British law designed to guide the reconstruction of that nation after World War II, the State Land Use Law provided for the zoning of all of the land in the Hawaiian Islands. It was the first such statewide measure in the United States, leading one scholar to call the law "the most sophisticated and complete system of land-use planning and control in the United States and perhaps the world." Hawai'i's history of having a centralized government, the state's still-concentrated ownership of land, and Hawai'i's relatively small size encouraged a statewide approach to land use. Adding urgency was the fear that unless a broad zoning measure were adopted, agricultural land on O'ahu would be gobbled up in resort developments. Two principles ran through the State Land Use Law: first, to preserve as much land as possible for conservation and agricultural purposes, and, second, to keep urbanization concentrated in relatively few areas.[8]

Although the State Land Use Law was revolutionary in providing zoning for an entire state, the measure built on earlier territorial laws. In 1957 the territorial legislature enacted legislation establishing the Territorial Planning Office, whose main goal was economic stimulation for Hawai'i; in the same year it passed a companion law defining standards for the exercise of zoning powers by the counties. According to this act, the counties were to use zoning to help stimulate economic growth. Zoning was to be employed as one part of a general territorywide economic expansion package. The 1957 zoning law called on the counties to "encourage the most beneficial use" of their "land consonant with good zoning practices."[9]

Maui County officials had already initiated limited regulation of land use.[10] In early 1956 Supervisor Hannibal Tavares, who would become Maui's mayor in 1979, persuaded the Board of Supervisors to create a County Planning Commission. With the passage of territorial zoning legislation in 1957, Maui's board of supervisors enacted an interim zoning ordinance in 1958. The county plan adopted a year later called for the adoption of "a comprehensive zoning ordinance" for Maui County, and just such an ordinance, the first in the Hawaiian Islands, was put in place in 1960. Maui's zoning ordinance divided the county into sixteen zoning districts and laid down basic specifications for land uses, building heights, lot sizes, lot frontages, and yard sizes in each district.[11]

The State Land Use Law of 1961 superseded these county efforts. The law set up a nine-member State Land Use Commission, appointed by the governor, to zone all of the 4.1 million acres in the Hawaiian Islands; in 1964 the commission designated its first land districts. Zoning was revisited every five years as part of the preparation of statewide development plans in the 1960s and 1970s, and every ten years in the 1980s and 1990s. The commission established four land use categories — agricultural, conservation, rural, and urban — and designated most of the land as agricultural or conservation.[12] Composed of 465,800 acres in 1995, Maui County had 42 percent of its land (193,634 acres) classified as conservation, 53 percent (247,770 acres) as agriculture, 4.4 percent (20,640 acres) as urban, and less than 1 percent (3,759 acres) as rural.[13] These classifications were important. Land was taxed at different rates according to its designation, with lower rates applied to agricultural and conservation lands than to urban and rural lands. Moreover, it was often difficult to have land moved from one classification to another, requiring lengthy appeals to state and county agencies.

Giving clout to the work of the State Land Use Commission was state legislation adopted in 1978. With the passage of Act 100 in that year, Hawai'i's state development plan, including its land use categories, was written into law. That is, a plan drafted by the state government for Hawai'i's economic development became legally binding. Everyone in the islands had to follow the plan. What was usually a guideline or policy document in other states was a legal document in the Hawaiian Islands.

Prepared once a decade, the Hawai'i State Plan had three major parts: goals, objectives, and policies; planning implementation and coordination; and priority guidelines. It was, moreover, backed up by twelve functional plans covering items from conservation lands to higher education. At its heart lay land use matters. Nor was this the end of it. Each county prepared its own development plan, much of which dealt with land use topics, and the county plans had to be in consonance with the state plan. Like the state plan, the county plans were drafted every ten years and, once accepted by the state government, had the force of law. Planning also operated at the local level and, again, dealt largely with land use matters. Every ten years, citizen committees for the different regions of each county — there were nine in Maui County — prepared plans for their areas. Appointed by the mayor and the county council, and advised by professional planners, members of the committees held extensive public hearings as part of their work. Once approved by the county councils, these local plans were supposed to have the force of law.[14]

The Democrats have sometimes been criticized for not accomplishing enough in the way of land reform in the Hawaiian Islands; in fact, their efforts did not radically alter land ownership patterns. Through the 1990s land ownership remained more concentrated in Hawai'i than in most other parts of the United States. Instead of reforming land policies root and branch, many Democrats became deeply involved in land development for tourism from the 1960s on. As they profited from such ventures, their ardor for thorough-going land reform waned. As one leading Democrat later explained, "Many of these new men did not really want to change things or destroy anything. They just 'wanted in.'"[15] The policies of the State Land Use Commission have also been criticized. The policy of allowing only contiguous urban expansion and of restricting even that type of growth encouraged upward rather than outward expansion in the interest of maintaining farm lands and open spaces. This policy had the unfortunate effect, critics maintain, of contributing to housing shortages and soaring housing prices.[16]

As the neighbor islands developed, tension mounted between the state and county governments on land use matters. County governments could initially modify state policies only slightly. The arrangement that placed most of the power in the hands the State Land Use Commission made sense when Hawai'i first became a state, for the counties lacked the planning experts and apparatus needed to deal with land matters. However, by the 1980s and 1990s the counties had fairly well developed planning departments and wanted a greater voice in land matters.[17] And, in time, the counties won increasing control. Most importantly, in 1985 the Hawaii legislature revised the state's land laws to allow county governments to take actions with regard to parcels of less than fifteen acres in size, as long as those parcels were not conservation lands. This represented a major step in the direction of empowering county governments.[18]

Land Development Issues on Maui in the 1960s and 1970s

Nowhere were the changes caused by the transition of Maui's economy from plantation agriculture to tourism more apparent than in debates about land. With state and county governments sharing, and increasingly contesting, zoning responsibilities, the politics of land use was often a hot potato. The thrust of decisions made during the 1960s and 1970s, especially those at the county level, was to bring land to the market, develop it, and put it to use. Most of Maui's residents saw land development as the handmaiden of tourism, a way to bolster their county's economy. Only toward the end of the 1970s were doubts expressed about this line of development. Eddie Tam and Elmer Cravalho, two Democrats, headed Maui's government from the late 1940s through the late 1970s. Both were proponents of land use policies conducive to economic expansion, but they differed considerably in their personalities and in how they pursued development.

A consistent ally of Harold Rice, Tam easily won election in 1948 as Maui County's chairman and executive officer, roughly the equivalent of the later position of mayor of the county, and held that office until his death eighteen years later. Tam had gotten his start in politics as Rice's "right-hand man." Tam "would warm up the crowd" at political rallies for Rice. Known as "Friendly Eddie," Tam was actively pro-growth and did just about anything he could to publicize Maui's attractions for businesses and tourists alike. At his request a sign bearing the saying "You can't sell peanuts at the end of a parade" hung over the meeting room of the Board of Supervisors. Known as "a showman," Tam "pretty much welcomed new developments on Maui," Ramil later recalled. Wherever he went, Tam "kept singing the praises of Maui." He was actively involved in getting governmental funding for infrastructure improvements needed in the early stages of the West Maui developments. As James Apana, Maui's mayor in the late 1990s, remembered, Tam was "Mr. Aloha himself," a leader who "started the concept of tourism . . . for Maui especially."[19]

If Tam started the ball rolling, it was Cravalho who, more than any other political leader, shaped modern-day Maui. Cravalho's grandparents immigrated to Maui from San Miguel Island in the Azores off the coast of Portugal. As Cravalho later recalled, "My grandparents settled in the country areas; we were country people all the way back." Cravalho's father was a schoolteacher, his mother a housewife. Born in Pā'ia, Cravalho attended school there

through the first semester of fifth grade. Then he went Upcountry, when his
father was transferred to teach at the Kēōkea School, a "three-room school."
After graduating from Maui High School in 1944, Cravalho attended the
University of Hawai'i for a year on a territorial scholarship, studying agriculture and education. Returning to Maui, he taught school for eight years,
becoming the acting principal of the Keāhua School, a small, rural school
halfway between Kula and Kahului.[20]

Cravalho left his career in teaching to become chairman of Maui's Democratic Party and a representative in the Hawaii legislature in 1954. As he later
observed, he was part of the "Democratic sweep of fifty-four," in which the
Democrats won control of the state government. Reelected to both positions
periodically, Cravalho became speaker of the house in 1966, the year Tam died.
Cravalho was attracted to state politics, he explained, because that "was where
the action was, where decisions were made; and, like many, many others, I
felt there was a need for change." His objectives, like those of many Democrats, were deceptively simple: "minimum wage, land availability, job opportunities, education, and proper funding and support for education." Land
reform was important to Cravalho, "one of the motivating factors that got
us involved."[21]

Chosen chairman and executive officer of Maui County in a special election following Tam's death in the fall of 1967, Cravalho held that position until
1969, when revisions to Maui's county charter created the position of mayor.
He then served as Maui's mayor for a decade.[22] Cravalho could, perhaps, have
been lieutenant governor of the state. "That was not for me, however. I wouldn't
be satisfied," Cravalho later stated. "I wasn't ready to go to that type of experience." He did not "want to give up the chance to walk the streets, the super-
markets . . . being able to be called by my first name, stopped by people to
just talk — I did not want to give up that privilege. And so, I came home."[23]

Cravalho was part of an emerging middle class that was coming to make
up Hawai'i's Democratic Party. In addition to his work in politics, he was
deeply involved in a number of business interests, especially in Upcountry
ranching and agriculture. Like Tam, Cravalho favored the development of
tourism. Upon taking office, Cravalho visited financial institutions on the
mainland to discuss Maui's bonding potential, the county's ability to bor-
row to finance sorely needed infrastructure improvements — roads, sewers,
and water systems. He then met with the officers of Maui's leading com-

panies, many of whom he knew from his time in the state legislature, to work on development plans. Looking back in the year 2000, Cravalho observed, "I think we had an understanding of each other, not necessarily of approval, but an understanding of where each was coming from and what needed to be done." Most could agree on the need for certain types of economic development then, Cravalho later stressed. One of the most important business leaders with whom Cravalho worked was J. Walter Cameron, Colin Cameron's father. He "was on the opposite side of the fence politically, but we got along very well," Cravalho remembered. "I found in him an echoing wall."[24]

While laboring hard for the development of a visitor industry on Maui, Cravalho also wanted his county to have a diversified economy. Cravalho was, as he put it then, "insistent that Maui work toward a more balanced economy and not put all of its eggs in the tourism basket." Questioning by leaders like Cravalho led, as we have seen, to the conference on Maui's economic future in 1981. Cravalho also insisted that private-sector developers contribute something to Maui — parks, low-income housing, community centers, and so on — in return for the county's support of their development efforts. An acute 1968 analysis of Cravalho's work concluded that "three key words may well describe his philosophy — 'balanced growth' and 'leverage.'" Another observer made much the same point six years later. "Articulate and benevolently powerful," Cravalho was able to wring concessions from developers in the forms of "roads, green belts, parks, extra set backs and sewage schemes."[25]

Cravalho ran county politics for more than a decade with an iron fist. He got things done and, by all accounts, cared deeply for people, including rising ethnic groups. In return Cravalho expected complete loyalty and adherence to his wishes. "When people say I was a strong leader," he later noted, "they are being polite. . . . [I am] adamant and hard-hitting." All, he thinks, benefited from his approach: "This is the way; not only requesting and inviting and almost compelling [business leaders] to cooperate, but in return being damn sure we [county officials] kept our word on what we were going to do." Cravalho's motto was: "You will perform, we will perform; this is a joint venture." As a result, Cravalho believes, Maui can now "stand on its own feet — where there is greater opportunity, greater security, greater financial capacities than in other areas."[26]

As tourism developed into a big business, the Maui County Council worked with the mayor's office to facilitate its growth. Economic development was the watchword. In 1976, for example, council members unanimously called upon the federal government to construct a monorail through the 'Īao Valley, which later became a nature area and state park, as a way to connect Kahului and Wailuku to burgeoning resorts in West Maui. A monorail would, they averred, reduce traffic congestion and automobile accidents. Only when the federal government demurred was the plan dropped.[27] Thwarted on that front, the county council grappled with a host of related land use issues: how new subdivisions might be created, what the proper densities for apartment districts should be, and how zoning and rezoning matters should be handled.

The county council approved a new comprehensive zoning ordinance in 1969. This measure set countywide standards for infrastructure requirements for developers working in four types of areas: business, industrial, hotel, and apartment; residential; rural; and agricultural. The council laid down detailed standards for the construction of streets, the provision of utilities and water supplies, the construction of drainage systems, the sizes of lots, and the provision of parks.[28] However, when some developers complained about the rigidity of zoning and the long time needed to effect the rezoning of land, council members eased up on the requirements. Moreover, at the same time, they decided not to set any hard-and-fast rules for financial contributions from builders for infrastructure improvements, such as new roads and sewer plants, constructed to serve their developments. Council members thus modified their ordinance in the interests of rapid business development.[29]

In the spring of 1974 the council went further in this direction by passing a set of ordinances to increase the flexibility of land use.[30] The first ordinance allowed a 10 percent increase in the density of land use in residential districts. Pushed especially by Alexander and Baldwin, which was expanding Kahului and entering resort development at Wailea, this ordinance allowed the creation of smaller lots in some subdivisions. Hannibal Tavares, then a lobbyist for Alexander and Baldwin, presented the firm's arguments, claiming that higher densities were needed to make low-cost housing available to Maui's residents. Mayor Cravalho had vetoed a similar measure in 1970, saying that denser housing was undesirable because it might create social problems, but in 1974 the ordinance won approval.

Two other measures permitted developers flexibility in designing and winning approval for their plans. One allowed the creation of "mixed-use" areas in what had been residential districts, making it easier for developers to establish new areas for planned developments. Favored especially by the owner of the Kula Lodge, who wanted to expand her Upcountry hotel and restaurant to include condominiums, this measure, like the one allowing housing density increases, won unanimous approval. A third ordinance, which was strongly backed by Alexander and Baldwin, allowed the creation of "project districts" for large housing and resort developments. Within these districts developers were given "flexibility" in meeting the county's zoning requirements. As a county council member later explained, "The project district approach provides for flexible and creative design of large parcels of land under a single ownership." In other words, the measure limited the amount of planning initially needed to secure the approval of county authorities for a new development and thus speeded the development process. The high-technology park was developed as a project district.[31]

A final ordinance created the new zoning designation of "rural residential." Intended to ease the building of resorts, this measure — incorporating amendments proposed by representatives from Alexander and Baldwin — permitted the construction of such infrastructure improvements as sewage plants in areas in which they had previously been prohibited and designated golf courses and tennis ranches as types of land, along with parks and playgrounds, that could be counted as green space in developers' plans.[32]

Responding to complaints from developers that county officials took too long to approve their plans, the county council in 1977 empowered the Division of Land Use and Codes within the Department of Public Works to act as a Central Coordinating Committee with the authority to approve all aspects of development plans. Previously, a number of different agencies had handled various aspects of the plans. Strongly backed by Maui's architects and builders, this change was desired, as a representative of the Contractors Association and Home Builders Association explained, to "speed up the process of obtaining permits and the furtherance of the construction."[33] The alteration was also urged as a way of increasing county control over planning and limiting state control.[34]

Rethinking Land Use Policies

The recession of the early 1980s and the accompanying slump in tourism led Maui's residents to partially reassess the roles the visitor industry should play in their county's development. The county development plan adopted in 1980 stressed the importance of finding a balance between economic growth and the maintenance of established ways of life for Maui's residents and emphasized the virtues of economic diversification. These points had consequences for land use policies. County officials moved away, at least temporarily, from the easy acceptance of the largely unrestrained encouragement of tourist developments. In his annual message in 1979, the chairman of the county council voiced increasingly common sentiments: "It is imperative that the large landlords and major developers understand the concept of mutual benefits by and between the community and themselves." Echoing the State of Hawai'i's motto, he concluded that "the life of the land is preserved in righteousness, and that which is good for the community as a whole is right."[35]

Maui's residents were led by Tavares, their new mayor. Known as "Mr. Big" because of his large size, his political power, and, as one newspaper put it, "the largeness of his heart," Tavares succeeded Cravalho as mayor in 1979 and served in that position for a decade. Tavares had spent his early childhood in the small town of Pā'ia. A Portuguese immigrant to Maui in 1881, his father had risen to become the manager of the Kama'ole Ranch in 'Ulupalakua. When his father was killed by a kick to his head by a calf, Hannibal moved to Honolulu with his mother. After graduating from high school, Tavares briefly attended San Diego State College and then returned to the Hawaiian Islands to register for the draft during World War II. During the war he worked as a policeman in Honolulu's Chinatown and, from 1942 on, in Maui County. Promoted to district commander, Tavares served in Hanā and, after the war, on Moloka'i. From police work he went into teaching at Maui High School and then into work for Alexander and Baldwin.[36]

A Republican in deference to his father, Tavares was backed in politics by Colin Cameron. Tavares won election to Maui's Board of Supervisors in 1954, the only Republican to do so, and again in 1956. Dismayed by "hodgepodge" growth on Maui, which he labeled "chop-suey" development, Tavares spearheaded nascent planning efforts in the late 1950s. Losing in bids to become Maui's mayor in 1958 and 1960, Tavares moved to Honolulu as the chief lobbyist for the Hawai'i Sugar Planters Association, returning to Maui in 1972 to become the chief spokesman for Alexander and Baldwin. Even though he was a Republican, Tavares had the political support of Cravalho; as James Apana later explained, "He continued in Elmer's plans." Tavares worked with

Cameron to hold the 1981 Kapalua conference, which explored economic futures for Maui and led to the formation of the MEDB and the high-technology park.[37]

Breaking with long-established policy of the State Land Use Commission, the general plan adopted by Maui County in 1980 called for the encouragement of "the 'most reasonable and beneficial use' of land by discouraging practices that promoted 'the highest and best use' concept of land use." That is, the most intense use of the land was not necessarily to be mandated.[38] Change along these lines was also occurring at the state level. In the late 1960s and early 1970s Gov. Jack Burns, one of the architects of the Democratic revolution, set up task forces to explore many aspects of Hawai'i's future prospects. One examined land use policies and concluded that forcing the most intensive use, the so-called highest and best use, of land was not necessarily the most fruitful approach for long-term growth.[39] Giving this idea concrete form, Maui's 1980 general plan called for the development of land use policies reflecting "the individual character of the communities and regions of the County of Maui." The county government was to "encourage land use practices that would be consistent to and enhance, preserve and protect the surrounding areas." Quality-of-life issues were coming to the fore. In addition, the plan called on county officials to do more in the areas of watershed protection and the preservation of Native Hawaiian plants, animals, and fish — issues that would soon impinge on land development schemes.[40]

The county plan was ambivalent with regard to the use of land for tourism. Resort areas were to be clearly defined "to prevent their overflow" into neighboring communities, and in the original draft of the plan Wailea, Mākena, Kā'anapali, Kapalua, and Kahului harbor were designated as resort areas. Nonetheless, after considerable discussion, the county council decided not to specify any particular places as resort areas, thus allowing their sprawl to continue. Efforts were made by Mayor Tavares and Linda Lingle, who served as Maui's mayor in the 1990s, to limit sprawl and to contain urban developments to an urban core on Maui. In this way the countryside could be preserved and costly infrastructure improvements could be kept within reasonable bounds. However, as events in some areas showed — in South Maui, for example — urban growth was not easily contained. South Maui boomed in the 1980s with the building of a number of major resort hotels, and development sometimes took on a life of its own.[41]

Ambivalence was also apparent in how the 1980 plan treated infrastructure developments needed for resorts. County council members called on developers to pay for new streets, sewer systems, and the like and concluded that "all segments of the visitor industry should become more involved with the community in meeting the concerns of the County." Yet the final draft of the plan did not require such payments, and how infrastructure improvements were to be financed remained a thorny issue. Only in the 1990s, in conjunction with resort developments in South Maui, did the county council firmly establish what it called a "principle of concurrence." Council members finally decreed that resorts could not be built in advance of infrastructure additions needed for them and specified that most of the improvements had to be financed by developers.[42]

Over the next two decades county authorities found themselves returning to many of the issues raised in their work on the 1980 plan, as they dealt with the question of how to balance requests of developers for changes in land use patterns with the desires of many county residents to maintain established lifestyles. Council members moved in the direction of limiting development. As one observed in 1983, "The people of the County of Maui are not all developers"; the council, he believed, needed "to weigh the social, economical and environmental effects of future development on the community."[43] The council restricted the building of time-sharing condominiums and other transient vacation properties to specific districts on Maui and provided property tax relief for residents who found appraisals of their real estate, and thus their property taxes, soaring.[44]

As a prelude to renewed planning in the 1990s, county and state officials met with businesspeople and planners from across the United States at a conference hosted by the MEDB in late 1988. After three days of meetings the conferees agreed on recommendations to guide the future use of land in Maui County: that the county needed to define a realistic growth management policy, that agricultural diversification should continue to be encouraged and farm lands protected, that the county should impose impact fees on real estate developments to offset expenses in providing infrastructure improvements, and that the county should develop a public transportation system. Colin Cameron spoke for many of the participants in summarizing the conference: "As a representative landowner, I have seen our own thinking evolve from the early concept of 'Yes, it is my land, I will do just what I want to do,' to a concept of being stewards of the land with the ability to guide and direct some of the things we would like to see happen."[45]

The general plan adopted for Maui County's development in 1990 repeated many of the provisions of the plan of a decade before, showing a rising concern for quality-of-life matters. As its most general land use objective, the plan reiterated a desire "to preserve for present and future generations existing geographic, cultural, and traditional community lifestyles" by making use of land "in accordance with the individual character of the various communities." Each community was to define carefully its urban and rural limits; historic and cultural sites were to be preserved; programs to provide affordable housing were to be encouraged; and agricultural land was to be protected. In particular, the 1990 plan called on county authorities to "discourage the conversion, through zoning or other means, of productive or potentially productive agricultural lands to nonagricultural uses, including but not limited to golf courses and residential subdivisions."[46]

Land Subdivisions

Land subdivision issues, which attracted considerable attention in the 1990 plan, had occupied the county government throughout the 1980s. Over time, the county council increased its requirements of what developers had to provide in new subdivisions — how much land had to be dedicated to parks and playgrounds, for example. Even more important, and more annoying, to developers was the length of the permitting process. Some developers continued to complain that it took too long to have their land approved for subdivision. Families trying to cash in on Maui's growth as a tourist destination by developing their land found waiting especially frustrating. As one council member noted in the 1980s, something needed to be done "to expedite small subdivisions," for the council was "deluged by requests from these different small subdividers who want to subdivide their family lots." Establishing the Division of Land Use and Codes as a clearinghouse for such matters in 1977 was not enough.[47]

Such issues were statewide in scope and led to the passage of legislation in Honolulu. A key example lay in what was known as 'ohana zoning ('ohana, it will be recalled, means "family"). Before 1981 Hawaiian state law decreed that the minimum lot size for the construction of a dwelling on land classified as rural was half an acre. However, to speed the building of affordable housing, encourage the maintenance of extended families, and, perhaps, permit families to profit from tourism, the state legislature amended land laws in 1981 to allow two dwellings to be built on such lots. Modifications came in legislation passed in 1988 and 1989, but the basic principle remained intact: The counties should adopt reasonable standards permitting the construction of multiple housing units on plots of rural land.[48]

Rural subdivision issues came to a head on Maui in the late 1990s. Small landowners who wanted to divide their lots petitioned the county council to make subdivision easier. They asked the council to grant an automatic rural designation to any lot that had been designated rural by the State Land Use Commission but that was classified as interim by the county. The classification of interim resulted from an anomaly. When Maui County adopted comprehensive zoning ordinances in the late 1960s and early 1970s, there remained, nonetheless, considerable amounts of land that were not given a designation by the county. These were classified as interim. As matters then stood, residents had to petition the county council individually for the designation of rural. Nothing was automatic; each request was reviewed separately by the county. One member of the Maui County Council estimated that the long process of rezoning was costing Maui landowners $37 million annually. Worse, while landowners could often secure building permits for land designated as interim, they could only rent, not sell, the completed dwellings.[49]

The county council seesawed on requests for automatic rezoning. A motion favoring automatic rezoning won approval in a county council vote in 1996 but lost upon reconsideration a year later. Some council members feared that historic sites, especially those important to Native Hawaiians, might be lost in hasty rezoning and construction. Then, too, they believed that automatically granting the rural designation would increase population densities too much in some areas. Council members often singled out Hanā, a rustic region with numerous Native Hawaiian sites, as needing continued protection and oversight. However, renewed landowner requests brought about another reconsideration. Pushed by Mayor Lingle, the county council eventually got rid of interim zoning in most cases, allowing the easier reclassification of lands for subdivision. When she left office in early 1999, Lingle counted this as one of her main accomplishments.[50]

The Preservation of Agricultural Land

Nowhere was the county council's changing opinion about land use more apparent than in its treatment of agricultural land. Reflecting the desires of many of Maui's residents, and acting increasingly against the wishes of large developers, the council moved to preserve agricultural land. At particular issue was the question of whether or not landowners should be allowed to carve up agricultural land into two-acre plots, the smallest size that could be classified as agricultural, for the formation of so-called gentlemen's estates — that is, for the creation of upscale vacation homes. Those opposed to such estates wanted to see lands designated as agricultural kept in actual farming use. In its efforts to preserve agricultural land from development, the county council was in line with national developments. In California, for example, state legislation, especially the Williamson Act of 1965, and local ordinances sought to prevent the conversion of agricultural land to other uses. Between 1945 and 1968 California had lost an estimated one million acres of prime agricultural land to suburban development.[51]

Dealt with sporadically during the 1970s, the issue of agricultural land was addressed more frequently on Maui in the 1980s.[52] The Maui County Plan of 1980 called for the preservation of agricultural land and the encouragement of diversified agriculture, and in 1981 the chairman of the county council asked his colleagues to reexamine agricultural land use matters. "Agricultural subdivision laws," he said, "should be reviewed with the understanding that limited land is available for agriculture, and, thus, these lands should be used for the sole purpose of agriculture and not the creation of rural estates."[53] A year later the council declared a moratorium on the creation of agricultural subdivisions while it reviewed zoning ordinances with the goal of amending them in ways "to conserve and protect prime agricultural land."[54] Even so, the moratorium was only temporary, and little was accomplished during the 1980s.

Pulled in different directions by developers — a group that included small-scale farmers eager to subdivide their lands to take advantage of the revival of tourism on Maui in the mid-1980s — and environmentalists, the council soon lifted its moratorium and allowed the movement of agricultural land into other uses. Indeed, in 1983 the council set up a committee to speed the reclassification of so-called unproductive agricultural lands for nonagricultural uses. A year later council members revised Maui's tax code in ways that eased the reclassification of small plots of agricultural land for new uses.[55]

Not until the 1990s, especially at the end of the decade, did the county council take meaningful steps to preserve agricultural land. The general plan adopted for the county in 1990 called on council members to "protect prime agricultural land from competing nonagricultural uses." As in closely related subdivision matters, council members found themselves tugged in various directions; in the end they approved an ordinance designed to preserve agricultural land for farming. In 1996 they reimposed a moratorium on the creation of gentlemen's estates. Too many such lots, council members believed, were really being used not for farming, but for the construction of vacation homes.[56]

Spurred by small landowners who wanted to subdivide their property, the Land Use Committee of the county council revisited the matter of agricultural land in earnest during the winter of 1998. The committee estimated that 48,500 acres on Maui would qualify for subdivision into two-acre parcels, if no moratorium existed. Environmental groups favored continuing the moratorium. The administrative director of Maui Tomorrow wrote to council members requesting an extension; only in this way, he argued, could land be "saved" for true agricultural use. The county council extended the moratorium on subdivisions through 1998.[57]

At the same meeting in which they approved continuing the moratorium, council members debated a measure, commonly called the "ag bill," designed to tighten standards for the zoning of agricultural land, with the goal of keeping land in farming operations. Passage of the bill was essential, proponents thought, before the moratorium expired. As council members composing the Land Use Committee explained to their colleagues, current state and county definitions of agricultural land were "vague, loose, and difficult to enforce." They concluded that as a result, many acres of agricultural lands in Maui County had been developed for residential uses as gentlemen's estates, which limited the availability of lands for legitimate agricultural purposes. The ag bill, therefore, proposed to impose strict regulations on how agricultural land might be used.[58]

In the making for three years, the ag bill was hotly contested. Two issues attracted the most attention. At its heart, the proposal contained a "sliding scale," a provision that progressively limited the number of lots that could be carved out of a piece of land the larger that parcel was. The impact of the ag bill on parcels of less than fifteen acres would be minimal, allowing families owning small parcels of land to continue subdividing their land. The impact of the proposed measure on large landholdings would, however, be pronounced. For instance, lots of thirty-one acres could be subdivided to form a maximum of seven lots, not fifteen or sixteen as before. Lots of ninety-two acres could be subdivided to form twelve two-acre lots, two fifteen-acre lots, and one twenty-five acre lot — not the forty-six two-acre lots previously allowed. Not surprisingly, large landowners such as Alexander and Baldwin, Amfac, and Wailuku Agribusiness opposed the sliding scale, for it would limit subdivisions on their large pieces of land. On the other hand, the provision won strong support from the Sierra Club, Maui Tomorrow, the Maui County Farm Bureau, and the state Board of Agriculture.[59]

A second issue that emerged was concerned with how best to protect *kuleana* lands. *Kuleana* lands, it will be remembered, were lands originally taken up by Hawaiian commoners in the 1850s. On Maui significant *kuleana* acreage remained in Native Hawaiian hands in the 1990s, and Native Hawaiians wanted assurances that their lands would be maintained intact under the provisions of the ag bill. They feared the consolidation of their lands with other small agricultural parcels by developers, the subsequent subdivision of the lands, and a consequent loss of land.[60] When one council member tried to amend the ag bill to make the alienation of *kuleana* lands easier, Native Hawaiians protested. Led by their council of elders, they testified against the amendment in three hours of hearings before the county council. One observer caught well the meaning of this action. "This Council meeting was a ceremonial occasion," he noted, "with many Kupuna dressed in traditional costume reserved for religious rites. . . . One after another, representatives of environmental and community groups and small farmers came forward to ask that the zoning bill be passed, with the offending amendments removed," he continued. "The elders of the Hawaiian community did likewise," he concluded, "some citing specific cases of Hawaiian family lands being improperly annexed into neighboring large landholdings."[61]

The ag bill won approval in late 1998. It affected about half of the land in Maui County, all of the agricultural land and all land having state rural zoning and county interim zoning. The measure incorporated the provision for a sliding scale and also contained provisions protecting *kuleana* lands. The ag bill went even further to protect agricultural lands. It specified that neighbors of small farms had to accept certain inconveniences such as farm odors, noise, dust, and sprays, and it outlawed certain activities on farm lands: heliports, drive-in movies, motor sports clubs, and camping, among others. In this respect, as in so many others with regard to agricultural land, Maui conformed to national trends. As early as 1980–81 the American Farm Bureau Federation called for state legislatures to enact laws giving farmers "bills of rights" — that is, protection from lawsuits from those who might dislike the noises of farm machinery, farm odors, and so forth. In early 1999 Mayor Lingle signed the ag bill into law, saying that it was needed "to protect ag lands from unplanned, ad hoc urban development."[62]

Open-Space Issues

Accompanying discussions about zoning and subdividing rural and agricultural land were considerations of proposals to preserve open spaces. As early as 1984 the Maui County Council considered an ordinance "to create a zoning district to establish open space areas and to preserve park lands, wilderness areas, beach reserves, scenic areas, and historic areas, water sheds and prime water source areas, and to promote open space areas." Nothing came of the measure at the time, however. Nor did a proposal that the state create "open space" as a fifth category of land distinct from agriculture, conservation, urban, and rural come to fruition a few years later.[63] In their open-space proposals, advocates on Maui were playing catch-up with efforts on the mainland. Beginning in 1958 People for Open Space worked for the creation of a ring of parklands in the San Francisco Bay Area, achieving some success over the next few decades. Also, from the 1960s New England states led a movement in establishing conservation commissions to foster the acquisition of open spaces.[64]

Open-space issues were revived on Maui in the late 1990s. In early 1998 Maui Tomorrow proposed that the county council create a "land bank." The council, in turn, had a bill setting up a Maui County Open Space and Community Lands Acquisition Program introduced into the Hawaiian legislature. The program would buy lands for parks and other community purposes with revenues generated by a surcharge levied on all land transactions. Strongly backed by the Maui County Council, which was strapped for funds with which to purchase desired parklands, the measure was twice defeated in legislative committee — killed by opposition from real estate agents who objected to the land transfer tax. Learning from the continued opposition of these agents, and aware of similar opposition to land bank legislation on the mainland, Maui Tomorrow members began considering different approaches in the summer of 1999. They worked with private national foundations, such as the Trust for Public Land, and political leaders to try to find new sources of funding for the preservation of open spaces. Open spaces were needed, they averred, for tourists as well as residents. "Our visitors clearly indicate," one proponent observed, "that their most important reasons for coming here are our beautiful natural areas."[65]

A proposal to build an antenna farm on the southwest ridge of the mountain Haleakalā brought open-space issues into public discussion. In 1998 the State of Hawai'i wanted to put up four 199-foot-high antennas for the commercial broadcasting of television and radio signals to Maui and parts of O'ahu and Hawai'i. This action would allow broadcasting facilities then in use higher up the mountain to be relocated to a lower altitude. The high-altitude facilities were, it was said, interfering with scientific work being conducted on the summit. This proposal for new broadcasting towers evoked immediate opposition from Native Hawaiian and environmental groups. Mary Evanson, president of Friends of Haleakalā, observed that the mountain was "a very spiritual place." Referring to the construction proposal, she said, "We cannot let this happen. There are limits to the places that we give over to development." Charles Maxwell, the Native Hawaiian leader, spoke in a similar vein: "I'm drawing a line in the lava. I vowed there would be no more construction on Haleakala, and I'll put my okole [ass] on the line to protest." No construction had occurred by 2000.[66]

Native Hawaiian Land Issues

Native Hawaiian claims greatly affected land issues. As part of the Native Hawaiian Renaissance, Native Hawaiians sought to regain lands lost as a consequence of the 1893 revolution and the acquisition of Hawai'i by the United States in 1898. When it ceded sovereignty over the Hawaiian Islands to the United States in 1898, the Republic of Hawai'i conveyed title over all public lands to the federal government. These lands included the Government Lands and Crown Lands, which taken together became known as the Ceded Lands and totaled about 1.75 million acres. The Organic Act of 1900 establishing the Territory of Hawai'i confirmed the cession of the public lands to the federal government but also specified that any proceeds from the sale or lease of Ceded Lands should go to "such uses and purposes" as would "benefit the inhabitants of the Territory of Hawaii." There was a sense of trusteeship attached to the Ceded Lands. Some Native Hawaiian activists have argued that the Ceded Lands never really became an integral part of the federal domain; as one has put it, while "the United States received legal title to the lands, the beneficial title rested with the inhabitants of Hawai'i."[67]

The Organic Act had other provisions important for land ownership. It stated that Hawaiian land laws — those inherited from the days of the Kingdom and the Republic — not federal government laws, would govern land ownership and use in Hawai'i, thus making the situation in the islands different from those in most other western American territories. The Organic Act also contained two restrictions. Public lands could be leased for no longer than five years at a time, and no corporations, not even sugar plantations, could own more than 1,000 acres.[68]

Congress made some effort to help Native Hawaiians with the passage of the Hawaiian Homes Commission Act (HHCA) in 1921. This act set aside about 200,000 acres of public lands for homesteading by Native Hawaiians. For years Native Hawaiian leaders had been calling for homesteading as a way to reverse the decline in the numbers and quality of life of their people. By hiking food prices, World War I made matters worse by raising the cost of living for Native Hawaiians, especially the growing proportion of them living destitute in Honolulu. Only returning to the land, Native Hawaiian leaders believed, could improve living conditions for their people. As finally passed after a year of negotiation, the HHCA was a compromise. Native Hawaiian leaders had to accept provisions that made it palatable to Hawai'i's sugar interests. The HHCA exempted all cultivated sugar cane lands from inclusion in those lands available for homesteading. The law also lifted the restrictions on lease lengths and landholding sizes in Hawai'i's Organic Act, allowing planters to acquire larger landholdings and leases of more than five years in duration. Moreover, the legislation repealed a law passed in 1910 that had allowed groups of twenty-five people to obtain title to lands for homesteading in any given area. Finally, Native Hawaiians had to show a blood quantum of 50 percent, much more than had originally been contemplated, to qualify for coverage by the act.[69]

Even so, the HHCA was a significant accomplishment. Under its terms, lands were to be provided for homesteading under ninety-nine-year leases at a dollar per year. A Hawaiian Homes Commission (HHC), made up of the governor of Hawai'i and four others, three of whom were to be Native Hawaiians, oversaw the program. Any lands not allotted for homesteading could be leased for agricultural purposes to the highest bidder, with income from these leases going to support homesteading efforts. Specifically, loans of up to $3,000 would be made available to Native Hawaiian homesteaders at 5 percent interest for the construction of buildings and the purchase of farm machinery and seeds.[70]

When Hawai'i gained statehood, the task of managing the Hawaiian home lands was transferred from the federal government to the state government. In 1960 the state legislature established the Department of Hawaiian Home Lands (DHHL), headed by the new state HHC, to administer the home lands program. Like the earlier federal agency, the DHHL was supposed to provide leases for residential, agricultural, and pastoral (grazing) purposes at $1 per year for ninety-nine years. The new state agency was, moreover, to provide financial and technical assistance for would-be homesteaders. Any land not taken up by homesteaders could be leased to the highest bidder, with the income, once again, going to support the homesteading efforts.[71]

Whether administered by the federal or the state governments, the HHCA benefited only a few Native Hawaiians. Native Hawaiians faced many obstacles to effective land leasing. Government officials failed to provide the infrastructure needed to make the lands economically viable — roads, water systems, and so forth. The most important impediment, however, was simply that much of the land designated for homesteading was poorly suited for farming. On Maui 25,000 acres were set aside in Kahikinui, which was described in 1921 as "third class grazing" land, which "can be grazed only a few months of [each] year due to frequent dry spells." Another 6,000 acres were specified for homesteading in Kula; this land was "second class agricultural land" where "crops can be expected one year out of three." As late as 1989 only 5,778 leases had been awarded in the Hawaiian Islands, and there remained a waiting list of about 19,000 Native Hawaiians for homesteads. In June 1996 only 40,500 acres were in actual homesteading use.[72]

A closely related issue was that the amount of land actually set aside for Native Hawaiian homesteading was considerably less than that envisioned in 1920–21. The legislation passed by Congress called for sequestering 203,500 acres "more or less" for homesteading, but over the decades thousands of acres were lost from the homestead land trust. After years of negotiation the governor of Hawai'i made a commitment in 1994 to transfer 16,500 acres of state land into the trust, restoring it to its intended size. More than that, in legislation passed a year later the state agreed to pay $30 million annually for twenty years into a trust fund to settle all Native Hawaiian claims for home lands that had arisen between 1959 and 1988. In return, Native Hawaiians would give up any rights to sue the state for additional claims. Even so, in 1999 three Native Hawaiians brought suit for claims in actions taken beyond the deadline for filing lawsuits.[73]

While the loss of their lands sorely troubled Native Hawaiians, so did the failure of the federal and state governments to act as effective trustees for income derived from Hawai'i's public lands. A new state constitution adopted by residents of Hawai'i in 1978 began addressing some of these Native Hawaiian issues. The state established the Office of Hawaiian Affairs (OHA) in 1980 to hold in trust for Native Hawaiians some of the income flowing from the Ceded Lands. Between 1980 and 1989 that income came to $12.5 million. In 1990 the trustees of the OHA and the governor of Hawai'i agreed that in the future 20 percent of the income from the Ceded Lands would go to projects designed to help Native Hawaiians. Further negotiations led in 1992 to the payment to the OHA of $112 million for the settlement of unpaid benefits in the past.[74]

Even so, many Native Hawaiians, especially activists like Haunani-Kay Trask, greatly distrusted the OHA. They did not want to surrender their rights to land in exchange for cash payments. As we have seen, the group Ka Lāhui Hawai'i, formed in 1987, sought nation-within-a-nation status for Native Hawaiians and called for the full restoration of land to them.

In the eyes of many Native Hawaiians, more was involved than simply the loss of land in their material dispossession. While this study is not the place to review all aspects of twentieth-century Native Hawaiian life, it is worth noting, at least briefly, some of the impacts of land loss and economic change. A detailed report prepared for Congress by Native Hawaiians in 1983 concluded that "dispossession and defeat" had had "psychological, social, and cultural consequences for Native Hawaiians." Native Hawaiians had the lowest life expectancy, the highest infant mortality rate, and the highest suicide rate of any ethnic group in the Hawaiian Islands. Native Hawaiians suffered from the highest rates of academic and behavioral problems in school. Only 4.6 percent of Native Hawaiians had completed college, compared with a statewide average of 11.3 percent. About 30 percent of all Native Hawaiian families fell below the poverty line, and those working labored in mainly blue-collar, not professional, jobs. In fact, the report concluded, "by all major indices — health, education, employment, income — Native Hawaiians display distinct disparities with their fellow citizens."[75]

Native Hawaiian Land Leasing on Maui

The failure of the federal and state governments to make suitable land available, with proper roads and water systems, for leasing to Native Hawaiians angered members of the Maui County Council. Throughout the 1970s they repeatedly requested that "Hawaiian Home Lands be made available to people of Hawaiian ancestry." One councilman pointed out in 1974 that while 6,000 acres had been designated for such use in the Kula area, no land had actually been made available.[76] A residential Hawaiian Homes project came into existence at Paukūkalo on North Maui in the 1960s and 1970s, and had 181 families resident by 1997, but little more was accomplished until the 1990s.[77]

In the 1990s the DHHL started several new housing projects on Maui. It developed the Waiehu Kou subdivisions just north of Wailuku and Kahului, not far from the earlier Paukūkalo development. Thirty-nine families took up leases on Waiehu Kou homes in phase one, and about one hundred families planned to assume leases in phase two, with the first group of houses in phase two expected to be ready for occupation in April 2000. The DHHL put up $7.4 million for infrastructure improvements needed to get phase two under way, with the private contractor Everett Dowling actually building the homes. In late 1998 Charles Maxwell offered prayers at Waiehu Kou, calling the second phase of the subdivision "a sacred place to all Hawaiians." A third phase was in the planning stage.[78]

At about the same time, plans were made to develop home sites for Native Hawaiians on the Kula lands. Some 318 lots were planned for 668 acres at Waiohuli, with an additional sixty-three lots planned for nearby Kēōkea.

Building the homes had been delayed for a decade by the lack of roads, sewers, and water lines. To cost an estimated $22 million, the Waiohuli project was expected to open for occupancy in 2000. "Glory hallelujah," shouted the president of the Kēōkea Hawaiian Homesteaders at ground-breaking ceremonies in early 1998, "they've come to the land, they've touched the land."[79]

Kahikinui

If construction at Paukūkalo, Waiehu Kou, Waiohuli, and the like promised help for Native Hawaiians looking for residential housing, a development begun in Kahikinui was more revolutionary. After years of effort, a group of Native Hawaiians banded together as Ka Ohana o Kahikinui and led by Earl "Mo" Moler, won permission from the DHHL to live together according to *ahupua'a* principles on land at Kahikinui. Eventually to embrace 23,000 acres, the Kahikinui project included subsistence farming as well as housing.[80]

Kahikinui is located on the arid south side of Maui. In precontact times Kahikinui had supported numerous villages, with a population totaling perhaps 1,800. The DHHL leased Kahikinui to ranchers in the 1970s and 1980s; with those leases about to expire, the agency held a series of public meetings in 1992 to gather ideas about how to manage the land in the future. Sensing the possibility of persuading the DHHL to move in new directions, Moler formed his group in the fall of 1992 and urged that Native Hawaiians be allowed to live and farm on the land with a minimum of state aid. It was the financial inability of the state to provide the needed infrastructure, he realized, that had kept most land designated for homesteading from actually being put to use. However, more was involved than economics. As Moler envisioned developments, those settling at Kahikinui would preserve Hawaiian culture. They would wear traditional dress and would, Moler explained, "work together, play together, sing together." All the state and county had to provide would be a rough track branching off from Maui's Pi'ilani Highway. No electric connections, sewer systems, or water systems would be required from the government.[81]

The DHHL worked with Moler's group over the next few years to devise a workable plan for Kahikinui. The DHHL instituted what it called a Kuleana Homestead Program — a throwback in terminology to land use terms of the 1850s — for Kahikinui. The DHHL would bulldoze an unpaved road into the

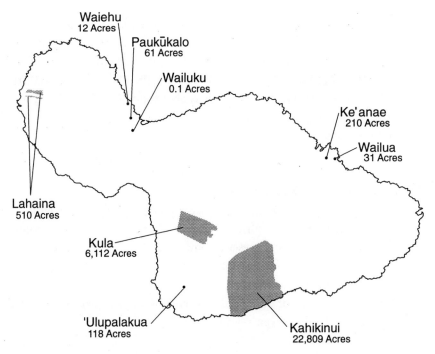

Waiehu
12 Acres

Paukūkalo
61 Acres

Wailuku
0.1 Acres

Ke'anae
210 Acres

Wailua
31 Acres

Lahaina
510 Acres

Kula
6,112 Acres

'Ulupalakua
118 Acres

Kahikinui
22,809 Acres

Land was set aside for Native Hawaiians at various locations on Maui, the largest being Kahikinui.

area and survey house and farm lots. The rest was up to the homesteaders.[82] Kahikinui was, in fact, a pilot project, the first Native Hawaiian Home Lands project to involve farming and land uses according to *ahupua'a* principles, a pioneering venture that might serve as a model for similar efforts throughout the Hawaiian Islands. Even as Kahikinui was beginning operations, a similar 60,000-acre project was in the planning stages on the island of Hawai'i.[83]

At Kahikinui, families would lease plots of land for ninety-nine years, on which they would engage in dryland agriculture, growing dry taro and sweet potatoes. They would also gather food and fish. Solar heating, composting toilets, wind energy, and water-saving techniques would permit a reasonably comfortable life in this isolated section of Maui. Already in 1998 a pilot program provided Kahikinui with 1,500 gallons of water per day through a system of screens that caught the mist from clouds on Haleakalā, condensed it, and channeled the resulting water to agricultural plots. Members of Ka Ohana o Kahikinui hoped to do more than simply farm their land. They wanted to restore the Kahikinui Forest, which had been damaged by overbrowsing by cattle, goats, and pigs. "Hawaiians just want to be caretakers of the land again," observed Moler. "These people don't want to live in the city, but in the country where their ancestors used to live. This is about going back to the basics, culturally, physically, and spiritually."[84]

A ceremony to celebrate approval for leaseholding by the DHHL at Kahikinui in 1998 revealed just how much developments there meant to Native Hawaiians. Stressing "love, faith, and hope," about forty members of Ka Ohana o Kahikinui gathered at Kahikinui. A large bear of a man, Moler oversaw a program of luau, hula, singing, and speeches, all pervaded by a feeling of warmth and a genuine aloha spirit of love. Emotions ran high. At one point, Native Hawaiians asked those present to kneel down and touch the 'āina, the land. Throughout, Moler and the others present stressed that they were going to live at Kahikinui and develop farming there, not just for themselves, but for future generations, "for our grandchildren." In the late spring of 1999 the DHHL awarded the first seventy-four leases.[85]

Continuing Questions about Native Hawaiian Lands

It was not always easy to decide on Native Hawaiian claims, as revealed by an incident involving a nature reserve on Maui. In 1997 the brothers Randolph "Boogie" Lu'uwai and Robert Lu'uwai of Mākena submitted a request to the Hawaii Department of Land and Natural Resources (DLNR), which oversaw the use of all conservation lands in the islands, that their Native Hawaiian family be allowed to conduct subsistence fishing in the 'Ahihi-Kina'u Natural Area Reserve. Composed of Cape Kina'u, which jutted out into the ocean several miles south of Mākena, the reserve encompassed about 2,000 acres. One of only two areas closed to fishing on Maui, Cape Kina'u was a favorite area for snorkeling and scuba diving. Established as a Natural Area Reserve in 1973, the first such Hawaiian area created under a law passed by the state legislature several years earlier, 'Ahihi-Kina'u served as a reserve for flora and fauna native to Hawai'i. 'Ahihi-Kina'u was home to rare brackish ponds and was the site of Maui's last lava flow.[86]

At public hearings Native Hawaiians noted that commercial tour operators took kayaking groups into the area (indeed, sometimes so many groups

Earl "Mo" Moler (far left), shown here with two of the land commissioners at Kahikinui, led the fight for Native Hawaiian homesteading on Maui.

that scuffles developed over the use of scarce coves and beaches) and asked for gathering and fishing rights in the reserve. Dana Naone Hall observed that the Lu'uwais were "not asking for the world. They're just asking to continue the traditional cultural practices that have been used for a thousand years or more." Charles Maxwell made much the same point, noting that more was involved than fishing: "It's a cultural and spiritual experience." For their part, the Lu'uwais said that they would act as "stewards," overseeing and protect- ing the reserve.[87]

The request of the Lu'uwais divided state natural area resource managers. Some reserve commissioners feared that granting the request would make their jobs more difficult, set an unwanted precedent for their state's seven- teen other Natural Area Reserves, and unduly favor Native Hawaiians over other Hawaiian residents. Bill Devick, acting administrator of the DLNR's Division of Aquatic Resources, expressed these views in a March 1998 letter. Devick praised the foresight shown in setting aside the reserve. While the near- shore resources of many of the Hawaiian Islands were in decline, he observed, those in the 'Ahihi-Kina'u Reserve were flourishing, allowing the reserve to serve as "a reference point showing how spectacular these resources could be elsewhere." Others wanted to give the request serious consideration. Bill Evanson, the Maui district manager for reserves, observed, for instance, that "a lot of our talk and ideas have been using a Western yardstick, which hasn't necessarily been in sync with the Hawaiian yardstick" and concluded that "we could get more support for preservation while not just taking a biological focus."[88]

In late 1998 the Lu'uwais proposed a compromise to a working group — the group included the Lu'uwais, commissioners from Natural Area Reserves, and Maui residents and was headed by the superintendent of the Haleakalā National Park — to consider their request. Any Native Hawaiians who could show that their families had been connected to Maui's Honuaula District, which included Mākena, since 1892 and who could demonstrate that their families had used the area for fishing purposes would be allowed to fish in the 'Ahihi-Kina'u Natural Area Reserve. However, there would be strict limitations on such fishing. Native Hawaiians could fish for only four days each year and then only by traditional methods. Fishing methods would be limited to the use of Hawaiian sling spears, casting nets, squid lures, hand lines, and hand gathering (such as the use of the 'opihi knife to take limpets). In the summer of 1999 the working group and then the DLNR accepted the Lu'uwais' proposal.[89]

Native Hawaiian land issues extended to include the preservation of burial sites. In a celebrated case on Maui in 1988, Dana Naone Hall and others belonging to Hui Alanui o Makena opposed the unearthing of some one thousand ancient burials during resort developments at Kapalua. Called back from a vacation in Europe by the burial discovery, the developer, Colin Cameron, worked out a satisfactory compromise by resiting a hotel. In 1990 Congress passed the Graves Protection and Repatriation Act, which helped Native Americans, Alaska Natives, and Native Hawaiians protect the remains of their ancestors, and the Hawai'i legislature passed accompanying legislation to stiffen state efforts to preserve Native Hawaiian burial and historic sites in the same year. Under the terms of the state law the DLNR through its State Historic Preservation Division (SHPD) set up burial councils for the major Hawaiian islands, including one for Maui and Lāna'i. The councils had the power to "determine the preservation or relocation of previously identified native Hawaiian burial sites" on lands subject to real estate developments.

The 'Ahihi-Kina'u Natural Reserve Area in South Maui was a site for conflicting notions of land use.

Developments in the Hawaiian Islands inspired similar actions elsewhere in the Pacific: The Chamorros of Guam and the Northern Mariana Islands took steps to protect gravesites and repatriate the bones of their ancestors in the 1990s.[90]

An event occurring in 1998 showed just how important the power to protect burial sites was. With the Hawaiian Islands struggling in a recession, Gov. Benjamin Cayetano proposed that state funding for the SHPD be slashed by half as part of a statewide governmental cost-cutting effort. Eight positions, including those of five archaeologists, would be eliminated. Native Hawaiians on Maui were among those who quickly opposed this suggestion. Leslie Kuloloio, a charter member of Hui Alanui o Makena and vice-chair of the Maui/Lāna'i Burial Council, observed that "we might as well get rid of our history then." Dana Naone Hall, who chaired the burial council, added that "there's been some movement in the development business community to weaken the [state historic] process" and wondered if Cayetano's proposal reflected this feeling. Not all developers favored the cutbacks, however. Everett Dowling, who sat on the burial council, opposed cutbacks on practical grounds: "I think it's bad for developers because it would delay projects that would otherwise get under way, allow construction and hire people to get us out of this economic slump." In the end, no cutbacks occurred.[91]

Land Use on Maui and the American West

In their growing concerns for open space and the protection of farmland, residents of Maui County shared concerns similar to those of mainlanders. In the 1970s Oregonians approved statewide measures imposing boundaries on Portland and other major cities as antisprawl devices. Californians probably led the nation, however; by 1989 they had placed nearly 150 "no-growth" measures on the ballot. At the same time, private groups such as the Nature Conservancy and the Wildlands Conservancy spent considerable funds to protect large areas from development. As early as 1981 some 400 private land trusts had been formed in the United States to protect land from private development.[92]

Still, changes in attitudes came hard, in the Hawaiian Islands as elsewhere. Possessing a frontier heritage, most Americans, but especially those in the Trans-Mississippi West, wanted to put land to use well into the twentieth century, to exploit it for their private gain. Whether as fur trappers, miners, ranchers, or farmers, Americans had gone West in hopes of wresting quick profits from the land. In fact, few pioneers expected to stay in the West very long. Land speculation and land development, whether in farmlands or town plots, were integral to the development of western American frontiers. Conversely, planned developments were few. Even when they had real chances to develop planned cities, for example, most westerners chose not to do so.[93] It is not surprising, then, to find a desire for rapid development running through Maui's land use policies well into the 1970s. The achievement of statehood by Hawai'i in 1959 and the Democratic revolution of the 1950s and 1960s contributed to this emphasis. As new groups came to the fore, they wanted a larger share in their state's economic advance. With the economic power of the Big Five companies weakened and with the Big Five's hold over politics eroded, new ethnic groups demanded a major share of their islands' economic pie.

Even so, there was always concern about how best to use land and, especially from the 1980s on, how to preserve at least some of it as farmland and open space. Over time Maui's residents came to realize that development could go too far. The Maui County Council found itself pulled in different directions by competing groups, but from the 1980s onward the balance of opinion on Maui, as in much of the rest of the United States, shifted in the direction of preservation. Certainly land development would continue, but with stricter public supervision. The input of Native Hawaiians was important here, for it showed a possibility different from that of land development for tourism. Like Native Americans on the mainland, Native Hawaiians won public recognition for some of their claims. In the 1990s, especially, Native Hawaiians finally won rights to lease some of the land set aside for them decades earlier. Perhaps most exciting was the experiment under way at Kahikinui. Subsistence homesteading along the principles of *ahupua'a*, if successful, promised to revolutionize lifestyles for some Native Hawaiians.

4

Water Controversies

Closely related to land use issues were questions about water in the Hawaiian Islands, for without water land was worthless for agricultural and visitor industry developments. A fundamental challenge faced Maui's residents: Water was not often found where it was most needed. Lots of rain fell on Maui — hundreds of inches per year on the West Maui Mountains and the windward slopes of Haleakalā. However, much less rain fell on Central and South Maui, home to sugar cane and pineapple lands, major towns and cities, and fast-growing resort areas. Rainfall over much of this part of Maui amounted to less than thirty inches per year, and in some sections less than ten inches annually. Moving water to where it was needed was crucial to Maui's economic growth. As a report prepared by economists at the University of Hawai'i observed in 1967, Maui's "development has been largely dependent on the degree to which water could be diverted from the windward northeastern portions of the island to the leeward and central plains."[1] Herein lay the crux of the problem: There existed no inexpensive way to transport water and have it available on demand. "Water controversies" are "in my estimate *currently* more along the lines of who will pay for developing water and not so much that we have run out," noted David Craddick, director of Maui's Department of Water Supply in the winter of 1999.[2]

Maui possessed a large amount of fresh water derived from surface runoff and underground aquifers. Generally speaking, agricultural water needs were met by private companies' development of surface water resources and by the tapping of underground water via shafts and wells. The county government supplied most of Maui's domestic water needs — that is, the demand for household water, especially drinking water — from both surface and

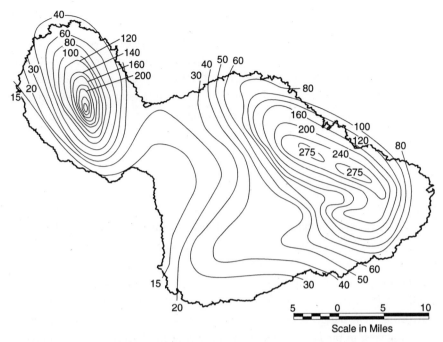

Average annual rainfall on Maui. Rainfall varied tremendously, from the wet northern windward side to the dry leeward southern side.

underground sources. On Maui the annual purchases of water from the county rose from 7.4 billion to 11.5 billion gallons between 1984 and 1996.[3] Even so, there was enough water on the island, if it were wisely used and if it could be transported to where it was needed. In the early 1990s the island of Maui fully used its 333 million gallons per day (mgd) of surface water. However, of the island's potential 452 mgd of underground water only 56 mgd were actually being used. There was, thus, considerable room for future development, enough to meet Maui's likely needs for at least twenty years, according to a 1990 county report.[4]

There were, however, warnings that not all was well. Growing demands strained distribution systems for water, putting pressures on state and county agencies to limit the building of new houses and resorts. In 1990 the mayor of Maui County declared a building moratorium for Wailuku when it was found that the aquifer supplying that city with water was being overdrawn. Nor was Maui alone in its problems. On parts of O'ahu shortages also be-

came apparent, particularly for housing developments near Honolulu. Re-
solving water issues was complicated, involving changing relations between
public and private water systems and shifting relations between the state and
county governments. Competing conceptions of how best to allocate and pay
for water were important in determining and implementing water policies.
Solutions to water issues became increasingly difficult to find as inexpensive
water was used to its safe limit.

Aridity, Culture, and Water

In some respects, water issues on Maui mirrored those of the American West.
While there exist tremendous variations among the different parts of the region, much of the Trans-Mississippi West is arid, becoming increasingly drier
as one travels westward. At around the one hundredth meridian — that is, at
about 100 degrees west longitude, a point on the western Great Plains — the
climate becomes too dry to farm by conventional means.[5] Less than twenty
inches of rain fall each year. Even dry-farming methods, hailed by settlers
moving west in the late nineteenth and early twentieth centuries, often prove
ineffective. Today some believe that much of this land is simply unsuited for
farming, and a few easterners have recently suggested that it should be abandoned by humans, to be turned back into a national bison range.

The aridity of much of the Trans-Mississippi West helped define the experiences of those moving into the region. New farming practices had to
be developed, including innovative long-distance irrigation. The historian
Donald Pisani has stressed in a number of important studies that "the aridity
model is too nebulous, and too subject to qualification and exception, to serve
as a paradigm for the entire West." Pisani has rightly emphasized the importance of values, culture, and institutions, along with local economic conditions and the actions of individuals, in determining how westerners sought
to shape their physical environments. As we shall see, local circumstances ran
through efforts in the Hawaiian Islands to deal with water issues. Yet, at the
same time, it is worth stressing that water problems were key challenges for
those eager to develop the land. The aridity of parts of the islands mattered,
just as it did in much of the West.[6]

Legal concepts about water ownership changed in the West, and these alterations would be important for developments on Maui. Most Americans

living in the well-watered East and Midwest adhered to the riparian rights concept of water use. Inherited from Great Britain, the doctrine of riparian rights held that the use of water was limited to people who owned land along the sides of streams. Rights to water were incidental to land ownership; in legal terms, water rights were "correlative," part of a bundle of land and water rights. Riparian owners could use water from their streams, but they had to return the water to the streams, so as not to diminish the flow or quality of the water to downstream users. Moreover, it was generally accepted that water would be used only on land next to the stream. In much of the arid West the doctrine of prior appropriation replaced or modified that of riparian rights. According to the legal construct of prior appropriation, the first person or company to take water from a stream could claim whatever amount could be put to beneficial use (or whatever amount might be put to good use in the future). In addition, the water could be transported some distance from its source before being used.

The legal doctrine of prior appropriation was a function of culture as well as of the aridity of western lands. Over several decades it defeated competing riparian rights ideas and Spanish and Mexican concepts current in the Southwest to become the law of the land. Spanish and Mexican legal concepts treated water as a common good and placed community rights over individual ones. Water for irrigation belonged to the state, not to individual settlers. Water masters doled out water in each community and supervised the maintenance of irrigation systems by inhabitants. Farmers contributed work and money to keep up the systems according to how much land they irrigated. While some water rights could be bought and sold, they gave people only the right to use water and did not convey ownership rights. Community controls were important in much of the Southwest, including parts of California, well into the nineteenth and even the twentieth centuries. However, most such controls gave way to the doctrine of prior appropriation in the 1880s and 1890s.[7]

In line with other U.S. legal doctrines of that day, that of prior appropriation favored individual enterprise over community rights as the most effective way of releasing energies needed for economic development.[8] Water should, most westerners thought, be put to its most productive use in mining and farming. With the passage of the Reclamation Act by Congress in 1902, the federal government sought, halfheartedly, to assert some control over western waters as a way of insuring that the irrigation projects in which it was involved had adequate supplies of water. For the most part, however, the concept of prior appropriation triumphed over state and federal governmental efforts to put forward ownership rights. Only much later, in the 1960s and subsequent decades, did new views challenge this dominant outlook. Pieces of congressional legislation, such as the Wild and Scenic Rivers Act of 1968, suggested alternative ways to view the most beneficial use of water.[9]

Some residents of Maui shared common outlooks with westerners in how they viewed and used water, but differences existed as well. Like westerners who transported water long distances, planters on Maui constructed elaborate and expensive systems to ship water from the rainy mountains to their companies' sugar cane fields. Later on, resort owners needed to bring water to their developments. As in much of the West, the key questions became who had legal rights to water and who should pay for the development of water systems. After World War II Native Hawaiian rights came to loom large in water matters on Maui, especially after a seminal decision by the Hawaiian Supreme Court in 1973. To be sure, the assertion of Native American rights influenced the use of water in the Trans-Mississippi West, but not to the extent that Native Hawaiian rights came to affect water usage in the Hawaiian Islands.

Water Issues to the 1970s

In precontact times the distribution of water was not the challenge it later became. Hawaiians who needed water to irrigate taro fields lived near streams and built systems of dams and ditches to carry water to their plants. Some of these were quite extensive; one ditch on Kaua'i was 3.7 kilometers long. Water masters appointed by chiefs oversaw the operation of the systems. Hawaiians viewed water as belonging to nearby land, as being, in later legal terms, an "appurtenance" to the land — a concept very similar in important ways to the doctrine of riparian rights. If a stream produced more water than was needed for the production of taro, that "surplus" water might be diverted to dry land to grow secondary crops such as sweet potatoes. Community rights ruled over individual rights, much as had been the case in the Spanish and Mexican Southwest. Overall, Hawaiians understood water to be a bounty that should be made available to all landholders, with the rights of those downstream respected by those upstream. Most water used in growing taro returned to streams, available for reuse. All taro growers were entitled to water from an irrigation system, provided that they helped maintain that system.[10]

Sugar cane required much more water than did taro. Nor could water once used for sugar cane be reused for other crops downstream. As the scholar Carol Wilcox has noted, "Sugar is a thirsty crop." Even with the institution of water conservation methods after World War II, especially some use of drip irrigation from the 1970s, it took five hundred gallons, or about two tons, of water to produce one pound of sugar! One million gallons of water a day were required to irrigate one hundred acres of sugar cane.[11]

Companies growing sugar cane obtained their water in several ways. Sometimes they purchased *ahupua'a* and in doing so claimed ownership over all surplus waters originating in or flowing through the *ahupua'a*. Any water not being used for the traditional cultivation of taro went into growing sugar cane. Sugar barons also bought water rights directly from the Hawaiian monarchy. On Maui it was through such purchases that Samuel Alexander and Henry Baldwin obtained water rights in 1876 and that Claus Spreckels won his rights two years later. These purchases sometimes involved chicanery. In one of the most notorious acts of his reign, King David Kalākaua met with Spreckels and others in a hotel late into the evening of July 1, 1878, to work out the details of Spreckels's water deal. When his cabinet balked at the terms, the king dismissed it and installed a new cabinet. Within a week Spreckels had his agreement: a thirty-year lease, renewable for an additional thirty years, for water taken from Maui's windward side, for which Spreckels was to pay $500 annually. In addition, Spreckels granted the king four $10,000 loans payable in two to five years at a 7 percent annual interest rate.[12]

Concepts of water changed as the economy of the Hawaiian Islands became commercialized. Water became commodified, turned into private property, similar to what was occurring at about the same time in the Trans-Mississippi West. Commodification took place piecemeal. In 1859 Hawaiian legislation recognized that water could be withdrawn from streams and transported some distance for urban use, to supply a growing Honolulu. This legislation eroded the idea that water was to be used only in its *ahupua'a* or watershed. Legislation passed in 1876 permitted the government to grant thirty-year leases to companies desiring to divert water from streams, legislation quickly seized upon by sugar cane growers.[13] There were some halfhearted protests against these actions, and into the early twentieth century Hawai'i's courts upheld some riparian rights to water. Then, too, some efforts were made to protect *kuleana* lands, which were seen as having rights to water. As revised in 1925, the Kuleana Act of 1850 specified that "the people also shall have a right to drinking and running water" and that "the springs of water and running water . . . shall be free to all."[14]

Nonetheless, the main thrust of public policy was to move water into profitable private use, especially for the irrigation of sugar cane fields. This mind-set was apparent in an observation made about Maui by a *haole* visitor in 1890: "On the sandy isthmus connecting East and West Maui, and on a plain which was formerly an arid desert, where neither a tree and scarcely a blade of grass could formerly be found, can now be seen green pastures, beautiful flower gardens, avenues of trees and twelve thousand acres of growing sugar cane." Only in the 1970s and 1980s did Hawaiian law return to treating water as a common good, as a bounty for all. For about a century the sugar companies effectively owned much of the water of the Hawaiian Islands, increasingly by securing long-term, inexpensive leases from the governments in Hawai'i. Only in 1986 did the last of state-issued water leases to the East Maui Irrigation Company, a subsidiary of Alexander and Baldwin, expire. Since then, the state government has issued revocable annual permits to East Maui Irrigation and other firms, for which the companies have paid flat monthly fees.[15]

Owning water rights did not solve all of the problems the sugar companies faced, for they needed to build extensive irrigation systems. To supply their fields on Maui's sunny central plains, the sugar companies set up subsidiaries to build long ditches to bring water around from rainy East Maui. Completed in 1878 by Alexander and Baldwin, the Hāmākua Ditch transported water seventeen miles from Maui's windward side to irrigate cane fields in more arid country. Building the ditch included crossing the steep-sided Maliko Gulch. Doing so involved heroics, well-remembered into the 1990s. The plan was to carry water down one side of the 450-foot-deep gulch and then up the other side through an inverted siphon constructed of twenty-four-inch iron pipe. Setting the pipe required workers to descend into the depths of the gulch by rope, which they at first refused to do. Finally, Henry Baldwin, who had recently lost a hand and part of an arm crushed in rollers in a sugar cane mill, clutched the rope with his one good hand and legs and went down. The workers followed and laid the pipe.[16] The Hāmākua Ditch could deliver about 40 mgd of water. Even larger was a thirty-mile ditch built a few years later to irrigate the lands of Claus Spreckels. Crossing thirty gulches and including twenty-eight tunnels, this ditch could deliver 60 mgd.[17]

Additional ditches followed, operated by East Maui Irrigation. As Wilcox has noted, "On the East Maui mountains many hundreds of men were employed almost continuously for fifty years building the 74 miles of canals and ditches." By far the most important was (and is) the Wailoa Ditch, which carried more water than any river in the Hawaiian Islands. Capable of transporting nearly 200 mgd, this ditch operated at the 1,450 to 1,100 foot level on the side of Haleakalā to carry water twenty-three miles to sugar cane lands. Altogether, East Maui Irrigation's ditches delivered an average flow of 160 mgd and had a peak capacity of roughly 400 mgd. The largest privately owned water company in the United States, East Maui Irrigation had a replacement value estimated at $200 million in the early 1990s.[18]

Wells tapping underground water supplemented the ditches. The first artesian well was sunk on Maui in 1881. By the early 1930s Hawaiian Commercial and Sugar — like East Maui Irrigation, a subsidiary of Alexander and Baldwin — could pump 144 mgd from wells tapping aquifers in Maui's isthmus. The wells featured inclined tunnels or shafts that penetrated far beneath the surface, ending in cavernous pumping rooms overlying sumps. Saturation tunnels led off from the sumps to collect underground water. Hawaiian Commercial and Sugar's pump 18 was, for example, located in a chamber 500 feet underground. The wells drew on water that fell as rain, soaked into the ground, and ran underground through porous rock until it met the salt water that saturated Maui's base. Lighter than salt water, the fresh water "floated" on top of the salt water in a lens-shaped body (it "floated" inside rock, not as a large pool of underground water).[19]

The achievements on Maui were part of a larger accomplishment throughout the Hawaiian Islands. In the 1920s irrigation systems built by the sugar companies diverted about 800 mgd. By 1934 Hawai'i's sugar companies had invested $39 million in water improvements. This was an investment averaging $304 per acre of sugar cane land — much higher than the irrigation investment per acre of irrigated land in any state on the mainland. In Arizona, the next highest, the investment averaged $99 per acre in 1940.[20]

Built for agricultural purposes, the ditches and artesian wells initially did little to provide household water for Maui's communities. The untreated water was unsuitable for drinking, and potable water was frequently in short supply. Kīhei faced a major water shortage as early as 1948. The two tanks supplying water to the town held 70,000 gallons, but residents were using 100,000 gallons per day. Water was a pressing problem for much of Maui County when Eddie Tam took over as chairman; the *Maui News* noted in 1949 that "the water supply is very bad on Maui." Maui's Chamber of Commerce responded by setting up a committee to study the situation. That committee recommended creating a Board of Water Supply, and the Board of Supervisors endorsed this recommendation. In 1949 the Territorial Legislature created the Maui County Waterworks Board and appropriated money to improve water systems.[21]

However, just six years later the legislature, influenced by county "home-rule" desires of Democrats, disbanded the Board of Water Supply. In its place the Maui County Board of Supervisors sponsored a charter amendment establishing a Department of Water Supply for Maui County. Run by a manager and chief engineer appointed by the chairman of the Board of Supervisors with the approval of the board, the Department of Water Supply oversaw Maui's water matters for a decade and a half. The Board of Supervisors also appointed a waterworks committee to advise the manager of the Department of Water Supply. In 1969, a decade after statehood, further alterations took place. Under Maui County's new charter, the Maui County Water Department, overseen by a County Board of Water Supply, became an agency operating, for the most part, independently of the county council. With some administrative changes in 1979, this situation continued through the 1990s. Altogether, these arrangements set up a system that was thought to be more responsive to county residents than the more centralized 1949 structure had been.[22]

Still, water problems persisted. The authors of the master plan adopted for Maui's development in 1959 observed that "the expansion of the water system for the Kihei, Makena, and Wailea areas must be considered," because the region was "served by a water system unable to take care of any material expansion of residential or agricultural activity." Appropriations by the Territorial Legislature were woefully inadequate, judged the authors of the plan. A report prepared in 1967 made much the same point: "Kihei, with its ideal climate and beach areas, has great agricultural and residential potential if an adequate water supply is available." That same report observed that Upcountry Maui — composed of small but growing towns and agricultural areas located about 1,000 to 4,500 feet up on the side of Haleakalā — was "ideal for diversified agriculture" but that an "inadequate water supply to this area has always been a limiting factor."[23]

The Impact of Growth: Water Issues in the 1970s and 1980s

Funding for water improvements continued to be inadequate in later decades. Water problems dogged Maui's development into the 1980s, as the growing demands of tourism and residential developments severely strained distribution systems. This situation was hardly unique to Maui. "Of primary concern is the availability of fresh water for human use and consumption," wrote two scholars looking at O'ahu. "As tourism booms," they observed, "the transient population needs to make use of the same water resources that serve residents."[24] As in so many respects, the growth of a visitor industry was a mixed blessing on Maui and throughout the Hawaiian Islands.

Upcountry Maui suffered the most, as more homes were built in the area. Between 1966 and 1979 the number of Upcountry water hookups doubled, reaching a total of 2,530. A water shortage dried up the region in 1972 and 1973, leading homeowners to petition the county council to "stop all building and all connections to any and all water supply lines in the Makawao District, including Pukalani and Kula." A water system had been put in place in Lower Kula around 1967, but by the early 1970s many of its lines had become clogged with dirt and gravel and were unable to deliver enough water. The immediate water crisis eased over the next few years, but shortages of drinking water continued. Throughout most of the 1970s many Upcountry residents often had to boil their water or bring in water from Kahului and Wailuku.[25]

A moratorium on most new water hookups in Kula, a so-called Kula rule, promulgated by the Board of Water Supply in 1977, briefly slowed residential developments. However, amendments to the rule reduced its effectiveness by giving land developments subdivided for family members access to water. Between 1979 and 1990 the county granted an additional 2,572 water hookups in Upcountry Maui. The Kula rule expired in 1993. Given authority by the Board of Water Supply, David Craddick, who had just become Maui County's water director, declared the Upcountry water system inadequate and halted most new water connections. In 1994 only thirty-seven hookups were approved.[26]

Water shortages extended to South Maui, and even to the Hānā area. Located in an arid region, Māʻalaea found itself chronically short of water, leading residents to oppose the construction of additional condominiums there. Similarly, water shortages led to a temporary building moratorium for much of Kīhei, Wailea, and Mākena in 1979. In Hānā the problem was not a shortage of water — frequent rains drenched the region — but, as in Upcountry Maui, a lack of sufficient tanks to hold the water and pipes to distribute it. Upon inspecting Hānā's water system, one council member found "that the lines out in Hānā are over 50 years old, full of leaks." The storage area was, he thought, "a disgrace."[27]

The county government played a never-ending game of catch-up in providing household water. In the late 1960s and early 1970s the county water board set standards for water systems for subdivisions and established rules for water connections within the county. Generally backed by Maui's realtors — once perceived inequities in assessments to pay for the water systems were ironed out — the standards and rules were seen as "vital" if development were to continue.[28]

While the county water board had most of the authority to set water policies for Maui County, the county council was not about to be left out of the picture. In 1977 one council member observed that "water is such an important item in our lives that I feel that the Council should attempt to examine all avenues that might be available to us to solve some of these problems." Too often, he thought, the council "had taken an ostrich-like viewpoint" on water matters.[29] Two years later another council member suggested that the county council establish an ad hoc committee to deal with water issues, which was done in 1982. The committee recommended that the county water board determine what parts of Maui it would serve with water and what standards of service it would provide. Perhaps most importantly, the committee recommended that the board should put in water systems in advance of development, with the county, not the developers, picking up the cost of those systems. Few funds were available to do so, however.[30]

The State Water Code of 1987

Even with the creation of the Board of Water Supply and the growing assertion of power by the county council, most of Maui County's surface water lay in the hands of private water companies, such as East Maui Irrigation. Over the decades the sugar cane producers had developed many of the water supplies on Maui and the other Hawaiian Islands, and the firms considered the water they controlled to be their private property. The State of Hawai'i challenged that view in the 1970s and 1980s, resulting in the redefinition of all water in Hawai'i as public property, a return in some senses to precontact Hawaiian concepts. In establishing state ownership of water, residents of Hawai'i also resembled their counterparts in some areas beyond the United States. People in both Canada and Australia had declared water public property in the late nineteenth and early twentieth centuries, as they wrestled with the settlement of arid lands.[31]

In Hawai'i the redefinition began with a crucial decision made by the Hawaiian Supreme Court in 1973. In *McBryde Sugar Co. v. Robinson* the court rejected the concept of private ownership of water. Looking back to the Great Mahele of 1848, the court concluded that the king of Hawai'i had intended to reserve the right to use water to himself in trust for the common good. In other words, observed the court, no right to private ownership of surface water existed in the Hawaiian Islands. In fact, concluded the court, the State of Hawai'i, as the successor to the king, was the owner of all water flowing in natural water courses. In its elaboration of this decision, the court combined ancient Hawaiian concepts of water use with principles of riparian rights. The court decreed that owners of lands adjacent to streams had the right to use water from those streams on lands next to the watercourses. However, landowners could claim no property interests in the water itself. Nor could landowners transfer water from the locality in which it was found to serve lands far away. Thus, sugar companies could claim no ownership rights to divert water, not even so-called surplus water, to irrigate cane fields outside of the watersheds in which streams ran.[32]

In a second major legal decision, the *Reppun* decision of 1982, the Hawaiian Supreme Court extended its ruling in *McBryde*. The *Reppun* case resulted from actions of the Honolulu Board of Water Supply. Eager to slake Honolulu's thirst, the board extended wells and water development tunnels far into the surrounding countryside. Over time, the board increased its pumping of ground water so much that some farmers, referred to collectively as Reppun, found that the surface water upon which they relied for irrigation had dried up. The farmers then sued the board and won. In *Reppun* the court decided that it could rule on underground, as well as surface, water matters. In finding for the farmers, the court cut to the heart of the situation: "We therefore hold that where surface water and ground water can be demonstrated to be physically interrelated as parts of a single system, established surface water rights may be protected against diversions that injure those rights." This ruling would have implications for Maui, as Native Hawaiians sought to reestablish rights to surface water depleted by the pumping of underground water.[33]

The State of Hawai'i soon moved to put its control over water rights into practice. In 1978 the citizens of Hawai'i amended their state's constitution in many ways, including how it dealt with water rights. The amended constitution provided for the creation of a state agency to "establish criteria for water use priorities while assuring appurtenant rights and existing correlative and riparian uses and establish procedures for regulating all uses of Hawai'i's water resources." A new state agency would determine how all of Hawai'i's water, from above-ground and underground sources, would be used. However, legislation to create such an agency was stalled for a decade. Considerable opposition came from county governments, which reasoned, correctly, that the establishment of such a state body would greatly erode their control over water. County officials testified in legislative hearings in Honolulu against the proposed law. Members of the Maui County Council, for example, argued that "the establishment of a centralized State agency would undermine the home rule powers of the political subdivisions of the State of Hawaii" and would "have a negative impact on the county's effort to develop and administer an effective water resources program responsive to the county's needs."[34]

In the end, lawmakers worked out a compromise. In 1987 the state legislators passed the State Water Code and created a six-member State Water Resource Management Commission to administer it. All private water users, such as the sugar companies, had two years within which to apply for water permits from the state. Almost all such applications were approved, with actual water use, if not ownership, continuing as before. The companies received water use leases from the state, for shorter lengths of time and at greater expense than before. The code reserved considerable powers for the counties. The counties were to determine how much water existed within their boundaries and whether there was enough to accommodate planned developments. Moreover, county agencies such as Maui's water board were to oversee the use of that water.[35] However, the State Water Code reserved for the state one very important power. The state water commission could step in and designate any part of Hawai'i as a water management area, if the commission determined that overuse was threatening water resources in the area. In such a situation the commission could take management of a designated area away from the county and mandate regulations designed to remove threats to water resources in the region. The state government now had ultimate authority over water usage.[36]

The two areas on Maui most affected by a growing imbalance between water production and consumption, and weaknesses in distribution systems, were South Maui and Upcountry Maui. How water matters worked out in each area illustrated well the tensions that developed as tourism became the island's economic mainstay. Their resolution showed, as well, some of the strains that had grown up between the county and state governments, stresses similar to those in jurisdictional conflicts over land use issues.

The 'Iao Aquifer

Initially, most of the water for South Maui came from local sources, but these quickly proved inadequate as the arid region developed as a tourist destination. As developers began looking outside of the region for water, they turned their thirsty eyes to underground sources in the 'Iao aquifer. Fed by rain falling on the West Maui Mountains, this aquifer contained a large amount of fresh water flowing underground in porous volcanic rock.[37] Intense exploitation of the 'Iao aquifer began when companies building resorts in South Maui reached an agreement with the county's Board of Water Supply. Signed in 1975, this pact was known as the "Central Maui Source Development Agreement." Four companies — the Wailea Development Company; Seibu, which was planning to put up the Maui Prince Hotel just north of Mākena; Hawaiiana, which was owned by C. Brewer; and Alexander and Baldwin, the major backer of the Wailea development — agreed to finance jointly the drilling of new wells, at a cost of millions of dollars, into the 'Iao aquifer.[38]

In what seemed to be a classic "win-win" situation, everyone was expected to gain. The companies were to benefit by receiving water they needed for their new developments. The firms were to develop up to 19 mgd of water from the 'Iao aquifer. Moreover, the county, joined with the private joint venture members, would construct large transmission lines to carry the water

Resort developments in South Maui, such as this condominium complex in Wailea, required large amounts of water from the 'Īao aquifer.

twenty-five miles south from the wells to the resorts. The county was to benefit in several respects. The companies were to turn over the wells and the pumps used to lift the water to the county shortly after their completion at no charge. In addition, the county retained the right to any water from the 'Īao aquifer beyond the 19 mgd set aside for the private companies. That is, if the companies did not use all of the water the wells were capable of lifting, the county had the right to sell or otherwise use that water. The county could also sink its own wells into the aquifer to develop additional water supplies. It was thought at the time that the 'Īao aquifer could sustain a renewable withdrawal of at least 36 mgd, more than enough for everyone for decades to come. Most broadly, of course, it was expected that the county would benefit from economic growth in South Maui. As Elmer Cravalho, Maui's mayor during the 1970s, later observed, the agreement was "a *quid pro quo* kind of thing," exactly in line with his ideas of government and business working together.[39]

However, the estimate of 36 mgd proved to be much too high, for within a decade actual usage showed that the aquifer could support a renewable withdrawal of just 20 mgd. One matter that upset predictions was how the land on top of the aquifer was used. For years the land had been planted in sugar cane, and some of the water used to irrigate the sugar cane — perhaps as much as one-third of it — had dripped down into the aquifer, helping to recharge it. However, as part of the movement to specialized agriculture, much of the sugar cane was replaced with macadamia nut trees, which were not irrigated. Less water dripped down into the aquifer, which was, thus, depleted more easily.[40]

Controversy soon engulfed policies for the ʻĪao aquifer. The state water commission began monitoring fresh water levels in the aquifer in 1985 and within four years warned that it might have to intercede. The state agency threatened to designate the aquifer a water management area and order the county water board to take steps to equalize the production and consumption of water. The county board might then have to declare a moratorium on all new water hookups to lines dependent on the aquifer, bringing resort and housing development to a screeching halt. Under the gun, the county board agreed that the sustainable yield of the ʻĪao aquifer was only 20 mgd. Even so, as development continued, more water was taken out of the aquifer than was entering it, as withdrawals crept up to 20.5 mgd. Salinity levels rose, increasing the danger that salt water would mix with the fresh water to destroy the aquifer — raising again the specter of state control.[41]

Matters bubbled over in the 1990s. In mid-1997 Wayne Nishiki, a member of the county council from South Maui, spoke for many from his area when he labeled the consequences of the possible depletion of the ʻĪao aquifer "catastrophic."[42] The tapping of an aquifer by a well in North Waiheʻe made an additional 1.5 mgd available, but this was not enough.[43] Faced with the possibility of a drought due to the vagaries of El Niño, Maui's residents wanted action.[44] Pressure came from different sources. Many longtime residents of Central and South Maui feared having their water allocations cut back should overuse of the ʻĪao aquifer continue and wanted the county water board to cease issuing, at least temporarily, new water meters — in other words, to stop hooking up new developments to the aquifer. They also wanted the board to devise an equitable plan for water restrictions in times of emergency. On the other hand, resort and hotel owners, looking beyond what they viewed as a temporary slump in tourism, wanted to assure themselves of access to water for future developments. They backed conservation measures led by the water board but opposed restrictions on the issuance of new water meters.[45]

A climax came in 1997. The chairman of the Maui County Council proposed that the water board cease making new water connections to the 'Īao aquifer and was supported by testimony from several residents. In opposition, however, were Lynne Woods, president of the Maui Chamber of Commerce, and Terryl Vencl, executive director of the Maui Hotel Association. They urged, instead, greater public education and conservation in water matters. Receiving no support from other members of the county council, the chairman's resolution failed.[46] Few residents were satisfied. "I'm irritated," wrote Richard Larson of Kīhei to the *Maui News*. "The Iao aquifer is virtually all we have left, with forecasts dim to find more water in time to meet the developers' demands. If we pull more water from it now, we could damage it irrevocably."[47]

Although the county council failed to back any resolution calling for a halt to water hookups, one member of the county water board suggested that it might, indeed, be necessary to prohibit new connections.[48] Alarmed, hotel and resort owners responded. First, they formed a task force to study Maui's water situation. Second, they took the lead in establishing a Maui Water Roundtable to make recommendations to the water board. Composed of representatives of C. Brewer, Wailea Resort, Maui Land and Pineapple, Alexander and Baldwin, and Makena Resort, the roundtable also included representatives from Mayor Linda Lingle's office, the state water commission, the county water board, and several conservation groups, including the Nature Conservancy and the Maui Open Space Trust.[49] While opposed to even temporary cutoffs in water hookups, the roundtable endorsed a broad range of options to alleviate Maui's water problems, from the installation of low-flow showerheads to the development of new water sources in East Maui. Vencl headed the roundtable. Believing, as she later explained, that the 'Īao aquifer was "being pumped at its max," she thought that conservation measures were needed to avoid state intervention. "I am convinced we can do it ourselves," she later remarked.[50]

While considering the roundtable's proposals, the county water board acted. At the request of the state water commission, the board held a series of public hearings to air a proposal on how to deal with water emergencies. The scheme postulated three levels of cutbacks in water usage: "caution," a 5 percent reduction; "alert," a 10 percent cutback; and "critical," a 15 percent reduction. A draft rule drawn up by the board called for charging anyone who used too much water in emergency periods up to twenty times the normal rate for water. If that penalty did not bring about the desired cutbacks, the board could remove water meters, cutting off water to offenders altogether. Modeled on a rule that had long been in use in Honolulu, the board's proposal met with opposition from residents who thought it favored wealthy developers who could pay fines to keep water flowing. The rule was approved in early 1999. However, the board still faced the task of implementing conservation measures that would satisfy its members, the mayor, various groups of Maui's residents, and the state water commission.[51]

As a result, circumstances with regard to the 'Iao aquifer remained murky. The situation seemed to be improving, as conservation measures took hold. A continuing economic recession, which placed a hold on most resort and housing construction, also helped ease the water shortage. By 1999 withdrawals from the 'Iao aquifer had dropped to an average of just 17.4 mgd, well within the aquifer's sustainable yield.[52] Even so, new investigations in 1999 showed that salinity levels were rising and that fresh water-head levels were declining at an accelerating rate. There was speculation that water withdrawals from the nearby North Waihe'e aquifer were depleting water supplies in the 'Iao aquifer. Conservation groups continued to favor a state takeover. The Sierra Club consistently called for state management of the 'Iao aquifer as the only way to stabilize the water situation over the long haul. Similarly, the president of Maui Tomorrow observed that "we are a heartbeat away from overusing the 'Iao aquifer," and labeled the roundtable as "very self-serving."[53]

Upcountry Water Problems

Water problems continued Upcountry during the 1990s. With Craddick's actions in 1993, the number of new water hookups lessened but did not come to an end. An additional 1,129 hookups were granted between 1994 and 1999. Upcountry residents and farmers used water caught in local rain runoffs; as development proceeded, they became more and more dependent on water brought around from the East Maui watershed by ditches. Particularly important was the Wailoa Ditch. While most of this huge ditch's flow went to irrigate sugar cane fields owned by Hawaiian Commercial and Sugar, not all did. Beginning in 1977 some of the water was reserved for treatment at a plant built by the county at Kamole Weir for Upcountry domestic use, making the ditch the largest source of drinking water for Upcountry Maui. Some water from the ditch was also reserved for the Kula Agricultural Park.[54]

How the water came to be set aside is revealing about how county officials and businessmen could cooperate. In return for the county government's approval of Alexander and Baldwin's Wailea development, including the 1975 water agreement, Mayor Cravalho exacted a price: that the county receive a guaranteed 12 mgd from the Wailoa Ditch for use in Upcountry communities and another 4 mgd for the Kula Agricultural Park. Alexander and Baldwin, which owned the Wailoa Ditch through its subsidiary, East Maui Irrigation, complied. Thus, as he often did, Mayor Cravalho got something for the county in return for cooperating with developers. The trade-off is also telling about Maui's embrace of tourism. Alexander and Baldwin sacrificed water that might have gone to its cane-growing subsidiary, Hawaiian Commercial and Sugar. In giving up this water to the county, Alexander and Baldwin decided that resort development was more important than agriculture. Set up to run for twenty years, the agreement was renewed annually thereafter, although not without considerable dispute. During Mayor Hannibal Tavares's administration in the 1980s, the amount reserved for Upcountry residents was reduced from 12 mgd to just 6 or 7 mgd.[55]

William Hines, the director of the Department of Water Supply for Maui County, explained the importance of water from the Wailoa Ditch in 1981. Upcountry Maui, he observed, used surface runoff collected at two levels in the Waikamoi forest preserve. "In times of good tradewind rains, these intakes can adequately supply the entire area," he noted. However, "the rainfall is extremely variable," he continued, and in times of drought "the supply from Waikamoi drops to nearly zero." Then, he pointed out, it was "necessary to supply the entire system by pumping water in various high lift stages from the East Maui Irrigation Co. ditch at the Wailoa Forebay." Water had to be pumped uphill from the ditch at a 1,000-foot elevation on Haleakalā to communities several thousand feet higher up. The costs in 1981 ranged for $0.52 per thousand gallons for water pumped to Makawao and Pukalani to $2.13 per thousand gallons for water destined for Upper Kula.[56]

Droughts plagued Upcountry Maui. When rain failed to fall in East Maui, even the Wailoa Ditch ran low. Severe droughts led to 25 percent mandatory cutbacks in water use in Upcountry Maui in 1984 and again in 1996. The County Board of Water Supply continuously made efforts to address the

chronic Upcountry water problems but, as in earlier times, found itself playing catch-up. In 1994 a reservoir was completed at Kahakapau, adding 110
million gallons of storage capacity to the Upper Kula system. Two years later
the board made substantial improvements to the treatment plant at Kamole
Weir and was well advanced in upgrading a water treatment facility at Olinda.[57]
Nonetheless, another drought in 1998 showed how tenuous Upcountry Maui's
water sources were.

Bereft of rainfall, Upcountry Maui saw its water supplies dwindle to such
a low point that the county water board declared an emergency for the area
in the winter of 1998. All water users, residential and agricultural, had to cut
their consumption by 10 percent. New water hookups, and hence new residential construction, were put on hold. Particularly worrisome was a drop
in the flow of water in the Wailoa Ditch, a fall to just 27 mgd, 13 percent of its
normal flow.[58] The impact of the water cutbacks was immediate. Unable to
plant five hundred acres, Hawaiian Commercial and Sugar laid off one hundred workers. Stock raisers culled their herds of cattle. Upcountry growers
deferred planting vegetables, fruit, and flowers.[59]

As the drought continued, the county water board repeatedly asked Mayor
Lingle to declare a civil emergency for Upcountry Maui. After the third such
request she took that step. Her action allowed members of the county board
to approach state officials for help and to petition the state court system for
access to water that could be pumped into Upcountry Maui from a number
of little-used wells. For a variety of reasons the wells were not normally tapped:
One contained low levels of pesticides, another was provided by a developer
and was not yet complete, yet another involved litigation by a group trying
to stop development, and so forth. The wells could provide 30 percent of
Upcountry Maui's water needs. Only by using water from these wells, most
county officials thought, could a 25 percent reduction in water usage by farmers be avoided. Such a reduction, according to the manager of Maui Land
and Pineapple, would "kill farming."[60] In late March state officials visited
Maui to look into the Upcountry drought, but even as they toured the region long-needed rains fell. With reservoirs brimming and with the Wailoa
Ditch gushing 132 mgd, the drought ended.

Virtually the same scenario was reenacted in 1999. When rain did not arrive to replenish the Upcountry and East Maui watersheds, the county water
board asked for 5 percent voluntary reductions in water use in late May. By

mid-June a 10 percent mandatory reduction had been imposed, and within a week gloomy farmers reported that their crops were dying. As cutbacks continued, residents vented their anger at the county board. "We in Upcountry Maui should not go on flushing 10 percent less, washing clothes at the Central Maui washettes, and bathing once a month," wrote one. Many blamed county officials for allowing development to exceed the water supply. "Every time the county Department of Water Supply does make improvements," asked one, "why is development allowed to the point where we're right back where we started?" A third Upcountry resident stated, "Even more alarming to us is that development of subdivisions, shopping centers and private residences continues in the face of potential community water shortages."[61]

Still rains failed. In mid-July the county water board ordered a 25 percent reduction in Upcountry water use, although it gave farmers a one-month grace period within which to comply. Board members also asked Mayor James Apana to declare an emergency, as Mayor Lingle had done during the previous summer. Apana did so and requested that Gov. Benjamin Cayetano follow suit. A state declaration would allow environmental regulations to be held in abeyance for the duration of the emergency. Water from contaminated wells, if purified adequately, could be used for human consumption. With Upcountry reservoirs nearly empty and with the Wailoa Ditch a sickly trickle, water supplies were critical. At the end of July Governor Cayetano signed an emergency declaration for Upcountry Maui. Lifted temporarily in September, the order was reimposed a month later. The seesaw continued over the next six months, with restrictions ending in November, only to be put in place again for part of March 2000.[62]

Realizing that water shortages were a long-term problem for Upcountry residents, county officials mounted several responses. The Water Department built additional reservoirs and upgraded Upcountry water supply and distribution systems. There was little dissent from taking these steps; nearly all agreed that they would help. Many, however, thought that they were not enough, and David Craddick, head of the County Water Department, faced tough — indeed sometimes angry — questioning by Upcountry residents. Seven hundred people still awaited Upcountry water hookups in early 2000. Not surprisingly, the Kula Community Association maintained that the "Board and Department of Water Supply should establish as its highest priority the development of water source, storage, and delivery systems prior to actual demand."[63]

*As head of Maui's water department, David Craddick was often at the center of
controversies during the 1990s.*

Some proposed actions of the county water board were problematic. Environmentalists and Native Hawaiian rights activists believed that county
officials were unfairly taking advantage of the drought emergency to rapidly
develop water sources. Only during an emergency could pipeline construction from wells quickly proceed. Under normal conditions, public hearings
on how increased water removals from the wells and how the building of the
pipelines might affect Maui's natural environment would be required. Then,
too, only during an emergency could polluted water, even when purified, be
used for human consumption. Native Hawaiian issues were wrapped up in
these considerations. Pumping from the wells, some believed, reduced the
above-ground stream flow to which Native Hawaiians had established rights
in court decisions. Concerned about these issues, Isaac Hall and others formed
a Coalition to Protect East Maui Water Resources and obtained a court in-
junction prohibiting work on the wells and the pipelines until the county had
prepared an acceptable supplemental environmental impact statement. Conflict on this issue continued into 2000.[64]

Cooperation on Water Issues

Agreements seemed more likely on water matters by mid-2000 than in times past. The possibility of agreement owed much to the work of Elmer Cravalho, who was appointed a member of the County Board of Water Supply in 1999 and who was elected the chairman of that board in early 2000. At Cravalho's urging, the Board of Water Supply and Alexander and Baldwin entered into a new twenty-five-year agreement designed, as the *Maui News* explained, "to fix the Central Maui and Upcountry water problems for a generation to come."[65]

Based on a memorandum of understanding only four pages long, the agreement covered a multitude of issues. It promised help for Upcountry water users by increasing the County Water Department's allocation from the Wailoa Ditch to 12 mgd, back to the amount negotiated by Cravalho when he had been mayor in 1977. The plan also called for the county to provide major improvements in water storage and delivery systems for Upcountry residents and farmers. The county would also, the agreement specified, "pursue" groundwater sources in East Maui and Kula for Upcountry users, with some participation by Alexander and Baldwin. These sources would, it was anticipated, include water from the wells disputed by the Coalition to Protect East Maui Water Resources. The agreement embraced Central and South Maui as well. The county won increased water supplies from the 'Iao-Waikapū Ditch, which was owned by Wailuku Agribusiness but to which Alexander and Baldwin had some rights. The county water board also gained the right to take up to 2 mgd from the 'Iao Stream, whenever it ran at more than 55 mgd. These sources of water would, it was expected, reduce pressure on the 'Iao aquifer. More generally, the county board and Alexander and Baldwin agreed to renegotiate how much water each received from the 'Iao aquifer, a matter of considerable dispute since the discovery in the mid-1980s that the aquifer could support a renewable withdrawal of at most 20 mgd.[66]

Whether this tentative agreement could be worked out in final form and implemented remained to be seen. Maui County contained many groups, many constituents, who needed to be satisfied on any major issue, as we have seen with regard to land use matters. Legal and political challenges might well be expected before any resolution of water issues occurred. While the fate of the tentative agreement for water use was uncertain, cooperation already characterized efforts to preserve watersheds on Maui. In 1990 the Hawaiian

legislature mandated that private landholders develop watershed management plans in return for leases of water rights from the state. Such schemes
were to "prevent the degradation of surface water and ground water quality"
and were to be implemented jointly by the leaseholders and state officials.[67]

How well such plans could work was illustrated by the management of the
East Maui Watershed. Covering 100,000 acres of rain forests on the windward side of Haleakalā, this area produced sixty billion gallons of water per
year, making it the single largest source of fresh water in the Hawaiian Islands.
Private and public bodies formed an East Maui Watershed Partnership in 1991
to manage the watershed. Composed of seven members — the Nature Conservancy, the Haleakalā National Park, the East Maui Irrigation Company,
the Hana Ranch, the Department of Forestry and Wildlife of the State of
Hawai'i, Maui County, and Haleakalā Ranch — the partnership recognized
that the East Maui Watershed was "an invaluable resource for the island of
Maui that must be preserved and protected . . . into perpetuity."[68]

Efforts to preserve the East Maui Watershed were longstanding. In the early
1900s what was much later recognized as a natural dieback killed about 8,300
acres of native trees in part of the watershed. Working together, the Hawaiian Sugar Planters Association and the Territorial Division of Forestry re-
planted the region. Lacking knowledge later available, they reforested much
of the land with alien species such as Eucalyptus trees, leading one scholar to
aptly observe that the efforts were "not only unnecessary but damaging."[69]
Misconceptions were capably addressed in succeeding years. In 1991 private
businesses and government organizations formed the Melastome Action
Committee to battle alien species in the East Maui Watershed and elsewhere
on the island. Particularly alarming was the discovery of miconia growing near
Hanā. Known as "green cancer" on Tahiti, miconia plants covered 70 percent of that island's forests. Reorganized as the Maui Invasive Species Committee in 1997, the group received $800,000 in funding in late 1999. The East
Maui Watershed was home to at least sixty-three rare plant species and a
higher concentration of rare and endangered birds than anywhere else in the
United States, and in late 1999 the East Maui Watershed Partnership received
the President's Conservation Achievement Award.[70]

Success in East Maui bred imitation. In 1998 the county water board, the
Bishop Estate, C. Brewer, Amfac, Maui Land and Pineapple, the Nature Conservancy, and the state Department of Land and Natural Resources (DLNR)

reached a similar agreement to protect the 50,000-acre watershed of the West
Maui Mountains, which fed the 'Īao aquifer. This agreement aimed at preserving flora and fauna native to the Hawaiian Islands and in doing so sought
to conserve water. Wild pigs were to be eliminated from the watershed, because they tore up the ground while rooting for food. The ground was thus
made vulnerable to erosion and to invasion by alien plants, such as miconia
and tibouchina. Shallow-rooted, the alien plants tended to crowd out Hawaiian
plants and trees that had deeper roots, thus opening the watershed to additional destruction. Erosion could then impair the ability of the watershed to
hold rain needed to replenish aquifers. In late 1999 another agreement was
established to protect hundreds of acres in rugged East Moloka'i. In the first
phase of preserving this watershed, fences would be built to keep out feral
goats that were browsing on native plants. This was the fourth watershed
group formed in the Hawaiian Islands. In addition to those for West and East
Maui, one had been set up on O'ahu.[71]

When needs converged — as they did on some watershed issues — Maui's
residents could, thus, cooperate through public-private ventures. Nor was the
situation on Maui unique. As many parts of the mainland felt the pinch of
water shortages in the 1980s and 1990s, residents increasingly hammered out
acceptable compromises on water usage problems. As on Maui, they often
did so by forming groups to regulate water use in specific watersheds. Farmers, ranchers, environmentalists, fishermen, and others found themselves
working together in organized ways to preserve watersheds necessary for their
livelihoods and recreation. They even moved away from the doctrine of prior
appropriation of water in their new joint efforts. By the summer of 1998 there
were an estimated 300 such watershed groups in the West, of which 200 had
been formed since 1995.[72]

5

The Question of Electric Power

If land and water were crucial to Maui's modern economic development, so was electricity. As state officials observed in a seminal report in 1995, "Energy is one of the key factors shaping Hawaii's economy, standard of living, and environment. Energy fuels Hawaii's economy."[1] Electricity was and is a very important segment of the energy supply of the Hawaiian Islands, essential for economic development. Residents of Hawai'i generally agreed on the centrality of electricity to their lives but came over time to differ on how best to generate and distribute it. Tourism, which created seemingly insatiable demands for electricity, lay at the heart of the disagreements. The construction of electrical generating plants to serve the visitor industry split groups of Maui's residents — just as water and land issues did — as they envisioned different futures for their island. The development of an environmental movement, with its emphasis on energy conservation and its stress on the use of alternative (nonpetroleum) energy sources, contributed to the cleavages. A complex interplay of economic, environmental, and Native Hawaiian issues resulted, as various groups contested matters.[2]

Electric Power Development before World War II

Electric power usage began on Maui in the 1880s and 1890s. Electricity was first employed on the island — and, indeed, in the Kingdom of Hawai'i — to light Claus Spreckels's sugar refining mill at Spreckelsville on September 22, 1881. A steam generator powered by burning cane trash called bagasse generated the electricity. As reported prosaically by the *Saturday Press*, "On the evening of the 22nd, the new electric light machine was tried in Mill No. 1 at

Spreckelsville. Six lamps were in operation and worked to the satisfaction of all concerned."[3] The development at Spreckelsville set a pattern: Sugar mills produced Maui's electricity through World War II, fueled by bagasse, coal, and oil. This electrical generation was an early form of what became known as "cogeneration," in which heat is generated mainly for industrial purposes and then used also as a byproduct to produce electricity. Electricity generated by water power was also of importance. By 1897 the Olowalu Company was generating electricity by hydro power for lighting and irrigation pumps.[4]

Still more sugar mills, along with some other companies in Kahului and Wailuku, began generating electricity in the early 1900s.[5] Particularly important were the efforts of Hawaiian Commercial and Sugar. In 1917 Hawaiian Commercial and Sugar built its Central Power Plant on a spur of the old Haleakalā Highway near today's Kahului Airport. This facility would be Maui's single largest source of electricity through World War II. By 1924 the Central Power Plant, originally powered by steam but later by diesel, was producing eleven million kilowatt hours of electricity each year. Hawaiian Commercial and Sugar also developed hydroelectricity; by 1929 the company was generating sixteen million of its twenty-nine million kilowatt hours of electricity from that source. The firm's production topped sixty-five million kilowatt hours in 1943. Not regulated by governmental bodies, the sugar mills acted as private firms contracting with other private parties to supply them with power.[6]

Thus, Maui, like the other Hawaiian Islands, developed a mainly decentralized electrical power system in the years before World War II. Various sugar mills generated electricity for their own use and for the nearby communities that housed their workers. This stood in marked contrast to what occurred on much of mainland America, where more centralized systems grew up, whereby utilities supplied factories with electricity by World War II. Mills at Lahaina, Hanā, and elsewhere, in addition to the mills of Hawaiian Commercial and Sugar, were important generators of electricity on Maui. At this point, beyond Central Maui and Pā'ia sugar mills there was little interlocking of power grids; rather, each mill and its community stood apart.[7] A search for alternative fuels — other than oil and coal — would run through many efforts to produce electricity on Maui in the 1970s, 1980s, and 1990s. This search was already under way before World War II. Eager to boost their profits, the sugar companies expanded their use of bagasse as a fuel. Concerns about costs rather than the environment drove the early use of alternative fuels.[8]

Business leaders made some efforts to consolidate the production and distribution of electricity on Maui before World War II. In 1907 the Territorial Legislature granted a franchise for the establishment of an electric light and power plant for Wailuku and Kahului, and Island Electric began providing electricity for streetlights from a small 100-kilowatt, steam-powered generator five years later. "It will be possible to walk down the streets," the *Maui News* observed, "without taking a chance of falling over a cow or some other animal." Island Electric's power plant was in Wailuku, and the Wailuku Sugar Company tied its mill generator into Island Electric's facility, the first of many important links. Electrical generating companies in the Hawaiian Islands used surplus electricity produced by sugar mills as part of their power bases, a practice that continued through the 1990s. Even so, service by Island Electric soon deteriorated, especially after the firm's generator broke down because of overuse and lack of maintenance in 1919.[9]

The Maui Electric Company (MECO) replaced Island Electric in 1921 and had 400 customers by year's end. MECO initially generated no power of its own, relying instead on electricity purchased from Hawaiian Commercial and Sugar and several other companies.[10] MECO expanded its services in the 1920s, and substantial rate reductions encouraged the adoption of electrical power in that decade. MECO faced a decline in demand for electricity with the onset of the Great Depression of the 1930s. Recovery began late in the decade: MECO had about 3,500 customers by the end of 1935 and 4,140 two years later. World War II brought boom times to Maui, greatly increasing the demand for electricity, straining capacity, and leading MECO and other producers to think about expanding their generating facilities.[11]

Electric Power on Maui, 1945–1972

The history of electric power on Maui during the first three decades after World War II revolved around a large expansion of MECO's operations through acquisitions and by the construction of new generating capacity. As Maui began developing a visitor industry, MECO provided that industry with sorely needed electricity. In 1945 MECO's directors authorized building an independent power plant in Kahului. They had been considering such a move for at least a decade but had lacked the funds to do so during the depression years. The first generating unit of the Kahului plant came online in 1948, and by the mid-1950s three oil-fueled, steam-powered generators were in operation. In the 1960s MECO added two more generators. Even as it developed its own power plant, MECO maintained contracts with the sugar companies to buy surplus electric power from them. Most importantly, in 1959 MECO entered into a twenty-year contract for the interchange of power with Hawaiian Commercial and Sugar.[12]

As MECO expanded its generating capacity, it began knitting Maui together electrically. MECO extended its power lines to serve additional communities. In 1940 lines reached Mā'alaea, which had fifteen customers. Lines followed to Upcountry Waikamoi in 1943 and to South Maui in 1946–48. MECO began sending power over the West Maui Mountains to Lahaina in 1957. MECO also extended its reach through purchases of existing power systems. It bought Hana Light and Power in 1964 and Lahaina Light and Power three years later. In 1968 MECO itself became a wholly owned subsidiary of the much larger Hawaiian Electric Company on O'ahu, a position it maintained through the 1990s.[13]

As MECO expanded, it encountered its first environmental challenges. Scattered complaints about smoke from the Kahului plant were heard in the 1950s. MECO's officers took some measures to correct the problem by burning more low-sulfur fuels, only to encounter complaints resulting from hikes in electric rates. Low-sulfur oil cost more than high-sulfur oil, and MECO passed on the increased costs to its customers. Faced with protests, MECO returned to cheaper operations, with smoke from its Kahului plant occasionally casting a pall over the nearby sky. MECO's management was beginning to learn just how difficult it was to balance economic and environmental matters, a learning process that would continue for decades.[14]

Electrical Power and Environmental Issues, 1973–1990

The scramble to keep up with the demand for electricity that characterized MECO's expansion in earlier decades became more hectic during the 1970s and 1980s. As in so many issues on Maui, the growth of tourism exacerbated the demand for electric power. As tourism boomed, the demand for electricity soared. Between 1970 and 1985 the amount of electricity sold by MECO more than tripled, far outpacing the increase in electricity sold by Hawaiian Electric on O'ahu. Electricity sales, as measured in millions of kilowatt hours, skyrocketed:

	Maui	O'ahu
1969	131	3,000
1975	281	4,600
1979	413	5,200
1985	538	5,300

By 1988 MECO had 33,317 residential customers who consumed 221 million kilowatt hours and 5,672 commercial customers who took an additional 230 million kilowatt hours. The impact of tourism was clear. Seventy-four large commercial users, mainly big hotels, resorts, and shopping centers, consumed 221 million kilowatt hours, as much electricity as that taken by all residential customers on Maui combined.[15]

At the same time, rising oil prices — in the wake especially of price hikes by the Organization of Petroleum Exporting Countries (OPEC) in 1973 and 1979 — spurred efforts to conserve oil and made alternative fuel sources increasingly attractive. Between 1970 and 1974 the price paid by MECO for its fuel oil jumped 124 percent. In response, MECO hiked its rates 17 percent in early 1974, hard on the heels of earlier boosts in 1973. Additional hikes in oil prices and electric rate increases soon followed. Between 1975 and 1981 the cost of electricity to consumers on Maui nearly doubled. The State of Hawai'i, Maui County, and MECO all responded with energy conservation programs. Maui's program covered everything from limiting nighttime use of public tennis courts to new procurement methods for machinery using electricity to provide for "life cycle costing for energy efficiency." Throughout the state of Hawai'i, and certainly on Maui, the provision of electricity became more complicated than ever. MECO sponsored programs to educate its customers in energy conservation.[16]

Lacking adequate generation facilities, MECO had at times to resort to brownouts and rolling blackouts. At other times Maui's electrical system simply broke down, leaving much of the island in the dark. A meeting of the Maui County Council in April 1974 reported, for example, that "electrical power has been virtually eliminated from the entire community except for isolated cases." In 1974 and again in 1978 major power failures led the council to give the mayor of the county emergency powers over the allocation of the island's supply of electricity.[17]

To try to stay abreast of demand, MECO built a new power plant at Māʻalaea on land acquired from Alexander and Baldwin in the early 1970s. There was some opposition to this plant, as part of opposition to plans by the Army Corps of Engineers to increase the size of Māʻalaea's harbor, locate an oil refinery there, and develop nearby Keālia Pond. Dick Mayer, the Upcountry community activist and faculty member at Maui Community College, and others protested against these plans. The possibility of thermal pollution of Keālia Pond, should the power plant use steam power, especially attracted the ire of environmentalists, for hot water would be discharged into the pond. Plans to enlarge the harbor were dropped, as was the plan for an oil refinery there. The construction of a power plant went ahead, but initially on a smaller scale than that desired by MECO. In a "very heavy meeting at the Land Use Commission in 1971," Mayer later explained, the "Land Use Commission told [MECO's officers] to scale back their plans" and gave them permission to build on twenty-five acres.[18]

Over the next two decades, MECO built up the Māʻalaea plant and looked for additional energy sources. Three diesel generators were in operation at Māʻalaea by late 1972, and twelve generators were producing electricity there fifteen years later. By 1980 the Māʻalaea plant was the largest diesel-powered generating facility in the United States. At Māʻalaea MECO pioneered in the use of waste heat to generate electricity, with a system employing heat from two combustion-turbine generators to power an additional steam-turbine generator. The use of diesel generators was unusual: Most mainland urban utilities keep several diesel generating sets as emergency backups but rely mainly on steam generators. On Maui, however, opposition to the building of a large-scale, traditional plant led to reliance on a diesel plant. At the same time, MECO maintained its ties to Maui's sugar mills. In 1980 Alexander and Baldwin and MECO signed a new ten-year agreement by which Hawaiian Commercial and Sugar would increase its generation of electricity for MECO to fifty million kilowatt hours per year by 1984. To accomplish this increase, the sugar company installed a large generator fired with bagasse at its Puʻunēne plant.[19]

As they wrestled with soaring consumer demand, MECO's officers also had to contend with the rising price of oil, their utility's major fuel, and with a growing number of environmental issues. While the vast majority of Maui's residents continued to favor the expansion of electrical generation facilities as essential for economic growth, more residents than in the past raised questions about various impacts that power generation had on their island. In these concerns Maui's residents resembled their counterparts elsewhere in the United States. Beginning in the 1970s, and especially during the presidency of Jimmy Carter, Americans grappled with how to lessen their dependence on foreign oil, how to conserve fuels, how to protect their nation's natural environment in the face of a continuing need to develop electrical power stations and grids, and how, at the same time, to lower energy prices. Elements of an emerging national energy policy varied over time but included incentives for utilities to develop energy alternatives to oil.[20] Many of those at MECO shared concerns about the environment and looked to alternative sources of energy for the generation of electricity as a possible solution to their dilemmas.

The officers of Hawaiian Electric and MECO considered nuclear power but soon dismissed that option. The problem was viewed as one of economics, not one of environmental concern. As Hawaiian Electric's 1976 annual report explained, "It appears that a nuclear plant probably cannot be used economically in Hawaii in the near future. . . . The islands are not electrically inter-connected," the report continued, "and the smallest commercial nuclear units presently being built are too large for Oahu's needs," much less needs on Maui. In other words, given the nuclear technologies of the day, such plants were too big for commercially efficient use in the Hawaiian Islands. Then, too, by this time the cost of building nuclear plants had climbed due to safety concerns; this ensured that the market in Maui was too small to support a nuclear plant given the high cost of building one.[21]

Interest in other alternative sources of energy waxed and waned with fluctuations in the price of oil, and with tax incentives allowed or removed by the federal government. More was involved than simple economics. Technical matters were also important: Droughts affected the availability of water for hydro power, for instance. Wind power attracted considerable attention. In 1974 the Maui County Council called upon MECO to conduct a feasibility study of the use of windmills to generate electricity.[22] In 1982 MECO hired American Wind Power as a consultant to install a wind machine at Mā'alaea. The goal was to produce enough electricity to power sewage treatment plants in Kīhei and Kahului. A 340-kilowatt machine was installed in 1984, only to be abandoned later, because of mechanical problems and physical deterioration due to salt in the air. In another experiment, MECO signed a contract with Zond Pacific for one hundred wind machines to generate power at Kapalua in 1985. However, high costs led to the abandonment of the Kapalua project just four years later. MECO's wind-power experiments were part of efforts made by Hawaiian Electric, which constructed a major wind farm on O'ahu's north shore. Dedicated in 1986, this wind farm was expected to generate enough electricity to save 62,500 barrels of oil annually. However, actual operations, like those on Maui, proved disappointing.[23]

Environmental issues extended to the question of air pollution. In late 1972 the State of Hawai'i Department of Health "found that personal injury and property damage were occurring in the Kahului Harbor area" as a result of sulfur dioxide emitted by MECO's power plant. Over the next two years MECO experimented with different blends of high- and low-sulfur fuel at its Kahului plant; in early 1974 the state reported that MECO had solved the problem, observing that the "air quality level for sulfur dioxide is well below State Standards."[24] Nonetheless, questions remained. With the hikes in oil prices that occurred in the 1970s, MECO sought to use more high-sulfur oil. While this oil caused more air pollution than low-sulfur oil, it cost considerably less, promising some rate relief for MECO's customers. This desire to use high-sulfur oil came into direct conflict, however, with clean air legislation passed by Congress in 1963, 1967, 1970, and 1977. Amendments in the latter two years were particularly important. The 1970 law mandated national rather than state air quality standards based on health criteria developed by the federal Department of Health, Education, and Welfare. The Environmental Protection Agency (EPA), a newly created federal government agency, was to implement the 1970 law. The 1977 law went even further, calling for the "prevention of significant deterioration" of air quality nationwide.[25]

When the EPA's air quality standards for Maui were announced, it was apparent that avoiding high-sulfur fuel, by itself, would not bring MECO into compliance. So, to meet the new standards, MECO agreed to raise the height of the Kahului plant's smokestacks to 185 feet, a feat accomplished in 1982 at the cost of $9 million. MECO also agreed to use medium-sulfur oil. Moreover, MECO agreed to rely more upon its new plant at Mā'alaea, where trade winds carried the smoke out to sea, and to purchase as much power as possible from the sugar mills. Taking these steps, it was hoped, would result in cleaner air over Kahului.[26]

A new direction in limiting air pollution was taken in 1991, when William Bonnet, Hawaiian Electric's environmental manager, explained that MECO would use water injection to control the emission of nitrogen oxides into the air. The EPA and the State of Hawai'i Department of Health had determined that water injection was the most effective way to limit nitrogen oxide emissions from combustion turbines and mandated its use by MECO.[27] Even so, air pollution problems continued to dog MECO. In 1998 the State of Hawai'i cited MECO for violating clean air laws for more than a decade. The seriousness of the violations was a matter of debate, but environmental groups seized on this finding to criticize MECO. The director of the Hawaiian chapter of the Sierra Club called the violations "staggering." When MECO agreed to a consent decree that stipulated that the utility spend $100,000 to create an educational display on air quality for the public, the program director of Maui Tomorrow labeled the penalty "wholly inadequate."[28]

Geothermal Possibilities

The most promising alternative energy source in the Hawaiian Islands was geothermal energy. Driving this quest were two closely related concerns, as in all searches for alternative sources for energy in the Hawaiian Islands. First, the rising cost of oil, the main source of energy, spurred efforts to develop geothermal energy, especially during the 1970s. Second, there was a more general desire to break Hawai'i's dependence on oil. The islands were much more dependent on oil for energy than was the U.S. mainland, and policymakers saw the use of geothermal energy as one way to lessen that dependence.

Tentative steps were taken to develop geothermal energy on Maui. In 1982 state investigations identified six areas with "some potential for a geothermal resource on Maui," and Mayor Hannibal Tavares called upon MECO to develop geothermal energy on the island. Responding to state and county actions, MECO issued requests for proposals for the development of up to thirteen megawatts of geothermal power on Maui as a way "to avoid installing additional oil-fired generation." Two years later the state's Department of Land and Natural Resources (DLNR) designated 'Ulupalakua as a geothermal subzone, and in 1985 MECO worked with the state government to complete a study of the region. In the end, however, nothing came of these efforts.[29]

MECO was no longer considering geothermal projects by the early 1990s. In 1992 MECO's president explained that a failure by the county government to establish reasonable drilling regulations had killed geothermal projects on the island. Then, too, public hearings had revealed opposition to the development needed to make geothermal power generation a reality — the drilling of wells, the construction of a generating plant, and so forth. Finally, it became apparent from initial investigations that the "probability of a commercially viable resource" at ʻUlupalakua was "extremely small."[30]

Geothermal possibilities in the Hawaiian Islands extended well beyond Maui, however, and some had the potential to help residents of Maui in their bid for new energy sources. In response to the hike in oil prices of the early 1970s, the State of Hawaiʻi began with private companies and the federal government to explore the possibility of constructing a geothermal plant on the Big Island of Hawaiʻi. Geothermal energy had been suggested as a potential energy source for the Hawaiian Islands as early as 1881, when King David Kalākaua met with Thomas Edison in New York City. Such thoughts were revived in the 1950s, and in 1961 a private company drilled four test wells on Hawaiʻi. Still more serious consideration began when the state established the Hawaii Geothermal Project in 1972. In 1975–76 a deep research well was drilled into the lower east rift zone of Kīlauea, an active volcano on Hawaiʻi. A three-megawatt wellhead generator installed in 1981 fed electricity into the Big Island's power grid for a decade.[31]

Encouraged, government officials and utility executives began to see geothermal energy as a way for their state to achieve energy independence. In 1984 the state's Department of Business and Economic Development (DBED) declared that it was a major objective of the state government to "accelerate the transition to an indigenous renewable energy economy by facilitating private sector activities to explore supply options." Many Hawaiian residents began thinking of a 500–megawatt plant to supply Oʻahu, which consumed 82 percent of the state's electricity, and Maui, as well as Hawaiʻi, with electric power. To be located on the Big Island, the facility would send power to Oʻahu and Maui via a deep-sea cable. It was anticipated that about fifty megawatts could be tapped for Maui, with smaller amounts available for Molokaʻi and Lānaʻi.[32]

Building on the experimental success of the three-megawatt wellhead generator, a twenty-five-megawatt commercial plant was established on the Big Island by Puna Geothermal Ventures. Using technologies similar to those developed in Iceland and New Zealand, this plant tapped geothermal energy in the form of steam from deep wells. The steam ran turbines, which in turn generated electricity. The facility was soon producing nearly one-quarter of the Big Island's electricity. Many hoped that this plant would soon be greatly expanded to provide electricity for most of the Hawaiian Islands. Serious technical, environmental, sociocultural, and economic challenges had to be overcome, however, for the proposed 500-megawatt plant to have a chance for success.[33]

Although daunting, the technical problems proved to be the simplest to solve. The greatest difficulty lay not in drilling the wells or generating the electricity but in transmitting the electricity to O'ahu and Maui. Up to this time, the longest underwater electrical transmission cable connected Norway and Denmark. Seventy-eight miles long, that cable reached a depth of 1,800 feet. By contrast, a Big Island–O'ahu cable would have to be twice as long and would lie at depths of up to 7,000 feet. A new type of cable had to be designed, and ways to lay that cable in deep water had to be devised. After analyzing 192 possible cable designs, Hawaiian Electric selected a heavily armored, pressurized cable built to last at least thirty years. Concurrently, cable-laying techniques were perfected to put down the cable in the steep-sided trench separating the islands of Hawai'i and Maui. Bonnet was the project manager for this undertaking, called the Hawaii Deep Water Cable Program.[34]

By 1990 solutions to the technical problems had been found, but by this time environmental issues had surfaced. The wells and the power plant needed to be constructed in the Puna rain forest on Hawai'i. Some 300 to 600 acres of land, of a total 60,000 acres, in the forest would have to be cleared. Critics argued that doing so would injure the habitats of animal and plant species native to the Hawaiian Islands and would allow alien species to invade the forest. A professor of biology at Stanford University testified that the proposed geothermal developments would "significantly degrade a unique and valuable lowland native rainforest." Not all agreed with this analysis, however. A University of Hawai'i biologist, who had studied Hawaiian plants for thirty-five years, pointed out that less than 1 percent of the Puna forest would be affected and that most of the land designated for clearing had already been "heavily impacted" by alien species.[35]

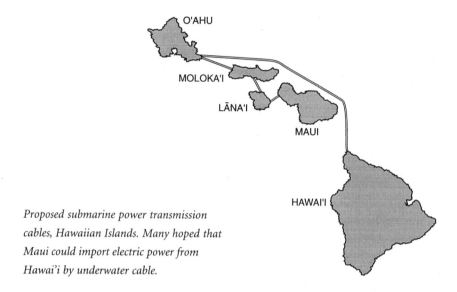

Proposed submarine power transmission
cables, Hawaiian Islands. Many hoped that
Maui could import electric power from
Hawai'i by underwater cable.

Native Hawaiian issues were also important. "Long before geothermal, there was Pele," the goddess of volcanoes, observed one investigator. "For Native Hawaiians, the world's most active volcano was the personification of the volcano goddess," he continued. "Kilauea was her sacred ground." Some Native Hawaiians in the Puna district believed that they were descended from Pele and revered Pele as an *'aumakua* or personal totem. The Puna rain forest was a place of Native Hawaiian renewal, and Native Hawaiians expressed dismay that the goddess Pele might be disturbed by the drilling and other energy creation activities. Native Hawaiians went to court to protect their rights but lost in a 1987 decision by the Hawaiian Supreme Court. Ruling that Pele practitioners had not used the Puna forest for religious purposes in times past, the court allowed development to proceed.[36]

An environmental review prepared by the state took notice of the opposition of some Native Hawaiians. "Hawaiians in Puna," the report observed, "are concerned with changes in their economy, and with access to land resources. They are also concerned with the general character of their region. . . . Many Hawaiians," the report continued, "are concerned with the State's responsibilities and attitudes towards Hawaiians as a group — geothermal development is only one of several topics where the State's commitment to

Hawaiian citizens can be measured." The report concluded, "The Pele prac- titioners anticipate grave impacts of geothermal development on their god and on themselves." The hiring of Native Hawaiians for construction jobs, the provision of educational programs, and the mounting of archaeological surveys might, state officials hoped, lessen opposition to the project.[37]

Economic matters also divided Hawaiian residents on the issue of whether to develop geothermal energy sources. While exact estimates of costs varied tremendously, there was no doubt that drilling the wells (about 150 would be needed), building the generating plant, and constructing an interisland power transmission system would be expensive. The state estimated the cost at $1.7 billion, but environmental groups put the price tag at between $3.4 billion and $4.3 billion. Opponents argued that the cost was too high and that build- ing such a system would, moreover, commit the state to just one way of gen- erating electricity for the foreseeable future. With oil prices falling in the early 1990s, opponents found this unacceptable. As one claimed, "Geothermal energy cannot be obtained at a cheaper cost than oil or certain other renew- able resources." Moreover, he continued, "by committing huge resources to the development of geothermal energy at this time, the government is mak- ing irretrievable commitments of irreplaceable resources."[38]

By the early 1990s opposing sides had become well defined. Favoring the development of geothermal energy were the Pro-Geothermal Alliance, com- posed mainly of Hawaiian Electric and several drilling companies; the Big Island Alliance, made up of labor unions, especially those in the construc- tion trades; the Hawaii Island Geothermal Alliance, which included labor unions and the Big Island's chamber of commerce; and the DBED. Opposing development were the Pele Defense Fund, a Big Island group representing Native Hawaiian views; the Rainforest Action Network, a mainland nonprofit body; the Big Island Rainforest Action Group, a local citizens' organization; and the state Office of Hawaiian Affairs, which found itself in opposition to the DBED.

Faced with growing opposition, and with a recession that limited the funds at its command, the state backed off from the geothermal program in the early 1990s, and it was soon abandoned. Private companies lacked the resources to go it alone. Particularly worrisome to Hawaiian Electric, moreover, was a successful challenge in the federal court system from the Sierra Club. The resulting legal decision mandated the preparation of a comprehensive environmental impact statement before any more work on the geothermal system could be done, thus adding yet another element of instability to business decision making. The geothermal project on the Big Island revealed just how divided citizens of the Hawaiian Islands were on energy matters. Solving technical problems, the controversy showed, was not enough. Economic, cultural, and environmental issues were even more important. In the end, geothermal projects failed to live up to their billing as energy saviors for the Hawaiian Islands, and no new electricity came by undersea cable to Maui.[39]

Integrated Resource Planning

The failure to unite the Hawaiian Islands with an electric grid powered by geothermal energy did not end efforts to achieve greater energy independence. Far from it. Beginning in the 1980s governmental officials worked with the officers of public utilities and with members of a concerned public to devise a comprehensive Hawaii Energy Strategy. As laid out in a final state government report in 1995, this strategy had three interrelated goals: "Dependable, efficient, and economical state-wide energy systems capable of supporting the needs of the people; increased energy self-sufficiency where the ratio of indigenous to imported energy use is increased; and greater energy security in the face of threats to Hawaii's energy supplies and systems."[40]

As several researchers noted in 1993, "Hawaii is unique among the states in its level of dependence on oil as an energy source." Altogether, oil produced 90 percent of the energy used in the Hawaiian Islands, compared to just 40 percent on the mainland. Imported oil supplied nearly all of the energy used to fuel the islands' cars, planes, and boats. Moreover, despite efforts to develop alternative sources of fuel, oil supplied about three-quarters of the energy used to generate electricity. Most of the rest came from the burning of bagasse and from hydroelectric power dams built by the sugar companies.[41]

Extending such observations, the state's 1995 report called for Hawai'i's public utilities to approach energy questions from both the supply and demand sides — that is, to consider ways to generate energy from nonoil sources and to find ways to reduce the demand for electricity by encouraging conservation. Combining the supply and demand sides of the energy equation in planning for the future was called Integrated Resource Planning (IRP). Comprehensive IRP quickly became the touchstone of the State of Hawai'i's energy strategy.[42]

Hawai'i's quest for IRP had begun in the 1980s. In 1987 state agencies involved in energy planning joined with the Hawaii Chamber of Commerce to sponsor a workshop on IRP issues. All of the participants, including the Public Utilities Commission (PUC) and Hawai'i's four electric utilities, one of which was MECO, agreed that comprehensive energy planning was needed and formed an IRP Task Force to explore options. After further meetings, the PUC instituted proceedings in 1990 for the utilities to begin IRP. Technical workshops on the subject, according to a state report, "developed a consensus among parties on key issues affecting the development of an IRP framework." In 1992 the PUC ordered all of Hawai'i's energy utilities to develop and implement IRP.[43]

In 1993 the utilities, including MECO, filed their first integrated resource plans for approval by the PUC. The PUC helped the utilities by ruling that they could recover the costs of demand-side management — that is, costs incurred in energy conservation programs — through rate increases. MECO responded by starting a pilot program to subsidize high-efficiency lighting for commercial customers and later began a program to help public schools use solar power. The utilities were to conduct major reviews of their plans every three years, in which they were to adopt twenty-year "time horizons." That is, as specified by the PUC, each plan was to detail a "utility's needs over the next twenty years to meet the forecasted energy demand for its service area." Advisory boards assisted the utilities in the preparation of their plans. Acting as "a sounding board," according to Bonnet, MECO's president from 1996, MECO's advisory board included a member of Maui County's Office of the Consumer Advocate, a representative of the Maui Hotel Association (MHA), the Maui County Energy Coordinator, and members of environmental groups like Maui Tomorrow.[44]

IRP extended beyond the Hawaiian Islands to the rest of the United States. As the congressional Office of Technology Assessment (OTA) observed in a 1993 report, IRP had been "a keystone of the [George] Bush Administration's National Energy Strategy." In fact, the Energy Policy Act passed by Congress in 1992 called on state utility regulatory commissions to consider adopting standards requiring utilities to go to IRP, which, of course, is exactly what

Hawai'i's PUC did. More generally, the Energy Policy Act aimed at improving energy efficiency in the United States, boosting the use of renewable energy resources (thus reducing America's dependence on foreign oil), and lessening the impact of energy generation on the physical environment—goals similar to those put forward in Hawai'i's energy strategy.[45]

All of this seemed reasonable enough. After all, who could argue with efforts at energy independence and conservation? However, major issues soon split residents of Maui on the implementation of MECO's integrated resource plan. Numerous questions arose. Was MECO doing enough to develop alternative energy sources? What was meant by enough? As a privately held company, MECO needed to return a profit to its stockholders, and experiments in alternative energy could be expensive. Hawaiian Electric, for example, had lost about $30 million in pioneering its wind farm on O'ahu. Nonetheless, some environmentalists repeatedly charged that MECO's efforts to develop alternative energy sources were inadequate. What were the trade-offs between costs to consumers and possible damage to the environment resulting from the use of various energy sources to generate electricity? Was MECO accurately figuring the costs of different types of energy sources? Was the company fully capturing external costs — that is, indirect or hidden costs — in its reckonings? Above all, what were the future energy needs of Maui? Upon what bases should those needs be forecast?

Power Generation on Maui in the 1990s

Even as the movement toward comprehensive energy planning began, MECO's executives once again perceived themselves as hard-pressed to supply Maui's energy needs. Even though the expansion of tourism and the growth of population slowed on Maui in the early 1990s, MECO's officers saw themselves as having to continue playing catch-up with consumer demand. With geothermal energy possibilities abandoned, MECO's officers feared that their company might fall behind customer demand for electricity.

Additions to the Mā'alaea power plant helped. More generators, including another one using waste heat as its fuel, were brought into service in the early 1990s. Still more proposed additions evoked opposition from the Mā'alaea Community Association (MCA). Members of the MCA worried that tidal waves might sweep over power plant additions built there at tide-water. MECO's officers agreed to look for a different location; however, when they found that they could not buy desired land elsewhere, they returned to the idea of expanding at Mā'alaea. MCA members argued into 1995 that the proposed plant expansion was unneeded, too costly, and environmentally hazardous. Eventually, a compromise was worked out: MECO would not expand the plant beyond twenty-five acres and would build a dike tall enough to contain all of the oil in the tanks there, should they fail at the same time. The MCA withdrew its complaints, and MECO put in three new generators with a total fifty-eight-megawatt capacity. Additional capacity, twenty megawatts, came online at Mā'alaea in late 1999, "just in time," according to MECO's officers, for MECO "has been running its units at maximum capacity."[46]

With the additions to Mā'alaea, MECO's generating capacity was boosted to 215 megawatts by 1993 and was slated to rise to 254 megawatts by 2001. MECO had 44,000 customers in Maui County served by twenty-two power-generating units. Compared to developments on the mainland, this was a very decentralized setup, made necessary by the fact that MECO served three major islands, each of which contained some isolated communities. By 1995 MECO produced 80 percent of the electricity generated on Maui, with the sugar mills accounting for the rest. Some 90 percent of the MECO's electricity was produced and used on Maui, with an additional 4 percent generated and consumed on Moloka'i and another 6 percent on Lāna'i.[47]

Continued conservation efforts, although falling short of what some environmentalists desired, accompanied additions to MECO's generating system. By 1995 Maui was saving the equivalent of nearly 800,000 barrels of oil annually through the use of renewable energy sources. As on the other islands, most of this saving came from the burning of bagasse in electrical generators, enough to produce energy equal to that produced by burning 675,000 barrels of oil. Hydroelectricity saved another 25,000 barrels, and solar power an additional 95,000. As part of a concern for environmentally friendly power generation, the first phase of a biogas plant using bagasse to generate methane was started at Pā'ia. A $10 million plant secured by the State of Hawai'i and the Pacific Center for High Technology Research, this facility had made promising experiments by the mid-1990s. A plan put forward in 1999 by Zond Pacific to build a twenty-megawatt wind farm on Maui also looked promising.[48]

Plans for an Electrical Generating Plant at Waena

None of these efforts were sufficient, MECO's officers thought, to handle Maui's projected electricity needs, and in early 1997 they revealed plans to build a large generating plant just off Pūlehu Road at Waena in Central Maui. Controversies surrounding the question of building this plant dominated many discussions of economic development and environmental issues on Maui into the year 2000. It became apparent quite soon in these debates that more than simple economic matters were involved, as quality-of-life issues moved to the fore. Emotions, often heated, were expressed, especially by opponents of the plant.

MECO's officers based their decision to construct a plant at Waena on two major factors. The first was their forecast that there would be continued growth in the demand for electricity on Maui. "The population of Maui has been increasing since 1970," MECO's officers observed in their initial environmental assessment of the Waena plant. Moreover, population increases and demands for electricity could, they thought, be expected to grow in the near future. "As Maui continues to grow in population and as industry continues to shift away from agriculture," they predicted, "demand for electricity will increase." Second, they concluded that neither alternative sources of energy nor conservation measures could, by themselves, meet Maui's forecast electricity needs.[49]

Bonnet explained that while his utility favored economic growth for Maui, MECO was "neutral" in forecasting future demands for electricity. "We neither favor nor discourage demand," he stated. "We simply provide electricity." As he further observed, "Our forecasting for load growth reflects our expectations for the *reality* of the future, not our hopes for it." However, given the considerable time required to secure permits for new power plants — it had required four years to secure air quality permits for generating unit number 17 at the Mā'alaea plant — Bonnet and other MECO officers wanted to proceed with the Waena plant as quickly as possible.[50]

William Bonnet was born in 1943 into a family infused with engineering. His father was a civil engineer in the Army Corps of Engineers and was at the time in Chicago managing construction of the aircraft facility that later became O'Hare Airport. At the age of five months, Bonnet moved to Oak Ridge, Tennessee, when his father became the director of production of the Atomic Energy Commission's facilities there. Bonnet went to Vanderbilt University, where he majored in civil engineering. His family lived at Oak Ridge through 1962, when his father was reassigned by the army to Las Vegas. During his summers home from college Bonnet found engineering work at the army's Nevada Test Site, which he remembered as "fascinating stuff." He worked for the company that restored the tunnels after underground nuclear blasts to prepare them for the next explosions. From Vanderbilt, Bonnet went to the University of Illinois, where he earned a master of science degree in civil engineering, with specialization in water and wastewater engineering. After military service as an environmental engineer in the army, Bonnet earned an MBA from the University of Texas–Austin, and moved to Hawai'i.[51]

Before joining Hawaiian Electric, Bonnet acquired experience in environmental matters with the engineering firm of Austin, Tsutsumi and Associates and then served as deputy director of public works and as director of transportation services for the City and County of Honolulu. He became the project manager of Hawaiian Electric's Deep Water Cable Program in 1985. Problems, Bonnet later recalled, had developed in the utility's relationships with its consultants and with the federal government. Bonnet was hired "to get this thing on its feet," with his position dependent on "my ability of maintaining continued funding for that program" from the government. He had also to work with "a whole raft of subcontractors." Bonnet was learning how to get along with many different groups.[52]

In 1988 Bonnet became the environmental manager for Hawaiian Electric, a position that he kept until he came to MECO as its president eight years later. Environmental management involved overseeing compliance with state and federal government regulations and led Bonnet to stress the need for long lead times in the construction of new power plants. In his professional activities, as in his positions at Hawaiian Electric, Bonnet combined an interest in the environment with an abiding knowledge of engineering, serving at various times as president of the Hawaiian Society of Professional Engineers, which named him its Engineer of the Year in 1996; president of the Engineering Association of Hawaii; president of the Hawaii Water Pollution Control Association; and a director of the Hawaii Association of Environmental Pro-

*William Bonnet, the head of MECO, was deeply involved
in electric power matters on Maui in the 1990s. (Courtesy
of William Bonnet)*

fessionals. He also acted as a director of the Maui Chamber of Commerce
and as a member of the Executive Committee of the Maui Economic Development Board (MEDB).[53]

Muscled and wiry, Bonnet exuded strength and confidence. Well-informed
and persuasive, he represented MECO in the many hearings on the Waena
plant. Bonnet was, observed Mark Sheehan, president of Maui Tomorrow, "very
polished, very sincere" — in short, a tough opponent. While very much aware
of the importance of environmental issues, Bonnet sought primarily engineering
solutions to MECO's environmental challenges. His critics thought that he was

too narrow-minded in his approach, believing, according to Sheehan, that there was "only one way to do it." If some disagreed with Bonnet's methods, though, others favored them. "It is not an issue with us — are we going to have power on the island or not?" Mayor Linda Lingle's chief aide observed in 1998. "You've got to find a spot and make it work."[54]

To be constructed on sixty-six acres acquired from Hawaiian Commercial and Sugar, the Waena plant would be located just above Maui's major landfill on ground formerly planted in sugar cane. MECO intended to build the plant in four phases, each consisting of a fifty-eight-megawatt addition, with the final phase to be completed in 2020 (or 2030, if electricity needs grew more slowly than expected). The first phase was projected to be finished by 2006 at a cost of $105 million (the first part of phase one, the construction of a twenty-megawatt unit, was planned to be finished in 2004). The completed Waena plant would add 232 megawatts to MECO's power-generating capacity, nearly doubling the utility's projected 2001 capacity. When finished, the Waena plant would consist of four diesel-powered, fifty-eight-megawatt, dual-train combined-cycle units. Very efficient, these units would make use of waste heat. The total cost was estimated at $417 million.[55]

MECO's officers chose the proposed site at Waena with considerable care. Removed from major population centers and located at an elevation of 350 feet, it would be well above the likely reach of tidal waves. A plant at Waena would have, MECO's officers believed, a minimal impact on Maui's natural environment. It would be constructed in an area already degraded by other industrial enterprises — the county landfill, a quarry, and so forth. Native Hawaiian issues, so important in many of the other controversies on Maui, would be, MECO's officers hoped, of minor concern in the siting of the new plant. Hawaiian archaeological sites would not be damaged, they thought. Sugar cane cultivation had, at any rate, dug up the ground to a depth of four feet, probably already destroying any sites in the area, they pointed out. If construction revealed Native Hawaiian sites, the State Historic Preservation Division would be called in, as required by law, to assess preservation possibilities. Rare or endangered plant, bird, and animal species did not appear to live at the proposed site, but MECO agreed to conduct field surveys to look into that possibility.[56]

Plans for the Waena plant at first met only scattered opposition and questions. Initial public hearings monitored by CH2MHILL, a mainland-based

consulting firm in charge of preparing an environmental impact statement
for MECO, revealed three concerns. Residents in nearby parts of Maui wanted
promises that the new facility would not consume scarce water resources.
MECO's officers assured them that the plant would use only brackish water
unfit for most other uses and that precautions would be taken to prevent the
brackish water from infiltrating the area's water table. Residents were also
worried about plant emissions. To be dispersed through four 150-foot stacks,
the emissions would, MECO's officers contended, be translucent and would
resemble heat waves. No smoke would be visible, they said. In response to a
third line of questioning, MECO's officers argued that the plant would not
add much in the way of truck traffic to the area, although when fully constructed the plant would, they conceded, require forty-four trucks carrying
oil from Kahului's harbor each day.[57]

Such assurances were far from satisfying to all on Maui, however, and in
written testimony and verbal presentations during the summer and fall of 1997
increasing opposition to the Waena plant developed. The executive director
of Life of the Land opposed removing sixty-six acres of "prime agricultural
land" from cultivation and questioned the economic models used by MECO
in forecasting demands for electricity. Members of Maui Tomorrow raised
numerous objections. Lucienne de Naie of the Sierra Club on Maui later recalled bringing the power plant issue to the attention of Maui Tomorrow.
She was then working part time in Mark Sheehan's real estate office and remembered, "That's how that the MECO power plant thing got started up."
Those in Maui Tomorrow thought that building the Waena plant would make
Maui too reliant on fossil fuel sources and believed that MECO should do
much more to develop alternative energy sources. Then, too, they thought
that MECO's estimate of the rate at which consumer demand for electricity
would continue to grow was too high, given the economic slump into which
their island had fallen. The economic slowdown, they argued, gave Maui's
residents a breathing space during which they might explore energy options.[58]

In its final environmental impact statement, issued in late 1997, MECO
addressed the concerns that had been voiced by those questioning the need
for the Waena plant. The utility reaffirmed the need for new generating capacity, asserted that conservation measures and the use of alternative fuel
sources would not be adequate to meet Maui's probable electricity needs, and
touted the Waena site as the best choice because a plant there would have a

minimal impact on Maui's environment.[59] The state quickly accepted MECO's environmental impact statement, but before building the power plant MECO faced the hurdle of securing permissions from governmental bodies. Public hearings before state and county agencies revealed pronounced differences among various groups. Controversies continued into 2000, revealing conflicting visions about Maui's future.

Even before public hearings were held, environmental groups voiced their opposition. Noting that the Waena facility would "release sulfur-dioxide emissions and worsen the already degraded air quality of the South Maui region," the Hawaiian chapter of the Sierra Club called for "reconsideration of greater conservation planning in lieu of expanded facilities."[60] Maui Tomorrow made effective use of its Internet Web site to urge Maui's residents to speak out against the proposal at the coming hearings.[61] At the behest of Maui Tomorrow, Richard Heede, a research scholar specializing in environmental economics at the Rocky Mountain Institute, wrote to the State Land Use Commission urging that the Waena plant not be built. His arguments emphasized that the plant was unnecessary given the economic slowdown on Maui and that, at any rate, alternative energy sources combined with conservation measures could solve Maui's energy problems. A few years earlier, testimony by members of that institute had helped to kill a proposal for two diesel-powered plants on Hawai'i, and it was hoped that this success could be repeated on Maui. In that case, institute representatives had succeeded in having the Hawaii Electric Light Company, like MECO a subsidiary of Hawaiian Electric, consider more carefully the external costs of the proposed power plants on public health, air quality, and the quality of life. When these costs were reevaluated, the PUC dismissed the application for the installations.[62]

Testimony at Public Hearings

Hearings before the State Land Use Commission took place in the spring and early summer of 1998. The commission needed to rezone the proposed sixty-six-acre site from agricultural to urban before construction of the Waena plant could begin.

Representatives of the Maui Chamber of Commerce, the MHA, the MEDB, Hawaiian Commercial and Sugar, the Wailea Resort Company, Maui Memorial Hospital, the Maui County Farm Bureau, and the International Brotherhood of Electrical Workers testified in favor of rezoning the land. They stated that they favored the proposed plant as a way of assuring that they would have an adequate, reliable supply of electricity in the future. The Waena site, they believed, was the best available. As one proponent argued, much of the area was already industrial, possessing as it did the Ameron Quarry and the county landfill. As Lynne Woods, president of the Chamber of Commerce, observed, Waena was far from residential areas and high above Maui's tidal wave flood zone.[63]

Still others supported the proposed power plant. Albert Lyman, the former Hawai'i County planning director and then the senior project manager of CH2MHILL, MECO's consulting firm, assured those concerned that the plant by itself would not lead to further economic growth on Maui. Witnesses for MECO also stressed that the power plant would not unduly increase demands for county services — roads, police, fire, and schools. Maui County planning director David Blane added that only a new plant could provide the reliable power supply that his island needed for further growth.[64]

Maui Tomorrow led the opposition. Its members raised numerous objections: that the power plant would pollute Maui's air with invisible heavy metals, that supplying the plant with oil by tank trucks would congest roads, that prime sugar cane land would be removed from production, and that the plant would contribute to global warming. Above all, they questioned whether the plant was really needed, since economic development had recently slowed on Maui. Nor was growth always to be desired. Steven Moser, a physician testifying for Maui Tomorrow, concluded his exposition by urging that the plant not be built as a way of limiting development on Maui.[65]

The question of alternative energy sources figured prominently in the testimony. Representatives of Maui Tomorrow criticized MECO officials for, as they saw matters, not looking seriously enough at alternative power sources and for not promoting energy conservation strenuously enough. De Naie, who had become the conservation organizer of the Maui group of the Sierra Club, condemned MECO's proposed use of "obsolete technology" that would quickly become a "fossil-fuel-burning relic" and urged the development of solar and wind power. Bonnet and others representing MECO replied that they thought Maui's economic downturn was only temporary and pointed out that they were required by law to plan twenty years out, by which time Maui would surely need substantial additional supplies of electricity. Alternative energy sources were welcome, they said, but were not reliable enough by themselves to supply Maui's likely future needs.[66]

Economic matters were also of concern. Noting that "most of the businesses contributing to this County's economy are small businesses and that "my family is part of that group," Celeste King, one of Maui's pioneering environmentalists and in 1998 a director of Maui Tomorrow, urged consideration of alternative energy sources as likely to generate electricity costing less than that coming from the proposed Waena plant. Dick Mayer claimed that only investors in Hawaiian Electric, not Maui's residents, would benefit from building the plant. Mayer thus raised the issue of who should control Maui's development, Maui's residents or outsiders — an issue being raised at the same time with regard to the question of whether or not to enlarge Maui's major airport.[67]

Throughout their testimony, Maui Tomorrow members emphasized that they did not see the discussion about the Waena power plant as an issue pitting environmentalists against businesspeople. Rather, they said that they agreed with businesspeople on the need for additional, reliable sources of electricity. Those sources, should, however, come from nonfossil fuels. Generating electricity from solar and wind sources might well, they suggested, benefit businesses in the long run by being less expensive than power generated by burning oil. About three hundred windmills could, they thought, supply Maui's additional power needs — a claim contested by MECO's officers.[68]

Individuals joined Maui Tomorrow in its stance. For many the issue of saving land for agricultural use was of most importance, just as it was in the land zoning matters then being debated by the Maui County Council. Jeffrey Parker, a commercial orchid grower, denounced the proposal for taking agricultural land out of production and as unnecessary if alternative power sources were developed. Roy Smith, a Ha'ikū resident who farmed in Kula, echoed his sentiments, stating that it was "a foolish and dangerous idea to allow the conversion of any prime agricultural land, ever!"[69] Clearly, land matters were emotional ones. The sixty-six acres required for the proposed Waena plant represented only a small portion of the 36,000 acres that Hawaiian Commercial and Sugar had under cultivation on Maui.

The State Land Use Commission decided in mid-1998 to rezone the necessary land as urban, clearing away state government obstacles to construction.[70] Only one commissioner voted against rezoning, although two others were absent from the meeting at which the vote was taken. The lone dissenting vote came from Casey Jarmen, a professor of law at the University of Hawai'i. "My primary concern," Jarmen stated, "is the loss of prime agricultural land to an industrial use without sufficient justification for making such a trade-off." She also believed that not enough had been done in examining alternative energy sources and noted that the Waena plant would do "nothing to increase energy-sufficiency or increase the ratio of indigenous to imported energy use." In fact, Jarmen concluded, the Waena plant would make "Hawaii more vulnerable to a shortage of fossil fuels."[71]

Hearings also occurred at the county level, first before the Maui County Planning Commission, later before the Land Use Committee of the Maui County Council, and finally before the full county council. At issue was whether or not to amend community plans to allow the land for the proposed Waena power plant to be rezoned. Without such permission, the plant could not be built; state approval was not, by itself, enough.

In hearings before the Maui County Planning Commission, many of the same arguments put forward before the State Land Use Commission were revisited. Maui Tomorrow again denounced "the irreversible loss of prime agricultural land, air quality impacts on health and agriculture, the cumulative impact of the de facto industrialization of the Pu'unene area, the economic costs to local businesses in the way of higher rates and added infrastructural and environmental burdens."[72] The Sierra Club stressed the need to concentrate on "energy projects that are sustainable, renewable."[73] Many business representatives spoke again on the need for the Waena power plant as a source of reliable energy. They said their case was strengthened by rolling brownouts suffered throughout Maui. Unable to meet peak demands for power on March 11, 1998, because of the simultaneous failure of several generators, MECO had to cut off some customers' electricity. Bonnet was quick to point out that his utility could have avoided this action had it possessed more generating units, including those proposed for Waena. He went on to assert that the plant was needed to meet Maui's future demands for electricity, with development sure to pick up once tourism revived. Peak demand for electricity on Maui, Bonnet pointed out, had increased 18 percent since 1992.[74]

In these hearings several new arguments were stressed as well — especially by opponents of the Waena plant, who voiced an increased sensitivity to local economic issues and the rights of Native Hawaiians. Claiming that MECO's planning process was "developed from the top down," members of the Sierra Club called for energy projects that would "rely on local resources, create local economic opportunity."[75] Similarly, a long message posted by Maui Tomorrow on its Web site featured written testimony from Michael Potts of the Solar Utilities Network in California in which Potts claimed that "Hawaii's energy for decades has been managed for the profit of a few mostly off-islanders." An expert witness in a court case involving Hawaiian Electric, Potts had at the request of a group of Native Hawaiians prepared a draft, "Energy Policy for an Independent Hawaii."[76]

More than in earlier testimony, opponents also emphasized the need to consider the likely external costs of building and operating the Waena plant. They estimated these "hidden costs," such as increased respiratory health care costs, as being as much as 30–50 percent of the total construction and operating costs. If such externalities were taken into consideration, they argued, the economics of competing alternative energy sources would be much more attractive. Bonnet and others at MECO replied that in fact they had taken full account of externalities in their various IRPs prepared over the years.[77]

Unable to reach consensus, the Maui County Planning Commission voted in early 1998 to pass on the request to build the Waena power plant to the Maui County Council with no recommendation for or against, a decision hailed by Maui Tomorrow as a victory. In effect, the commission passed the buck to the council. Commissioner Moana Anderson had strong reservations about Maui's dependence on fossil fuels, and Commissioner Joe Bertram III wanted more community input into energy planning than he thought had occurred. The planning commission urged the county council to consider a number of salient points: a need for "more aggressive demand-side management of energy" (that is, a need to encourage conservation measures), a need to look again at energy growth and demand projections, a need to shield consumers from possible increases in oil costs, and a need to "make a firm commitment to renewable energy with specific goals and dates for implementation."[78]

Attention then shifted to the county council. The council's Committee on Economic Development and Environment sponsored a workshop on energy conservation efforts, hoping to foster cooperation among groups on Maui, but no consensus emerged. A representative of Hawaiian Electric explained that since drafting its first IRP MECO had looked seriously at thirteen alternative energy sources and had found several that appeared promising. By 1998 MECO was involved in, as its officers viewed matters, four "aggressive, achievable and cost-effective Demand Side Management (DSM) programs designed to minimize the inefficient use of electricity by our customers." MECO's officers estimated that their firm's DSM programs would bring a seventeen-megawatt reduction in peak load demands on Maui by 2016. This was far from adequate, countered MECO's opponents. Mayer, who had become a member of MECO's IRP advisory board three months earlier, condemned MECO's IRP as "a sham." The utility, he thought, had neither looked seriously enough at alternative energy sources nor calculated carefully enough the externalities involved in using fossil fuels.[79]

Following the workshop, officers of Maui Tomorrow and the Maui group of the Sierra Club issued a joint press release denouncing the proposed Waena plant, stressing what they thought were its economic downsides: "Quite frankly, we believe that the operation of the proposed power plant will suck the power out of Maui's economy. To pay for imported oil, Maui dollars will flow out of the community instead of providing support for local businesses and jobs. Our dollars will be supporting foreign jobs instead of creating local jobs in the installation and maintenance of alternative energy technologies."[80]

Similar disagreement took place in hearings before the county council's Planning Committee two months later. Once again Mayer and others from Maui Tomorrow claimed that MECO had not done enough to look into alternative energy sources. Once again, Bonnet defended MECO's IRP record and asserted that building a diesel-powered plant would not preclude the development of using alternative energy sources should they become economically practical in the future. No providers of electricity produced from alternative power sources had, Bonnet pointed out, approached MECO with a request that the utility purchase electricity from them. By the terms of a 1978 federal law MECO was required to do so, but MECO was not required to pay more than the cost of generating electricity by conventional means.[81]

The county council made no final decisions on the Waena power plant in 1998. Council elections were held in November, and pending the outcome of those elections council members agreed to defer matters into the following year.[82] Hearings resumed in the late summer and fall of 1999, this time before the council's Land Use Committee. Bonnet, representatives of business groups, and labor leaders restated the need for the Waena plant as the best way to ensure Maui's energy future. Representatives of Maui Tomorrow and Life of the Land countered by stressing the need to consider more fully alternatives to fossil fuels. The county council had recently created a Committee on Alternative Energy, and members of the environmental groups urged the council to delay making any decisions on the Waena plant until this new committee had time to look into matters.[83]

After an intensive series of public hearings, members of the Land Use Committee took two important votes in the opening days of 2000. In one they approved amending the Wailuku-Kahului community plan to permit the building of the new power plant, if the rezoning of the land were approved. Three weeks later the full county council also voted its approval. However, in a second vote members of the committee decided to defer considering the actual rezoning of land for the plant until later in the year, by which time MECO would have prepared a new IRP. Council members and environmentalists called on MECO to recognize more fully alternative energy sources and conservation matters in that IRP. MECO officials seemed to be moving in that direction. Bonnet said that MECO would set aside seventeen acres at Waena for alternative energy technologies and that MECO would not develop more than twenty megawatts in any single phase of the Waena project. He pointed out, too, that Maui County could intervene in later, ongoing approval processes before the PUC for each phase. Faced with continuing questions, Bonnet pushed back the estimated time for the installation of the first power unit at the Waena plant from 2004 to 2006.[84]

Moving toward Decisions

While no final decisions about the Waena plant had been reached by mid-2000, compromises seemed more possible than before — just as was the case with regard to water issues. The actions of environmentalists were having an impact, leading MECO officials to look more closely than before at alternatives. The course of events encouraged rethinking matters. Shortly after the Land Use Committee votes on Maui, the Citizens for Clean Air on Kaua'i asked their circuit court to throw out county permits for Kaua'i Electric to build a twenty-six-megawatt power plant. On Maui, Life of the Land and Maui Tomorrow sponsored a public presentation by a senior staff scientist with the

Union of Concerned Scientists from the mainland on the viability of alternative energy sources. Held in the chambers of the Maui County Council,
this presentation was taped and later broadcast on Maui's community television channel.[85]

In early 2000 the county council adopted an ordinance that changed the
map for the community plan for Wailuku and Kahului from agriculture to
heavy industry for nearly sixty-six acres across from the county landfill. While
seeming to open the way for the Waena plant, this action was far from deci-
sive. The ordinance won approval only after the inclusion of an amendment
stating that the council had not yet determined what was appropriate for
construction at that site. Debates continued, as council members expressed
concerns about rising oil prices, the need to examine alternative energies, and
other matters. Finally, late in the summer of 2000 the county council voted
to permit the rezoning of the land for the power plant. However, as often
happened on Maui, the clash of viewpoints and interests led to compromise in
the political arena. The council decreed that Maui Electric could produce electricity from conventional fossil-fuel sources on only 32.5 acres; the remaining
33.2 acres had to be reserved for alternative energy research, demonstration,
and production projects. Quickly approved by Mayor Apana, this decision
went to the PUC for final sanction.[86]

Divisions on electricity had not always rent Maui's citizens. Maui's residents embraced electrical generating plants through the 1970s, because electricity was welcomed as making life easier and as bringing economic growth
to their island. There was no opposition to the construction of MECO's plant
at Kahului in the 1940s and only limited dissent from the building of the plant
at Māʻalaea during the early 1970s. However, in the 1980s and 1990s opposition to additional power plant construction developed as environmentalism
caught on. That opposition helped kill efforts to build a large geothermal plant
on Hawaiʻi, modified MECO's plans for Māʻalaea, and delayed and then altered the construction of the Waena plant on Maui. In the Hawaiian Islands,
as in the rest of the United States, public opinion played increasingly important roles in shaping business decisions.

In several ways, however, the Hawaiian Islands, including Maui, seemed
to differ from mainland America. The search for alternative energy sources,
although less successful than proponents desired, went further than in most
parts of the American mainland. The heavy dependence on oil spurred those

in the Hawaiian Islands to look very seriously at a variety of other energy sources. While they did not in the end embrace geothermal energy in a major way, significant starts were made in utilizing windpower and other nontraditional energy sources. This partial embrace of alternative energy sources came from the rapid expansion of tourism during the 1970s and 1980s. The explosive development of the visitor industry, with its tremendous demand for electricity, heightened the tension between competing desires for economic development and environmental protection. Then, too, each island had its own electric power generation and distribution system, with no interisland connections or interlocking power grids — leaving the islands with a more decentralized electrical system than that of mainland America. Each island stood or fell alone. There existed no way to shift electricity from island to island as needed. A brownout or blackout on Maui could not be mitigated by bringing emergency electrical supplies from Hawai'i or O'ahu. In part, this situation had long existed because of geography, but it also continued because of the decision to abandon the geothermal project on the Big Island, a project that would have connected most of the islands in one power grid.[87]

6

The Controversy over the Kahului Airport

From the 1970s through the 1990s Maui's residents considered major additions to their island's main airport near Kahului, including lengthening its primary runway from 7,000 to 9,600 feet and building a completely new runway 8,500 feet long. Longer runways would accommodate larger airplanes, allowing direct, nonstop service between Maui and many parts of the globe for the first time. When fully loaded, large airplanes cannot take off from a runway only 7,000 feet long. Longer runways would mean that passengers and freight would no longer need to be transferred in Honolulu. Tourism on Maui would be aided, and, proponents of the runway extensions claimed, Maui's economy would be boosted. Not all of Maui's residents favored the proposed airport expansion, however. Some mistrusted the impacts of runway extensions and increased tourism on their island's economy and environment. Even more was involved, as the rights of different groups, especially Native Hawaiians, to determine their future became wrapped up in the controversy surrounding airport expansion proposals.

Railroads and Ships

Controversies such as those about proposals to expand the Kahului Airport were rare in earlier decisions about transportation improvements in the United States, especially in the Trans-Mississippi West. Throughout the nineteenth century and well into the twentieth most westerners welcomed transportation links with open arms. Connections to the rest of the United States and to the world meant economic growth and an end to social isolation. Environmental concerns were of distinctly secondary importance. Only through

improved transportation networks, most westerners reasoned, could the resources of their region be put to productive use, ensuring the creation of
private profits. Railroads were especially welcomed. Faster and more reliable year-round than earlier forms of transportation, railroads linked different regions within the United States, connecting the West to the South
and Midwest.[1]

Railroads and ships were important for Maui. The first railroad on the island was the Kahului and Wailuku Railroad, which began operations in 1879
and was incorporated as the Kahului Railroad two years later. Reaching out
from Kahului's harbor to most of the mills on Maui by the 1910s and 1920s,
the Kahului Railroad had 443 freight cars by 1936. The line carried sugar from
the mills to docks at Kahului, from which the sugar, along with pineapple
from canneries, went to Honolulu or mainland America. Improvements to
Kahului's harbor, some made by the Kahului Railroad and others by the territorial government, allowed that port to handle 370,000 tons of freight by
1944.[2] The Kahului Railroad remained important through the 1950s; however,
as more and more sugar was carried to harbor by trucks, the line declined in
significance and was finally closed in 1966. For decades ships, such as those
of the Matson Line, provided Maui's residents with the only way to travel to
other islands. However, shipping service seemed slow to Maui's residents, who
eagerly took to air transportation as a way to go from island to island.[3]

Early Airports on Maui

With territorial government funds in short supply, private enterprise was
responsible for the first commercial airport on Maui. In late 1929 Inter-Island
Airways (which later became Hawaiian Airlines), Hawaiian Commercial and
Sugar, and the Kahului Railroad cooperated in building a paved airstrip near
Māʻalaea, just one year after the dedication of the John Rogers Airport serving Honolulu. To introduce Maui's residents to air travel, the airline gave
excursion flights to ninety-three of the island's residents on April 15 and 16,
1930. The *Maui News* caught the excitement felt about air travel then. "Sun-
day broke clear and bright and thousands turned out to inspect the new runway at Maalaea Airport and to watch the plane 'Maui' in her flights over the
island," observed a reporter for the paper. "The flights varied from 15 to 20
minutes," he noted, "the plane flying over the blue water of the Pacific and

then around the slopes of Haleakala, over the wastes of Kihei and Maalaea Bay to come swooping down like a huge hawk on to the macadam runway."[4]

Commercial operations began with Inter-Island's Sikorsky airplanes a bit later that spring. Airmail service started in 1934. Mā'alaea had drawbacks, however. It was troubled by high winds and was too close to the West Maui Mountains. It was also far, by the standards of that time, from Wailuku, then the island's main town. Only a rough, unpaved road connected the airport to Wailuku. In 1938–39 the Mā'alaea airport was closed, deemed inadequate for the larger airplanes that had come into use during the decade.[5]

In 1939 Maui's airport was moved to the Pu'unēne area, a region of wide, open spaces in the middle of the island's central plain. This location won approval over two other possibilities, a site up the bay from Mā'alaea, and an area near the old Kanahā fish pond at Kahului. Close to most of Maui's major towns, the Pu'unēne area had plenty of available land, something the Mā'alaea site lacked, and had no obstructions to airplane landings. Flight paths near Kanahā would have to have been routed around sugar mill smokestacks and electric power lines. Built as a New Deal project at a cost of $200,000, the Pu'unēne Airport opened in April 1939, with the arrival of sixteen-passenger Baby Clippers from Honolulu. A year later DC-3s began landing there.[6]

With America's entrance into World War II, military concerns led to the transformation of the Pu'unēne facility into a naval air station. A naval air station was also constructed near Kahului in 1943. The military left Pu'unēne at the conclusion of the war, and in 1947 Maui's general airport was moved to its current location just outside of Kahului.[7] Several factors dictated the choice of Kahului over Pu'unēne: It was closer to population centers, water supplies, and sources of electricity; it had three runways, compared to Pu'unēne's two; it had better terminal, repair, and refueling facilities; and air currents there were more predictable.[8]

Environmental issues did not figure in the siting of the Mā'alaea, Pu'unēne, or Kahului Airports. Constructed on the site of the naval air station there, the Kahului Airport converted additional sugar cane lands to airport usage, which did not seem troublesome at the time. Maui's residents were, in fact, enthusiastic to get new air connections to the outside world.[9] Concern for the preservation of Maui's natural physical environment was just beginning, and those few environmentalists who lived on the island were engaged in more pressing issues than those involving Kahului. Nor was much thought given to the rights of Native Hawaiians, with the Native Hawaiian Renaissance still several decades into the future. Economic growth, not protection of the environment, was on the minds of most residents of Hawai'i in the years right after World War II. With the economy of their island stagnant, Maui's residents favored economic expansion over all other matters.

Nor, it might be added, did environmental concerns loom large in the revamping of Honolulu's airport right after World War II. Complaining of noise and the danger of crashes, a few Honolulu residents urged that the airport be relocated from its site close to their city to a more distant area. Arguing that alternative sites were too far away and pointing out that federal funds were already being spent on improving the existing airport, territorial authorities rejected such suggestions out of hand in the 1940s and 1950s.[10]

The Emerging Debate over Airport Expansion

The debate over the expansion of the Kahului Airport dates back to the rapid development of tourism on Maui in the 1970s. Incremental additions and changes were made to the airport throughout the 1960s. In 1965, for example, the airport terminal was greatly enlarged. More far-reaching changes were considered during the 1970s, and with that consideration came the beginnings of conflict over airport development.

An announcement by American Airlines in 1974 that it wanted to start direct flights to Maui from the West Coast spurred thoughts of airport expansion. Members of Maui's county council discussed whether to petition the Civil Aeronautics Board to allow direct flights and whether to ask the state government to extend the length of the Kahului Airport's major runway to 12,000 feet. Council members were divided. Some saw airport expansion as the salvation of their island, as the best way to stimulate Maui's tourist industry, create new jobs for its residents, and thus stem the exodus of young people from Maui. Other council members, however, questioned the benefits. They raised concerns about noise pollution and the loss of agricultural land and asked whether the airport would raise housing costs on Maui. In the end, the county council referred matters to committee. Mayor Elmer Cravalho favored runway expansion at the time but lacked the funds to do much about it.[11]

Conflict arising over where to locate a small commuter airport to serve visitors going from Kahului to West Maui suggested some of the issues that would soon arise about the plans to expand the Kahului Airport. As resorts continued to develop in West Maui — Kā'anapali, Kapalua, and Lahaina — the small West Maui airport on Amfac's land near Kā'anapali was overburdened. Expanding it proved difficult because of the proximity of high-tension electrical wires and other engineering problems. Planners decided to build a new, larger West Maui Airport close to Lahaina. This decision provoked anguished howls of opposition. It might, feared one poetic opponent of the new location, "bother whales who frolic in the ocean near the airport site." Others were against the proposed location as likely to increase traffic congestion in Lahaina, especially in the town's historic district. Proponents of a new airport pointed out that it would be better for the whales to play elsewhere anyhow, farther away from humans, and that a little traffic congestion was a small price to pay for economic growth sure to result from the airport. David DeLeon, then a reporter for the *Maui News*, remembered the fight over the West Maui Airport as "horrendous." Nonetheless, a larger airport was constructed in the 1980s, and the controversy soon died.[12]

Capping airport discussions in the 1970s, the comprehensive plan prepared in 1980 by county authorities for Maui's development over the next decade recommended banning direct flights from the mainland or abroad to the island. This county plan called for a balanced approach to development through economic diversification.[13] Planners did not want to trade dependency on plantation agriculture for dependency on tourism. Hence, they did not favor airport runway extensions; such expansion would, they feared, increase Maui's growing reliance on the tourist industry.

Growing Conflict in the 1980s and Early 1990s

Owned and operated by the State of Hawai'i as part of a statewide airport system, the Kahului Airport covered about 1,450 acres by the early 1980s and was by far the most important airport on Maui. In 1982 the state put forward a master plan for the development of the Kahului Airport based on the assumption that it would handle only interisland flights, as specified in the county's development plan. The airport plan retained a 7,000-foot limit on the length of runway 2-20, the airport's longest runway, content to propose

The Kahului Airport handled increasing numbers of passengers during the 1990s.
(Courtesy of Wayne Tanaka)

a slight extension to a shorter runway and several other minor airport improvements. The deregulation of the U.S. airline industry quickly made this plan obsolete, however, as several airlines scheduled direct flights, mainly for the benefit of tourists, from the West Coast to Maui in 1983.[14]

As Maui developed into a premier tourist destination in the mid-1980s, the state revisited airport issues and in 1988 drafted a new master plan. This airport scheme consisted of a short-term plan for changes to be made through 1990 and a long-term plan for alterations through 2005. Based on the assumption that the Kahului Airport would handle both interisland and overseas flights — a real change from earlier airport plans — the 1988 plan called for extensions to the airport's two major runways. The plan to enlarge Maui's airport was part of a larger scheme to expand much of the state's airport system. In a plan approved in 1990, some $2.5 billion were allocated for the purpose, with most of the funding going to upgrade Honolulu's airport. At the time, political leaders projected a 33 percent increase in the number of tourists coming to the Hawaiian Islands by the year 2000, with most of them passing through Honolulu.[15]

The preparation of an environmental impact statement accompanied the 1988 airport plan. Objecting to what they thought would be environmental damage resulting from the implementation of the 1988 plan, individuals and environmental groups filed suit to block any airport changes, charging that the environmental impact statement was inadequate and calling for the preparation of a more complete one. This litigation resulted in a court-ordered stipulation in 1991 that such a study be made.

Over the next several years conflict shifted to the county level. Maui's residents adopted a new ten-year general development plan, which, like its predecessor, stipulated that the longest runway be restricted to 7,000 feet and that other alterations be limited. These limitations placed the county plan at odds with the 1988 state airport plan. However, in early 1992 Mayor Linda Lingle asked for an immediate reconsideration of the county plan. With Maui's economy slumping as a result of a falloff in tourism, Lingle called for airport additions, including an extension to the main runway. As the *Maui News* observed at the time, "A deepening recession, higher unemployment and concern about tourism and the economy set the stage for reconsideration."[16] At this point, supporters and opponents of airport alterations began mobilizing as organized groups, making their positions clear in public statements and hearings.

Leading support for the runway extension was the Maui Pueo Coalition headed by Jimmy Rust. A Native Hawaiian who lent the coalition the name of his family's *'aumakua* (personal totem), the *pueo* or Hawaiian owl, Rust was a heavy-equipment driver and representative of the Hawaii Operating Engineers on Maui. The Pueo Coalition was an umbrella organization composed of twenty major bodies including business groups (the Maui Chamber of Commerce, the Maui Visitors Bureau [MVB], the Maui Economic Development Board [MEDB], and the Maui Hotel Association [MHA]), labor unions (the International Longshore and Warehouse Union [ILWU] Local 142; the Laborers' International Local 368, and the Hawaii Carpenters Union Local 745), and several farm organizations (the Maui County Farm Bureau, for example).

Rust put forward the coalition's unwavering position. "We have to get people back to work," he reiterated in speech after speech. There were, he claimed, 4,000 unemployed on Maui, with "thousands more who have had their work hours cut or second jobs eliminated." Some of these were former sugar cane and pineapple workers trying to make the transition to a new type of economy on their island, a difficult task. Many could not, Rust concluded, "feed their families, pay their mortgage, rent or car loan." Economic growth resulting from an expansion of tourism would benefit them, he thought. Environmental problems, he was sure, could be minimized. Still more was involved. Rust and others disliked being lectured to by relative newcomers to Maui, especially members of environmental groups. "When you go to these hearings you see the opposition is almost always people from somewhere else," Rust complained. "They've left overgrown places to come here." Such people, Rust believed, did not understand the situation on Maui. "We ask," Rust observed, "what are we going to do with all these kids who are graduating every year?" Newcomers needed, he thought, to keep the job needs of longer-term Maui residents and their families in mind.[17]

Others seconded Rust's position. The executive director of the MVB claimed that other newly developed destination resorts around the world were taking business away from Maui and concluded that that business could only be regained through airport alterations.[18] The president of the Maui Chamber of Commerce, who was also a member of the Pueo Coalition, said that no compromise was possible. Proponents of airport extensions, he noted, had already retreated from their desire for the construction of two 10,000-foot-long runways. The MEDB issued a pamphlet touting a longer runway as absolutely necessary for Maui "to stay competitive and achieve greater stability and growth in its economy."[19]

Led by Dana Naone and Isaac Hall, many of the opponents of airport expansion formed the Maui No Ka Oi Coalition. As we have seen, Dana Naone Hall was (and remains) a Hawaiian rights activist. In fact, she had to return early from a protest meeting on Kaho'olawe to testify against the airport extensions. Criticizing Mayor Lingle for not upholding Maui County's general plan, members of the Maui No Ka Oi Coalition claimed that the expansion would bring too many new visitors to Maui, straining the island's already overstressed infrastructure of roads, sewers, water sources, and supplies of electricity. Then, too, unwanted pests — snakes, insects, and plants — might, they feared, hitch rides on planes from South Pacific islands and Southeast Asia, flourish on Maui, and threaten the island's native flora and fauna.[20]

Particularly feared was the brown tree snake, which had overrun Guam and which, many on Maui were afraid, might infest the Hawaiian Islands, if any ever got loose. There were no snakes in the wild in Hawai'i, but there were fears that planes from Guam might accidentally transport brown tree snakes to the islands. Planes stopping in Honolulu landed at an airport built on a reef out in the city's harbor. This physical isolation made it difficult, but not impossible, for snakes, which might hitchhike in airplane wheel wells or cargo holds, to escape into the countryside. Between 1981 and 1994 seven brown tree snakes were found in the Hawaiian Islands, all on O'ahu.

Other groups joined the Maui No Ka Oi Coalition in its stance. As early as 1986 the Hawaiian chapter of the Sierra Club had called upon the state legislature to take measures to keep alien plants and animals out of the Hawaiian Islands, fearing that they would "suffer biological, social, and economic losses" from an invasion by intruders, and opposed runway extensions at the Kahului Airport for that reason.[21] The president of the Spreckelsville Community Association pointed out that a runway extension and jobs did not necessarily go hand in hand, and labeled the carrot of jobs "a cruel hoax." More was involved in his opposition, however. Spreckelsville was a wealthy community near the Kahului Airport, and its residents, later actions would show, were concerned mainly about increased noise levels. In fact, the county council had listened to complaints about excessive noise throughout the 1980s. The head of Maui Tomorrow turned economic claims back on members of the Pueo Coalition. Employing an argument that would become increasingly prominent over the next few years, he observed that far from helping Maui's residents, a longer runway would "just perpetuate Maui's overdependence on tourism, which makes our economy more fragile and more vulnerable to recession."[22]

A climax came in ten consecutive hours of public hearings before the Maui County Council on August 24, 1992. Members of the Pueo Coalition, the Maui No Ka Oi Coalition, and other groups presented what were becoming well-known positions and dramatized their statements in colorful ways that were hard to ignore. They knew the value of symbolism in discourse. Wearing baseball caps emblazoned with "96 in '96," by which they meant the building of a runway 9,600 feet long by 1996, Pueo Coalition members brought cans of SPAM luncheon meat to the meeting, lamenting that all of Maui's residents would be hungry if the Kahului Airport's runway were not lengthened. Found in great quantities in grocery stores in the Hawaiian Islands, SPAM was viewed as the food of poor people. Maui No Ka Oi Coalition

Controversy engulfed the question of whether to expand the Kahului Airport in the 1990s, as can be seen in this photograph of a public hearing before the Maui County Council on August 24, 1992. (Courtesy of Wayne Tanaka)

members countered by filling the hearing room with Native Hawaiian chants and by presenting council members with woven coconut-frond baskets filled with fruit. Faced with vociferous differences of opinion, the county council put off making a decision by referring airport matters to the Maui Planning Commission, which, in turn, would report back to the council at some undetermined date.[23]

The 1993 Airport Plan

Conflict intensified with the publication in 1993 of a new master plan for the Kahului Airport.[24] The 1993 master plan looked at what Maui was like in 1990 and tried to predict changes through 2010.[25] The number of people passing through the Kahului Airport had risen dramatically, the plan pointed out, and would continue to increase in the future. The airport handled nearly 5 million passengers in 1990, up from 1.2 million twenty years earlier. Nonstop overseas passenger service had begun in 1983, and by 1990 nonstop service to Los Angeles and San Francisco provided 1.1 million of the passengers using the Kahului Airport. By 2010, if alterations were made, the airport would handle about 9.5 million passengers, the plan estimated, including 2.4 million coming from or going nonstop to the U.S. mainland and another 432,000 arriving from and departing nonstop to international (mainly Asian) locations. In 1990 Maui had a resident population of 91,000 with an additional average of 35,000 visitors on any given day. Authorities predicted that Maui could have 145,000 residents and 71,000 tourists by 2010. Tourism, the 1993 plan observed, "has been the primary force in Maui's economy over the past decade, while agricultural activities on the island have decreased." Tourism, the plan predicted, would become still more important in the future.[26]

By 1993 the Kahului Airport was already the second-busiest in the Hawaiian Islands, handling 5.4 million travelers that year. (Only the Honolulu airport, which took care of 22 million people, was busier. Honolulu International Airport was the fifteenth-busiest in the United States and the twentieth-busiest in the world in 1993.) Continuing incremental improvements allowed the Kahului Airport to handle more and more people. In early 1993 a new terminal building was completed, along with four new holding rooms for passengers and twelve new gates for aircraft, built at a cost of $72 million.[27]

To accommodate the growing number of passengers, the 1993 master plan argued that major additions were needed for Kahului's airport. Among the most important changes would be lengthening the airport's runway 2-20 from 7,000 to 9,600 feet and building a completely new parallel runway 8,500 feet long. These runways could handle the large planes used in nonstop trans-Pacific flights and nonstop flights to the Midwest and East Coast of the United States. Another already existing runway, runway 5-23, would be kept at 4,990 feet in length to handle commercial general aviation and interisland flights. The improvements should be phased in, the plan said, over two decades. During 1992–96 runway 2-20 would be lengthened to 9,600 feet. Only later, between 2003 and 2010, would the new 8,500-foot-long runway be built.[28]

The suggested improvements would be expensive, but possible, according to the 1993 plan. The plan estimated that total costs would reach $322 million, with $38 million used to extend runway 2-20 and another $107 million needed to construct the new parallel runway. New buildings, road improvements, and other infrastructure alterations accounted for the rest of the expenditures. The funds were, it seemed, available. The State of Hawai'i operated its airports as a single system, with concession and user fees as the main sources of income. Those fees paid the interest and principal on bonds sold to fund airport additions (the bonds were airport revenue bonds, not general obligation bonds). In 1993 the state had $746 million in authorized, but unissued, airport bonds — enough, it was then thought, to finance improvements to the Kahului Airport and to other airports in the state system.[29]

Mayor Lingle endorsed the airport plan in her 1993 State of the County speech, which proved to be an explosive step. Her chief aide later remembered that "it was like dropping a match in a roomful of kerosene." Opposition from environmental and Native Hawaiian groups brought a new court-ordered stipulation forbidding implementation of the 1993 master plan and halting hearings by the State Land Use Commission aimed at reclassifying land needed for the airport expansion. The court found an environmental impact statement prepared by the state's department of transportation in the summer of 1992 inadequate, in part because it did not address many of the new actions urged by the 1993 master plan. So in early 1994 the federal and state governments (represented by the Federal Aviation Administration [FAA] and the Hawaii Department of Transportation [HDOT]) began a new investigation designed to analyze all aspects of the impact of the 1993 plan.[30] Preparation of the new environmental impact statement took two years, with completion coming in 1996.

Conflict over the Airport Intensifies

The 1996 environmental impact statement embraced considerable input from Maui's many concerned business, labor, and environmental groups. In written correspondence and in public hearings the groups that had been emerging in the early 1990s elaborated their positions, with different views of what economic growth, environmental responsibility, and the "good life" meant coming to the fore during the intensifying debate.

Chaired by Rust, the Pueo Coalition led the charge for runway extensions, expanding on arguments made four years before. Its economic message was blunt. "Without one-stop flights to Maui from major world airports," Rust claimed, "we will see decreased tourism which will lead to fewer jobs and a reduced tax revenue base." Thousands of jobs were, Rust averred, at risk. Unless airport extensions took place soon, "the next generation will leave for other states." Toni Rust, Jimmy Rust's twenty-three-year-old daughter, lamented what many people her age were saying: that after completing her college education at the University of Hawai'i, she would have to go to the mainland, because there were "no adequate job opportunities" in the islands.[31]

Jimmy Rust argued that the proposed airport changes would diversify Maui's economy. The tourist business would become less dependent on a seasonal influx from the West Coast. "The ability to encourage direct flights to Maui from the Mid West and East Coast," he said, "will ensure more stability for our number one industry — tourism." Nor was that all. Farmers and high-technology businesses — Rust singled out "Maui's growing software, graphic design, and small manufacturing industries" — would also benefit from better air connections. Picking up on the point raised by the Rusts, Carolann Guy, who had just stepped down as president of the Maui Chamber of Commerce, wondered if there would be enough jobs available on her island in the future. Maui, she worried, "lacked the economic opportunities and diversity . . . to attract her children back to Maui's shores." Further, Guy queried, "Have we considered what a community built without young adults will become? The common term — brain drain?"[32]

Representatives of numerous business entities, including many belonging to the Pueo Coalition, rallied to Rust's support. The head of the MVB, who was also vice-chair of the Pueo Coalition, observed that Maui was in increasing competition with other destinations worldwide for tourists and business and that airport alterations "will help us counter the onslaught, enabling us to reach out to new markets domestically and internationally." The executive director of the MHA echoed such sentiments, saying that "we have to do what we can to keep [tourism] healthy" and noted that "even to diversify our economy, and we are certainly not opposed to that, we will need to be able to compete with other areas of the world with regard to ease of getting in and out for both people and products." The general manager of the Stouffer Wailea Hotel was outspoken: "Make no mistake about it: we are all part of tourism and tourism is part of us." The president of the Maui County Farm Bureau wrote that a longer runway was needed, "because exports represent such a significant part of the total market for our agricultural production."[33]

Members of the Pueo Coalition downplayed environmental dangers. Rust stated that his group was "deeply concerned about the introduction of alien pests" and supported "all creative ideas for intercepting alien species," without, however, putting forward much in the way of specific plans to do so. Rust argued that the arrival of more nonstop flights on Maui would benefit the island, for the number of interisland flights would fall, thus lowering the risk of the importation of insect pests from O'ahu. The president of the Maui County Farm Bureau added that he thought that "individual farmers should be responsible for pest management on their own farms." Claiming that "there is no evidence that existing flights have impacted bird life at Kanaha Pond" — by this time the former fish pond had become a nature preserve near the airport that was the home of three endangered species of birds — Rust doubted that the runway extension would have any negative impact, either.[34]

Opponents of airport alterations attacked on several fronts. The Halls continued to raise legal issues, objecting, for instance, that representatives of the FAA and the HDOT had met privately with members of the Pueo Coalition to listen to their views and that the agencies were beginning preparations to lengthen runway 2-20 even before the new environmental impact statement was issued. The Halls called for a full evaluation of all environmental issues, including the need to bolster Maui's inadequate infrastructure, and for a reassessment of the airport extension cost figures, which they thought were too low. They and many other opponents also asserted that the safety issue was bogus — proponents of longer runways argued that the extensions would increase the safety of airplanes using the Kahului Airport — because the Kahului Airport had been certified as safe by the FAA and would remain safe in the future, with or without longer runways.[35]

Environmental issues were at the forefront of the minds of many opponents, and of these the topic of alien pests generated the most discussion. Maui's residents recoiled in horror from the possibility of a brown tree snake invasion and from the possibility of unwanted insects getting loose on their island. "It is imperative," stated Isaac Hall, "that a program be developed in the [economic impact statement], that can be implemented *prior* to extending any runways and *prior* to internationalizing the airport to prevent the introduction of further alien species. . . . Any increased introductions," he observed, harm "Maui's farmers, endangered species and parks." Members of the Sierra Club raised similar objections. The superintendent of the Haleakalā National Park observed that his domain was "the home of more endangered and threatened species than any other national park" and concluded that "new introductions of alien species arriving aboard foreign aircraft" would greatly harm his park's integrity.[36]

Related environmental issues surfaced. The fate of bird life at Kanahā Pond, which the airport extensions seemed to threaten, took center stage. The head of the Hawaiian Audubon Society protested that contrary to what Rust had argued, airport expansions could hurt the Kanahā Pond Wildlife Sanctuary, home to the Hawaiian stilt, the Hawaiian coot, and the Hawaiian duck — endangered species all. Even more was involved. Built in the mid-1700s by a leading Maui chief, Kanahā Pond was by the 1990s valued by Native Hawaiians as a historical site and a part of their culture.[37]

Opponents also raised economic issues, many of which were intertwined with the environmental ones. Jeffrey Parker — owner of the Tropical Orchid Farm, the largest exporter of live orchids from Maui, and an outspoken opponent of the Waena power plant — greatly feared "the very real threats to Maui's eco-system and agriculture which could arise from direct overseas flights." Alien slugs and thrips were already damaging his flowers, he said. Similarly, the owner of a papaya farm feared "the insects and pests that come into the islands." Thus, far from all of Maui's farmers agreed with the Maui County Farm Bureau that runway extensions would help agriculturists. For growers of specialized fruits, vegetables, and flowers the prospect of unwanted insects was even more terrifying than their fears of brown tree snakes.[38]

Taking a different tack, the president of the Spreckelsville Community Association denounced the higher noise levels likely to come with larger planes and underlined that building a new runway parallel to runway 2-20 would require taking seventeen acres from Spreckelsville, destroying "one of Maui's most desirable communities featuring quality homes, sandy beaches, water recreation, and a favorite place for local residents." Beyond testifying at public hearings, those living in Spreckelsville took to the courts, charging that noise from the airport was damaging their property values and seeking $19 million in compensation. They lost their case in early 1998.[39]

For others the economic stakes were broader. Maui Tomorrow led much of the fight against airport alterations by stressing the need to diversify Maui's economy and pointing out that the airport improvements would not do so. Mark Sheehan, the group's president, argued that it had "not yet been shown that the net effect of the runway extension would be diversification of Maui's economic base." To the contrary, "if the runway extension is more of a stimulus to tourism than it is to agriculture," he observed, "the result will be a less diversified economy." Moreover, Sheehan pointed out that economic and

As the home for endangered species of birds, Kanahā Pond was involved in debates over the future of the Kahului Airport.

environmental issues were closely linked, for the importation of agricultural pests could "hamper efforts to diversify our economic base by making it harder (more costly) for diversified agriculture to succeed." Then, too, he argued that even tourism, far from being helped, might be hurt by airport extensions. The influx of too many tourists would, Sheehan feared, overwhelm the island. "Maui must be careful," he warned, "not to let the success of tourism degrade the natural environment and quality of life upon which that tourism depends." Dick Mayer added that "a particular issue is the question of home rule." Airport extensions, he feared, would "give much greater control to people off this island and even outside this state, even outside this country" — much the same argument he mounted against building the Waena power plant.[40]

For many opponents there was more at stake than economic or environmental issues. Cherished ways of life seemed to hang in the balance. For no people was this truer than for Native Hawaiians. As Dorothy Pyle, a faculty member teaching Hawaiian history at Maui Community College and head of the Maui County Cultural Commission, observed, the Hawaiian sovereignty issue was "important," with Native Hawaiians disliking "being dictated to by outside interests." One Native Hawaiian wrote, "The expansion of the Kahului airport will devastate the unique natural beauty of my island home, Maui" and concluded that "Maui's beauty and lifestyle is unparalleled and must be preserved." He stressed his fear the brown tree snake might enter Maui and then destroy Maui's native bird life. Another Native Hawaiian, a fisherman, objected to having public hearings at the airport. "Why couldn't we have the hearing down in the Maui Community Center, where it's common ground?" he asked. "Am I to be someone talking about spirituality, cultural resources, the environment where you choose it to be?" he wondered. Charles Maxwell, the Native Hawaiian leader, called the plans for the expansion of the airport "one of the worst things that's happened to Maui."[41]

Native Hawaiians and their supporters were not alone in their concerns. "Magic Maui," many were afraid, might be overwhelmed by construction projects and become another Waikīkī. With too many people, the island's infrastructure would crumble, and the quality of life for residents would decline. Airport alterations acted as a lightning rod for such fears. With more planes and people arriving on more and longer runways at the Kahului Airport, prophesied the head of Maui Tomorrow, "quality of life will deteriorate, property values will decline, and as the island becomes a less attractive place [in which] to reside and to vacation, the decrease in revenues will transform this thriving community into a morass of social and environmental ills."[42]

Continuing Conflict

In 1996 the FAA and the HDOT issued their long-awaited joint environmental impact statement in five volumes weighing twenty-two pounds. The statement made an effort, although not as much as was desired by most environmentalists, to explain the effects of the airport expansions on Maui's environment and to suggest mitigation methods.

The environmental impact statement focused on several major topics. Observing that airport expansion might disturb ancient Hawaiian burial sites, the statement called for careful monitoring of all construction by professional archaeologists, the avoidance of burial sites wherever possible, and proper reburial overseen by the County Burial Council where necessary. Noting that "the proposed airport improvements do not include any actions within

Kanaha Pond," the report called for no mitigation measures with regard to the wildlife sanctuary. Airport extensions, when completed, would result, the statement showed, in the loss of 690 acres of sugar cane fields and 170 acres of grasslands. However, when studies revealed that no endangered or threatened plants or animals lived within the boundaries of the proposed airport extensions, the statement concluded that "no mitigation is required." The issue of alien pests proved complicated. The statement admitted that air traffic accompanying the airport extensions might "increase the potential for the introduction of alien flora and fauna species (pests) to Maui." The report urged the HDOT to continue working with other state and federal agencies, as well as the airlines, to deter alien introductions but put forward little in terms of new mitigation measures. In the end, the statement concluded that "there are no significant impacts due to the Proposed Project and therefore no mitigation is necessary."[43]

Statewide measures to deal with alien pests had become more varied and intense over the previous two years with the establishment by the Hawaii legislature of the Alien Species Action Plan of 1994. This plan set up an Advisory Task Force consisting of representatives from state and federal agencies, community groups, and business organizations. By 1996 the Advisory Task Force had issued extensive recommendations. These included increasing the vigilance of established inspection agencies and coordinating the work of those bodies, mapping the incidence of pests and establishing a center for their control, retaining close inspections of all airplanes for the brown tree snake, and launching a public awareness program.[44] The brown tree snake attracted special attention. By the mid-1990s state and federal agencies were cooperating in a three-prong effort to keep the snakes out of the Hawaiian Islands: the inspection on Guam of all airplanes leaving for Hawai'i, the inspection in Hawai'i of all airplanes arriving from Guam, and the establishment of Snake Watch Alert Teams (SWAT) to seek out and destroy any brown tree snakes that got loose in the Hawaiian Islands.[45]

Opponents found many problems with the 1996 environmental impact statement. At a public hearing in May 1996 six people spoke in favor of it, with fifty-five criticizing it, especially, as they saw matters, for its failure to deal thoroughly enough with the alien pest issue. The Halls, in particular, condemned the report on this issue, calling it "as inadequate as the previous [statement] that was prepared." Dana Naone Hall asked, "Are we willing to sacrifice species for the sake of a third international airport in Hawaii?" In response to continuing challenges, the FAA and the HDOT prepared a revised, final environmental impact statement and issued it in the fall of 1997. This report contained more stringent measures to prevent the entrance of alien species to Maui.[46]

Meanwhile, disturbed by the long review process, Mayor Lingle reentered the fray. Speaking to the Maui Chamber of Commerce, she declared that "the delays in this project must stop." She and an economist for the First Hawaiian Bank pointed out that Maui's tourist industry was still in the doldrums. Moreover, they asserted that by building an 11,000-foot-long runway at the Keāhole Airport near Kona, the residents of the Island of Hawai'i had boosted tourism on their island. Direct flights from Japan, they speculated, were taking tourist business away from Maui.[47] Perhaps as a result of Lingle's prodding, the final environmental impact statement was soon forwarded to Gov. Benjamin Cayetano and the FAA regional office in Los Angeles. Governor Cayetano quickly said that he wanted to accept the environmental impact statement and start work on the airport.[48]

The FAA was slower to act. Continuing concerns about alien species led to further negotiations between the federal agency and several of Hawai'i's state agencies. Finally, in the fall of 1998 the FAA approved the 1997 environmental impact statement, seemingly giving the go-ahead to the airport expansions. Included in the final plan was a state-of-the-art quarantine and inspection facility at the airport, to be the first of its type in the United States. For a time it seemed as if the new airport plans might resolve the long-standing conflict. Hawaiian Airlines applied to the U.S. Department of Transportation to begin a daily flight between Kahului and Tokyo on January 1, 2000.[49]

Agreement, however, proved short-lived, if, indeed, it ever really existed. In the spring of 1999 the State Land Use Commission reopened public hearings on whether or not to rezone the land needed for the airport expansion from agricultural to rural — those hearings had been placed on hold in late 1993, pending preparation of an acceptable environmental impact statement — and testimony at the hearings revealed that people were still far apart in their thoughts. In often testy statements and questioning, the same issues that had been debated for over a decade were revisited: the roles a longer runway might play in Maui's social and economic development, the possible impact of a larger airport on Maui's infrastructure, potential problems resulting from the inadvertent introduction of alien plants and animals, and the rights of Native Hawaiians. Representing those opposed to the expansion of the airport, Isaac Hall led the offensive, often backed up by Dick Mayer, who sat next to him at many of the hearings. The devil lay in the details — for instance, to keep alien pests out of Maui, just where should inspection facilities be placed, who would fund them, and for how long?[50]

Resolution

Many of Maui's residents saw the question of whether to expand the Kahului Airport as the most disruptive local political issue of the 1990s. Sally Raisbeck, the retired scientist turned environmentalist, spoke for many when she called the airport controversy "very divisive."[51] The fallout from the debate on Maui reached to the other Hawaiian Islands. In the summer of 1999 consideration was given to lengthening the runway of the airport at Lī'hue on Kaua'i. Fearing that his island's residents would be divided the way those on Maui had been, one of the county council members for Kaua'i called upon the Center for Alternative Dispute Resolution to help those on Kaua'i reach consensus.[52]

Still, as the 1990s came to a close, compromise on Kahului Airport matters seemed closer than before, despite the continuing debates before meetings of the State Land Use Commission. The long recession on Maui may have led some of the island's residents to look upon airport expansion more favorably. Alice Lee, a member of the Maui County Council, thought so. Noting that while there were "very strong feelings on both sides," she believed that "the seven-year recession has changed people's minds about the extension of the runway . . . because now jobs are at stake, abilities to pay mortgages are at stake."[53] Reaching a satisfactory compromise was also more likely than earlier because grassroots environmental and Native Hawaiian rights groups had had a real impact on the airport plans. Efforts to mitigate the invasion of Maui by alien pests, resulting from pressures emanating from environmental groups, had become more stringent. Maui's experience with airport expansion shows just how important public involvement in the planning process can be. By participating in hearings on the various environmental impact statements and by the astute use of court challenges, opponents of airport extensions had a measurable impact on the outcome.

Like most of the other matters examined in this study, the debate about the Kahului Airport serves as a reminder about just how interlinked economic, environmental, and cultural issues are. The airport controversy reveals the complexity of the situation, showing that much more joined and separated people than simply economic issues. Economic matters merged with cultural and ideological concerns. Differing views about Native Hawaiian rights and the physical environment of the island divided groups of Maui's residents. At the root of controversy lay competing visions about the quality of life on Maui and the roles different types of economic changes might play.

In the end, however, it was economics that decided matters. With concession fees from shops in airports drastically declining and with airlines reluctant to pick up the shortfall in the form of higher landing fees, funds to expand the Kahului Airport were not available, and in March 2000 the state abandoned efforts to win approval for runway extensions. Had opponents won a major victory? Perhaps. "I am pleased that the runway extension plan has been cancelled," enthused Dick Mayer. "I believe this is a wonderful way for Maui to keep its reputation as the No. 1 tourist area in the world and it also means that housing prices and other difficulties that the people of Maui would have had if their airport had been extended will be kept under control." Still, there was more to the situation. A new generation of efficient, lighter airplanes such as the Boeing 777 could fly long distances. They could offer direct flights to and from places far from Maui, using the existing runway at the Kahului Airport, ensuring that debates over how best to mitigate the impacts of those flights would continue.[54]

7

Two Communities

Land, water, transportation, and electric power matters had direct and indirect impacts on community development on Maui, as shown by the course of events in two communities, South Maui and Upcountry Maui. One of the fastest-growing tourist areas in all of the Hawaiian Islands, South Maui faced difficult choices with regard to development throughout the late twentieth century. A more agricultural region, Upcountry Maui encountered challenges of growth during the 1970s and 1980s but was much more affected by development in the 1990s. Decisions made in these two communities illustrate well the complexities of economic and environmental issues in the Hawaiian Islands.

South Maui Developments in the 1970s

South Maui's early history gave little hint that the area would one day become a hot tourist destination. In precontact times numerous Hawaiians lived well in South Maui, fishing in the ocean, raising fish in fish ponds, and trading with upland people for agricultural goods. After contact, parts of South Maui were sites of efforts to grow cotton and sugar cane. Mākena Landing served as a shipment point for goods bound to the 'Ulupalakua Ranch and for cattle going from the ranch to markets beyond Maui. In the late 1930s and early 1940s the territorial government sold land by auction in parts of Kīhei at prices of between $110 and $455 per lot. The first house was built on Keawakapu Beach in what would become Wailea only in 1946. Some sixty homes went up in South Maui in 1948; even so, at mid-century South Maui was still largely an undeveloped area of scrub and cactus. Farmland could be purchased for $225 per acre, and residential lots went for five to ten cents per square foot.[1]

There were, nonetheless, signs that this situation was about to change. In 1950 Bill Azeka opened a grocery store in Kīhei, a forerunner of the commercial developments he would spearhead. Born on a Maui sugar plantation, Azeka was sent to live with his grandmother in Japan at age six. Upon returning to Maui a decade later, he worked in a restaurant owned by his parents in Kahului. His parents later opened a store, giving Azeka additional retail experience. Moving out on his own, Azeka bought the Tomokiyo Store in Kīhei in 1950. Because few people lived in the area, the store was at first unprofitable, grossing only $30,000 in its opening year. However, through hard work, persistence, and the good fortune of being in Kīhei just as it was starting to attract visitors, Azeka eventually succeeded. Using his store as a base, Azeka branched out into related activities, including the development of a neighborhood shopping center in the mid-1970s. In 1987 Azeka Enterprises grossed $7 million, and a year later the Small Business Administration honored Azeka as its "Small Business Person of the Year" for the state of Hawai'i.[2]

Azeka, known affectionately as the unofficial mayor of Kīhei, worked during two very different periods in Kīhei's history. As one astute observer noted in 1980, "Kihei, the development that stretches along a southerly portion of Maui, is the place he's made his mark. Once a quiet place where fishermen sought the evening meal in solitude, and returned to wives and children in tree-concealed houses, it has burgeoned into a parade of condominiums and hotels along a narrow two-lane road." The writer noted that "Azeka has managed to bridge the era of the solitary fisherman with that of the tourist carrying travelers' checks without losing friends in the process" and concluded that Azeka was "from a generation that believed in hard work, and combined it with the instincts of a businessman who sensed the pulse of progress, saw his local banker, found an architect, and went big time."[3]

South Maui possessed some of the finest beaches in the world, and the signing of the water agreement of 1975 made possible the rapid construction of world-class hotels and resort destinations, stimulating a building boom throughout that section of the island. What most characterized much of South Maui's development was a lack of adherence to planning. Existing plans, had they been followed, might have guided development, but, for the most part, the plans were ignored.

There existed considerable support for planning. The Maui Chamber of Commerce urged the adoption of a plan "that would restrict building heights and control density to assure the preservation of the open space concept and protect the esthetics of the Maui coastline." Members of the Kihei Community Association also wanted planning, because in its absence land parcels had been downgraded in their zoning, threatening the values of their properties. A questionnaire sent to Kīhei's residents in 1970 revealed that nearly all favored some sort of planning. "The desire to effect overall community improvement," officials summarizing the results of the survey concluded, "overshadowed desire for personal pecuniary gains."[4]

Financed by an urban planning grant from the U.S. Department of Housing, a Civic Development Plan was adopted for South Maui in 1971. This scheme sought to anticipate growth in Kīhei. The plan's goals were ambitious: "An almost totally undeveloped coastline with a population of under 1,500," the plan stated, has "to be planned to accommodate a possible fifty-fold increase in population within the next 20 years." The plan aimed, first of all, at preserving the region's "13 miles of white sand beaches along this coast for the future enjoyment of not only guests of the hotels to be built, but for all residents of the area," through the creation of ten miles of beach parks totaling more than 1,000 acres. Public access to the beaches was to be assured, and builders were to be given incentives to locate their "structures in such a way as to insure open vistas to the sea." Building height and density restrictions and setback requirements would, it was thought, result in "highly developed urban clusters . . . set off by graduated buffer zones of lower rising apartments and residential neighborhoods, as well as neighborhood commercial sites."[5]

Planning extended beyond Kīhei to Wailea and Mākena. Alexander and Baldwin was in its initial stages of developing Wailea as a planned community, and this scheme was subsumed into the regional plan for South Maui. South of Wailea lay Mākena. As described by planning proponents, "the plan would place strict development controls in Makena, with special emphasis placed on the conservation of Makena's historic sites . . . so that when maximum urbanization is reached in the rest of the planning area, Makena will remain as now, a quiet place of natural beauty and historic interest."[6] The plan concluded with high aspirations for the harmonious development of South Maui. "The overall plan was drafted in the belief that this Hawaiian

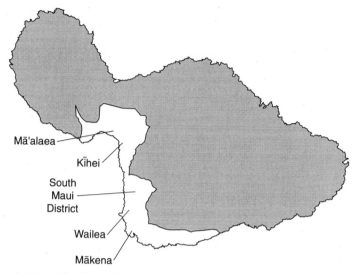

The South Maui Planning District encompassed a region of hotels, resorts, and towns.

coastal region of Maui; once the center of native population, enjoying an almost unparalleled mildness of climate; beside a sea that is a setting for the nearby Islands of Kahoolawe, Lanai, and Molokini," planners stated, "can once again become a major population center while still remaining a place for pleasant living." The planners believed that "orderly development will be as profitable for developers as uncontrolled growth" and thought that "in the final analysis, everyone, including the developers, will benefit."[7]

Despite sentiment in favor of planning and despite the adoption of a community development plan, Kīhei mushroomed in a largely unplanned manner. Several factors militated against close adherence to the community plan. The plan itself was modified throughout the 1970s to allow for larger business districts in parts of Kīhei; it was in one of these areas that Azeka placed his shopping center. Many residents favored this expansion of business districts, even though it ate up green space, because it increased the convenience of daily shopping. Some six hundred people signed a petition asking the county council to approve Azeka's building plans.[8] Not all residents favored Kīhei's business district expansion, however. Foreshadowing future debates, one lamented, "I see nothing in the plan that makes Kihei a more attractive place." Observing that "a town, just like a building, should have character and charm," he concluded that "we do not need another typical American town that stretches for miles without a beginning, middle or an end."

Changes in the plan, in turn, opened the door to the granting of numerous variances. In case after case, the county council approved variances that allowed the construction of high-density condominiums and apartments, as long as the projects were reasonably "compatible with the existing neighborhood development" and helped "meet the demand for housing in Kihei."[9]

Exacerbating the situation was the fact that, unlike circumstances throughout most of the Hawaiian Islands, land ownership was fragmented in Kīhei. By the early 1980s more than one hundred separate development projects had put up 8,000 condominium units in the Kīhei area. As each private developer tried to maximize his project's appeal, a wall of high-rise condominium complexes cut Kīhei off from the ocean, and urban sprawl came to characterize the area. The fact that many local politicians were heavily involved in the development schemes smoothed the way for the necessary variances, as has been amply documented by the scholars George Cooper and Gavan Daws. Thus, exuberant growth came to South Maui in the 1970s. Only in 1984 did the county council, after years of discussion, impose a moratorium on the issuance of building permit variances for structures exceeding the height, lot coverage percentages, and floor area/lot area ratios specified in the community plan.[10]

One exception to this state of affairs was the Wailea development, located just south of Kīhei. Acquired by Alexander and Baldwin in 1969, the Matson Line had been contemplating the development of 1,500 acres it had purchased from the 'Ulupalakua Ranch in 1957. Alexander and Baldwin employed the well-known firm of Grosvenor and Company to prepare a master plan for Wailea and, lacking the resources to go it alone in such a large project, brought in the Northwestern Mutual Life Insurance Company as a partner in the creation of the Wailea Development Company. Alexander and Baldwin bought out Northwestern Mutual's share in 1984, at which time Wailea Development became a wholly owned subsidiary of Alexander and Baldwin.

Having a single owner meant that Wailea could be developed in a coordinated manner. The development was intended initially to be free of cars. "It will be an entirely new town catering primarily to the tourist who wants to escape from the noise and bustle of city traffic," stated developers. A small boat harbor, facilities for children, and extensive landscaping were planned.

Condominium complexes came to block views of the ocean in parts of Kīhei.

A "central core area" would be "both a gathering place and commercial center." Many of the more idealistic concepts, such as excluding cars, were quickly dropped, and the economic downturn of the early 1980s killed other aspects of Wailea's development. A major beachfront development called "L'Abri" planned by Mike McCormick failed to materialize when McCormick could not secure adequate financing. The opposition of nearby residents on environmental grounds also contributed to the demise of the L'Abri proposal.[11]

Even so, achievements at Wailea were substantial. In 1973 the Wailea Steak House and a golf clubhouse opened. A year later condominium units were sold in the first phase of Wailea Ekahi, with units in phases two and three put on the market the following year. In 1975 the first condominiums in Wailea Elua went on the block, along with Fairway homesites. Wailea's first hotel, the Inter-Continental Maui (later the Aston Wailea Resort), opened its doors in early 1976, followed by the Wailea Beach Resort (later the Renaissance Wailea Beach Resort) in 1978. On April 15, 1978, some 1,200 buyers bid for 148 units to be constructed in the Wailea Ekolu Village in a frenzy similar to buying at Kā'anapali and Kapalua. Wailea Point sold its first luxury condominiums in 1986. By the mid-1980s Wailea consisted of three major condominium complexes, a number of housing developments, several world-class hotels, golf courses, restaurants, and a collection of shops at the Wailea Shopping Village. By agreement with the county, all beaches were open to the public, and a number of small parks were provided. Private green space abounded, as the condominiums were low-density developments, especially when compared with their counterparts in Kīhei.[12]

Yet the development of Wailea caused controversy, which highlighted unintentional difficulties resulting from the growth of tourism. Problems involved the creation of the infrastructure. The Wailea development strained Kīhei's sewer system. When the county greatly expanded that system, some of Maui's residents complained that Wailea was receiving special treatment not afforded their areas, even though much of the funding for the sewer system came from Alexander and Baldwin.[13] Also divisive was the relocation inland of the county road that had run along the South Maui shore to accommodate the Wailea development. Local residents feared that this action might cut them off from some of South Maui's beaches. Only when assured of beach access did they relent in their opposition to the relocation. Still other issues surfaced. Dick Mayer, a member of the Maui County Planning Commission, wanted developers to provide more affordable housing for employees and more open spaces for all. As a reporter for the *Honolulu Star-Bulletin* observed in 1973, "The major projects, especially at Wailea, have drawn an unusually large helping of criticism and opposition." Nonetheless, he concluded, "they have been welcomed by a large segment of the population because of the jobs and economic advantages they offer."[14]

By the early 1980s South Maui had changed dramatically from what it been just a decade earlier. Its resident population had risen from about 1,500 to roughly 6,000, and the nature of that population had changed. In the late 1960s Native Hawaiians had composed 56 percent of the area's population, but a decade later Caucasians made up 60 percent it. World-class resorts had been created, but urban congestion had also become a problem, especially in Kīhei. From the late 1970s on the president of the Kihei Community Association appeared before the county council whenever that body considered capital improvement projects. His refrain was uniform: that South Maui's infrastructure had fallen far behind what was needed for the booming region. "Kihei's repeated floods, open drainage ditches, lack of pedestrian walk-ways, and dangerous roads are among the items which need immediate attention," he noted in a typical presentation. "Other areas have been water problems, sewer problems, and other items." Beginning in the 1980s he observed that members of his association even favored a tax hike to address these problems.[15]

Not fully anticipated, the changes occurring were welcomed by some, condemned by others. Mayer later observed that "everyone was involved in land development. . . . The idea was turn the spigot, let's get in there, let's get development going." Mark Sheehan remembered the situation in similar terms: "You see how all the politicians and attorneys got in on it. . . . They all knew what they were doing, and they all got a piece of the action. And, it shows. That's why it looks like what it is, a strip where everyone got in on the game." Yet it is important to remember that for many of Maui's residents, especially non-Caucasians, the opportunity to be involved in the development of South Maui and similar areas in the Hawaiian Islands was one of their first chances to step out from beneath the shadow of the Big Five companies. No one knew this better than Elmer Cravalho, Maui's mayor during the 1970s. "Every condominium built represents a small developer," he explained. "Every one we allow to build diminishes the power of the great land companies. . . . When I help the small developer," he asserted, "I weaken the large companies and I help the community." He concluded, "What is lost aesthetically through small-scale development is gained in greater freedom — a small price to pay."[16]

Continuing Growth in South Maui during the 1980s

As part of Hawai'i's ongoing statewide planning process, renewed efforts to plan for South Maui's future began in the early 1980s. Aided by county officials and professional planners, a group of South Maui residents developed a plan to guide their region's growth through the year 2000, by which time South Maui was expected to have 23,000 residents. Three principles ran through this Kihei-Makena Community Plan, which was first put forward in 1981. All sought to address the chaotic growth then taking place in Kīhei. First, the plan called for "the creation of a pleasant community character" through "adequate setbacks, landscaping, and building massing and height controls." Second, the plan called for "sufficient variety in the location, density, type and price of housing." Finally, the scheme stressed "the importance of the shoreline and nearshore waters for recreational and scenic value."[17]

TWO COMMUNITIES [199]

From these principles flowed specific suggestions. Diversified economic activities were encouraged, including the creation of a light industrial zone just above the Pi'ilani Highway in North Kīhei. Resort and hotel developments were to be limited to areas south of Kīhei, that is, in Wailea and Mākena. Incentives were offered for the construction of housing for people of different income levels. Height and setback restrictions were set forth for different classes of buildings, including a three-story limit for commercial buildings and a six-story limit for apartments and condominiums. Shoreline protection measures were embraced. The plan specified that "existing dune formations should remain intact" and that "indigenous or endemic strand vegetation should remain undisturbed." An "open space system of parks" was to be established.[18]

However, as in the 1970s, construction outstripped planning. As put forward in 1981 the plan was only provisional, for it still needed the approval of county officials, and that approval was some time in coming. Pressed by other concerns, county officials took years to examine and then modify the plan. Into the mid-1980s they continued to grant variances for the construction of new buildings. Particularly disturbing to those involved in preparing the community plan was approval given for the building of a shopping center and condominium complex next to an elementary school in Kīhei, where automobile traffic was already heavy.[19]

As modified by county authorities, the Kīhei-Mākena plan disappointed many of those involved in its initial preparation.[20] Members of the community planning association, along with other area residents, criticized the plan for failing to control adequately commercial, industrial, and resort developments and for allowing the degradation of South Maui's physical environment to continue. "You have, you, the Council, seen fit to pile on an additional 100 acres for hotels, 58 acres for apartments, 175 acres for light industrial use, and approximately 275 acres for single-family residential development above and beyond the projected community needs," observed one critic.[21] Approved by the county council, the altered plan went into effect in 1985. While not going as far as some of Kīhei's residents desired in limiting growth, the final plan did retain building height and setback limits, provisions for park and shoreline open spaces, and some limits on resort and industrial development. In the end, the county council rejected a request from a family business group to rezone property on the South Kīhei Road for light industrial use, as a result of adamant opposition from the Kihei Community Association.[22]

Once the United States emerged from the recession of the early 1980s and tourism picked up again, South Maui boomed anew. Kīhei's resident population doubled during the 1980s to 15,365 people, with an additional 16,000 visitors on any given day. South Maui was the third-fastest-growing region of its size in the United States, after only St. Marys, Georgia, and Divide, Colorado. "Go Maui, young person, if you're searching for boom towns in the middle of the Pacific," advised the *Honolulu Star-Bulletin*. Particularly noticeable was the building of large resort hotels in Wailea and Mākena. As David DeLeon, an adviser to Linda Lingle, then a member of the Maui County Council, later recalled, "Money just ripped in there. . . . It just boomed the place." New hotels — the Kea Lani with 900 rooms and suites, the Grand Hyatt Resort with 814, the Four Seasons Resort at Wailea with 472, and the Maui Prince with 329 — turned the Wailea-Mākena region into a leading center for luxury tourism in the Hawaiian Islands. That growth again outran the area's infrastructure. As DeLeon observed, "Our infrastructure was so over-wrought; that was our battle front: sewers, water, roads, schools, police, fire; you name it, any type of public service was overwhelmed." Housing was especially a problem, with "people stacking up twenty people per house."[23]

More was involved in the minds of many longtime South Maui residents than the failure of their community's infrastructure to keep pace with resort developments. A way of life seemed to be vanishing — a lifestyle that was less hectic, more in tune with the natural environment and possessing a difficult-to-define, Native Hawaiian spirit of *aloha*, a way of thinking that stressed openness and sharing. At a community forum on South Maui issues in late 1989, Dana Naone Hall observed that "we are seeing the extinguishment of traditional life-styles," and Dick Mayer compared tourist-oriented development to drug addiction "fed by a lot of greedy people."[24]

Challenges Facing South Maui in the 1990s

The recession that hit the United States and Japan in the early 1990s, and which in Japan's case lingered to the end of the decade, slowed the development of South Maui. While some new housing opened, no new hotels went up during the decade. The slowdown gave residents a chance to rethink what they wanted their region to be and catch up with earlier hotel and resort developments. In the 1990s South Maui received a new library, community center, better roads, and an improved sewer system.

The pace of business picked up in South Maui as the 1990s progressed. Some liked the renewed hustle and bustle. Edward Ellsworth, a forty-one-year-old former Californian who started Media Wizards, a maker of CD-ROMS and other audiovisual products in Kīhei, spoke for many newcomers: "What I really like is the quality of life." Not all shared such sentiments, however. As they had in the controversies about the development of Mākena, older residents in South Maui expressed disappointment about their changing styles of life. "We used to put our fishing poles right on the beach," lamented Douglas Akina, who, ironically, was himself a tour operator, the owner of Akina Aloha Tours, in 1996. "It's gotten overpopulated. I don't go anymore." By this time the South Kīhei Road alone possessed eleven shopping centers and minimalls.[25]

Through community planning, residents of South Maui once more sought to shape their region. The community plan adopted in modified form in 1985 was up for review in the 1990s. In a plan finally adopted in 1998, residents of South Maui decided that tourist development would continue but that it would be more restrained. As in the 1970s and 1980s, the plan adopted in 1998 originated in the work of a citizens' advisory council, but there were many delays in considering the recommendations of this council, as various groups became involved in the planning process — to the extent that the citizens' council had disbanded well before the plan was finally adopted. Maui Tomorrow members, for example, expressed serious concerns about the impacts any additional developments might have on the beaches, wetlands, and infrastructure of South Maui.[26]

Designed to govern the region's growth to 2010, the plan resembled its predecessors in many respects but generally went further in trying to protect South Maui's physical environment. It did so, in part, by limiting hotel developments "to those areas presently planned for hotel use, such as Wailea and Makena," and not Kīhei.[27] While still allowing the development of hundreds of acres of land, the plan represented a reduction in development from what had been desired by some. The Wailea Resort Company, C. Brewer, and Alexander and Baldwin failed to win permission to move as much land as they wanted out of agricultural use into residential and commercial uses. Fears that resort development would continue to outrun infrastructure improvements, especially water supplies and street construction, prompted the restrictions. Stung by earlier experiences in South Maui, the county council put forth a "principle of concurrence" to govern developments. Council members decreed that "infrastructure and land use approvals go forward together." Land development could not proceed in advance of water, sewer, and street improvements.[28]

Particularly appealing to opponents of rapid resort development were provisions in the plan to preserve additional areas as open spaces and parks. After considerable wrangling, the county agreed to purchase Kama'ole Point as a park, a consideration dating back to 1969.[29] The county also hoped to turn about five acres just inland from Palauea Beach into a cultural park. The site of the remains of the largest known undisturbed Hawaiian village in the Kīhei-Wailea area, this park would keep intact what was described by its proponents as "a place where people can feel what it must have been like in precontact times." In the park there would be "a sense of suspension . . . an island in time."[30] Dana Naone Hall spoke for members of Hui Alanui o Makena when she approved the plan, saying, "This is a very wonderful plan. We have something to give to the future."[31]

However, controversy soon engulfed Palauea Beach, one of the last undeveloped beaches in South Maui, reminiscent of that which had surrounded Mākena Beach about a decade before. The county agreed in 1996 to purchase about five acres, but that land was not actually bought because of financial stringencies. When it appeared in the summer of 1999 that wealthy out-of-staters were about to purchase the undeveloped land in back of the beach and put up houses overlooking it, a public outcry for the county to buy all of the land immediately behind Palauea Beach arose. Many of the same people who had led the fight to preserve Mākena Beach, including members of Hui Alanui o Makena and State Park at Makena (SPAM), turned their attention to Palauea Beach, urging county officials to acquire the land without delay. In the end, the county bought enough land to give residents access to the beach, but not as much as many desired, allowing private building to occur just behind the beach dunes. Everett Dowling, one of the developers of land behind Palauea Beach, pledged in May 2000 to build on only twenty of his forty-four acres. The remaining twenty-four acres would, he said, become an archaeological preserve.[32]

Perhaps more promising were efforts at historical preservation. In the summer of 1997 the county and state governments cooperated in funding a citizens' group to preserve historical sites along a South Maui corridor. This effort grew out of earlier work. In 1992 testimony at public hearings on the community plan for South Maui suggested that as many as 1,000 archaeological features and 300 sites existed in the planning area. A 1995 workshop on greenways sponsored by the groups Kihei 2000 and Bikeways Maui again emphasized the need to preserve the region's heritage. Under the terms of the 1997 agreement, sites would be identified, preserved, and marked with signs. Among the sites were some of special importance for Native Hawaiians: a village and fish pond, a fishing shrine near the Kīhei public library, and the remains of a village at Keone'ō'io just south of La Perouse Bay. The old Hawaiian trail from Mā'alaea south to La Perouse would also be identified.[33]

Even though it placed restrictions on development, the 1998 South Maui plan allowed plenty of scope for new hotels, condominiums, and shops. In late 1997 developers won approval to raze the Wailea Shopping Village, a shopping center serving hotels in the Wailea complex, and replace it with a much larger Shops at Wailea, scheduled to open in late 2000. At about the same time, developers began construction of a fifteen-acre Pi'ilani Shopping Center just up the hill from Azeka Place II in Kīhei. More far-reaching was an announcement made by officials for the Makena Resort that they hoped to build a new 500-room hotel, along with 1,500 multifamily housing units. Supported by state and county officials, resort managers won approval in the late fall of 1997 for their request that 146 acres of their land be redesignated as urban and thus open for development. Water issues, however, intruded on these plans. Resort managers said that they would build a 700,000-gallon-per-day sewage treatment plant (expandable to 1.5 million gallons per day [mgd]). Reclaimed water from this plant, along with brackish water from wells on resort grounds, would irrigate the hotel's proposed golf courses. Even so, the new developments might require as much as 2.1 mgd of potable water. Just where this water would come from was unclear. The Makena Resort had rights to water from the 'Īao aquifer, but the amount due the resort was in dispute. As the economic recession lingered, no construction steps had been taken by 2000.[34]

Another area of contention was the northern entrance to Kīhei. By the summer of 1998 plans for a "gateway" to South Maui had passed through four renditions, each a scaled-down version of the previous one. To be built on twenty-nine acres just off the Pi'ilani Highway, the development was at one time to have included a small zoo, a rain forest, and 500,000 square feet of commercial space. Because of protests from people living in Kīhei, ideas for the zoo and the rain forest were dropped. As finally approved by the county council, the development was to include winding canals with boat rides, several new restaurants, thrill rides on artificial mountains, an "outback" camping area for local people, and 150,000 square feet of commercial space — all wrapped around a theme of "five villages of Maui." Those villages, complete with craft workers plying their trades, would be a Hawaiian village, a street from Maui's whaling era, a sugar cane plantation camp, Wailuku as it existed in the 1950s, and a "Maui of the Future." Thus was culture to be commodified and sold to Maui's tourists. Still, problems remained. One was flooding. Because so many condominium buildings had been put up near the site for the development, it was difficult to construct an outlet for all the rain that might fall during a major storm.[35]

Mā'alaea Harbor Plans

Located in the northwestern corner of South Maui, Mā'alaea was (and is) a small village with the only fully protected boat harbor in the region. A landing area for interisland ships until 1906, Mā'alaea Harbor needed improvements to become fully functional as a shipping point. How Mā'alaea evolved illustrates well changing attitudes and actions with regard to development and the environment on Maui.

Throughout the 1950s and 1960s governmental authorities worked to expand Mā'alaea's harbor for commercial use, reflecting what most residents on Maui desired. First developed by territorial officials in 1952, harbor facilities were improved in 1955 and 1959. In 1968 Congress approved a federal plan for additional alterations. The Maui County Council vigorously backed these harbor plans as likely to stimulate Maui's economy. Further, in 1976 council members unanimously called on the federal and state governments to look into converting nearby Keālia Pond into a marina "to take care of at least a thousand boat enthusiasts." By the 1970s, however, opposition developed to these plans. Mayer and other early-day environmentalists succeeded in having plans for Mā'alaea Harbor and its surrounding area scaled back. Federal plans for harbor improvements were put on hold because of concerns that they would destroy a wave known as the Maalaea Pipeline cherished by surfers, and no new civil works were undertaken for the harbor in the 1970s or 1980s.[36]

The issue of expanding the harbor at Māʻalaea was revisited in the 1990s. In 1989 Congress appropriated funds to reconfigure the shape of the harbor and to greatly increase its size. The proposed improvements would lessen the tidal surge within the harbor, reduce navigational hazards at its entrance, and increase the number of berths for boats within the harbor.[37] For $10 million the Army Corps of Engineers proposed to build a new breakwater for the harbor, redesign the entrance, and more than double the number of slips available for boats, many of which were commercial vessels catering to tourists. Both commercial boat owners and individual boaters strongly supported the proposed harbor improvements.

However, increasingly well-organized and vocal opponents mounted challenges, which halted the proposed work. The plans were opposed by surfers, including the Save Our Surf group and the Surfrider Foundation, and environmental organizations, such as the Sierra Club and Maui Tomorrow, which decried the plan as likely to destroy surfing sites, degrade water quality, damage coral reefs, and endanger whales and turtles. Native Hawaiian leaders joined in the opposition, pointing out that the stones used to build the original harbor had been taken inappropriately from the ruins of a nearby Hawaiian village and *heiau*. Charles Maxwell observed that "as kanaka maoli [a Native Hawaiian], whose ancestors used the ocean for sustenance, it is very disturbing." Joined together as the Protect Maalaea Coalition, opponents challenged the environmental impact statements prepared for the proposed harbor improvements as inadequate.[38]

Opposition to development at Māʻalaea owed much to Lucienne de Naie. Growing up in Southern California, she had been active in community development issues in Encinitas in San Diego County and had served on the board of directors of the town's Chamber of Commerce. There she developed organizational skills, bringing together diverse groups, including conservative businesspeople, to oppose successfully the building of a major freeway through Encinitas. After visiting Maui several times, de Naie moved to the island in 1985. Over time she became involved in environmental issues and in 1997 became the conservation chair for the Sierra Club on Maui.[39]

From the first, de Naie thought that the Mā'alaea Harbor issue fit in well with a new educational campaign the Sierra Club was mounting on environmental matters and turned her organizational expertise to it. She had gotten to know members of the National Surfriders Foundation by this time — she was herself an avid surfer — and at her invitation the president of the local Surfrider body made a presentation to the Maui group of the Sierra Club about Mā'alaea, emphasizing "how all the groups ought to work together." De Naie agreed and called a meeting of those opposing changes to Mā'alaea's harbor. They met at the Waterfront Restaurant in Mā'alaea, whose owners were opposed to the new harbor plan. Eighteen people attended, including a member of Life of the Land. Following this meeting, de Naie and others made Mā'alaea "into a Sierra Club issue."

Led by the Sierra Club, opponents gained in strength. In mid-1998 they presented Governor Cayetano with 500 postcards and a petition with 7,600 signatures against harbor alterations. At a public hearing a month later, some carried crosses with representations of sacrificial turtles and whales nailed to them. Police had to be called to the meeting to break up scuffles between those holding opposing views; with emotions running high, no decisions had been reached by 2000.[40]

More was involved in the development of the Mā'alaea area than harbor facilities. In 1997 Mā'alaea was slated by the county government to become the next town on Maui. Despite objections that the water supply would not support further development, the county council approved requests by C. Brewer and Alexander and Baldwin to redesignate about 910 acres zoned as agricultural to residential and business. Alexander and Baldwin planned to develop about 650 acres just east of the harbor complex, putting in about 1,500 homes, a golf course, parks, and open spaces. C. Brewer planned to build 1,140 houses on about 260 acres uphill and west of the harbor, along with parks and open-space buffers.[41]

Both projects were included in the Kīhei-Mākena plan of 1998, but they quickly came under fire. While the county council approved plans for Mā'alaea's growth, Mayor Lingle did not. "I strongly oppose and completely reject this plan's 910-acre expansion of the existing urban core into the relatively undeveloped Maalaea area," she wrote in early 1998. Maui's infrastructure of water, roads, and sewers was already stretched to the breaking point, and the Mā'alaea developments might, she feared, be more than it could take. Invoking the principle of concurrence, she vetoed the plan. The county council,

Opposition to developments at Māʻalaea mounted in the late 1990s.

however, overrode her veto by a vote of seven to two. Council member Alan Arakawa, chair of the council's Planning Committee, spoke for the majority when he stated that "we really want to see the area well planned" and asserted that most residents in South Maui backed the development proposals.[42]

Meanwhile, undeterred, business leaders opened a large aquarium in 1998 to attract tourists to Māʻalaea and began clearing land for the housing construction. The increased traffic from the aquarium, combined with dust, smoke, and mud from the housing projects, led to state intervention. When rain runoff deposited several feet of mud in the harbor, commercial boat operators complained that their livelihoods were being endangered. After conducting public hearings on this matter, the state's Department of Land and Natural Resources took action against those developing the Māʻalaea region, and the developers agreed to dredge the harbor.[43]

Upcountry Problems and Planning in the 1970s and 1980s

Many of the same concerns that surfaced in South Maui revealed rifts among Upcountry residents, those living in Kula, Makawao, Pukalani, and nearby areas. Located about 1,000 to 3,500 feet up the side of Haleakalā, these towns were long valued for their rustic, bucolic feel. While Hawaiians had used parts of Upcountry Maui for religious rites and dryland agriculture, relatively few had lived there. After contact, Upcountry Maui developed as an agricultural and ranching area. Makawao grew up as a cowtown, and even earlier as a center for lumber production, before all of the nearby trees, especially koa, had been cut. Pukalani served as a center for plantation agriculture and cattle raising. Kula became a vegetable-raising area, with its onions and potatoes reaching overseas markets by the 1850s. Unlike South Maui, cool Upcountry Maui was not a major tourist destination. The Kula Lodge and Hale Moi (later renamed the Silversword Inn) attracted only a few visitors, when compared to the throngs flocking to the hotels and condominiums lining the South Maui beaches.[44]

While not facing as massive an influx of people as that which hit South Maui during the 1970s, Upcountry Maui began experiencing growing pains at about that time. Beyond problems with its water supplies, the region found other aspects of its infrastructure strained: roads, sewer systems, athletic facilities, and the like. Particularly worrisome was the closing in the mid-1970s of a road connecting Mākena to the 'Ulupalakua Ranch. This dirt track had provided the only direct transportation link between South Maui and Upcountry Maui. Privately owned by the 'Ulupalakua Ranch, the road was offered to the county. When the county declined to accept the burden of maintaining the steep road, the ranch closed it to public travel. The county council also found itself trying to address the issue of land speculation, especially in Pukalani, which was home for many working in Kahului and Wailuku. As early as 1951 a private contractor developed 142 homesites in Pukalani. By the mid-1970s lots in Pukalani were selling at what were considered by many residents to be inflated prices, a situation that led one person testifying before the county council to assert that "I think this is going to continue to go and on . . . unless a good comprehensive kind of planning for the island can really, really happen."[45]

The town of Makawao was the focus for development issues in the 1970s. A one-time *paniolo* (cowboy) town, Makawao experienced a renaissance as a center for shops, art galleries, and restaurants catering to tourists. Old buildings were torn down and new ones constructed. At issue was whether or not to declare Makawao a historic district and place a moratorium on building demolitions and alterations. Some residents favored modernization. More than one

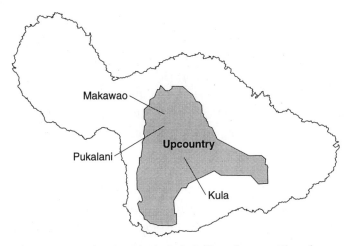

The Upcountry Planning District included lots of countryside and several small towns.

called the old buildings a "fire hazard" and condemned them as "dilapi-dated[,] ... dirty ... [and] ugly." Many, however, wanted to limit changes. A Wailuku architect found in a survey he conducted that "the leaders of the Makawao area" expressed "a great concern to keep Makawao as a unique paniolo-type town." Dick Mayer urged the county council "to preserve some [buildings] not as rat traps but perhaps where young people of Maui and visitors as well can visit and see what the culture of old Hawaii was like."[46]

As in the case of South Maui, there was a sense that a culture and way of life were in danger of vanishing. "If we fail to define the kind of community we want now," asserted one resident, "we can anticipate a slick, neon-lighted, chrome developer's shopping center type of community."[47] Another expressed the feeling of potential loss quite eloquently. "I was born and raised in the islands and my family has been here for five generations now," he observed. "I was born on Oahu and moved to Maui," he continued, "because I saw Oahu get ruined in my lifetime, and I chose Makawao as a place to live because it was in close similarity to the area where I was raised and had the same kind of outdoor life and charm. ... We're really blessed to be living here," he concluded, "and should be really careful in our development of the area and of all of Maui so that we don't ruin it and make the same mistakes that Honolulu did."[48]

Even as people debated the fate of Makawao, residents in Upcountry Maui sought to channel development through the preparation of a plan similar to that being drafted for South Maui. A citizens' advisory council working with the planning consulting firm of Donald Wolbrink and Associates devised a plan for the region's development. Presented to the public in 1976, this Makawao-Pukalani-Kula General Plan, often simply called the "Wolbrink Plan," embraced as its leading principle maintaining a "country atmosphere" for Upcountry Maui. From that principle derived several objectives: that growth should be limited to established towns and not be allowed to occur at random, that Makawao and Pukalani should be kept separate and not be allowed to grow together, that agricultural lands should be preserved from development, and that the construction of more low- and moderate-income housing should be encouraged.[49]

Debate on the plan revealed differences of opinion. While all agreed that some development was necessary for economic growth, heated disputes arose on just how much and what types of development should be allowed. A case in point lay in what to permit the owner of the Kula Lodge. She wanted to turn her establishment from a family-style restaurant into a cocktail lounge and upscale restaurant serving tourists. She also desired to build one hundred vacation units on her sixteen acres. "We can dream all the pastoral dreams that we like," she stated, "but it does not change the facts one iota," by which she meant the facts of economic growth. In the end, she was given permission to build only forty rooms, and her plans for a large cocktail lounge were killed by residents who complained that resulting noise would destroy Kula's tranquillity. Building densities were among the most heated planning issues. One resident even testified that he feared for his life, if he spoke up about parts of the plan. After considerable debate, house lots larger than those desired by many real estate agents were set as the minimum allowable sizes, 7,500 square feet in Pukalani and 10,000 square feet in Kula and Makawao. Moreover, severe restrictions were placed on alterations to any buildings in Makawao, and urban development was to be confined to existing towns. However, preservationists lost in bids to designate large tracts as "prime agricultural land" off limits to all development and failed to win inclusion for an "anti-speculation" clause in the community plan.[50]

Revised in the late 1980s, the community plan helped to shape growth into the 1990s. And growth there was: The population of Upcountry Maui nearly

The Kula Lodge was a focus for developmental controversies in Upcountry Maui at various times in the 1970s and 1980s.

doubled from 9,970 in 1970 to about 19,000 twenty years later.[51] Facing the pressures of growth, the county council granted variances to the Upcountry plans, when those variances were "not unreasonable" and when the proposals were "desirable in accommodating the needs and services required by the expanding Up-Country communities." Builders easily received variances to add 669 house lots to a development in Pukalani.[52] Even Makawao found its appearance changing, as the town was partly rezoned to accommodate a small community business district, its main street was widened, curbs and sidewalks were added, and a new drainage system was constructed. Still, a two-story limit on building heights was maintained, as specified in the 1981 plan.[53]

Development Comes to Upcountry Maui: The 1990s

In the 1990s developmental pressures intensified. Highway improvements allowed more people to live Upcountry and commute to work in Wailuku, Kahului, and South Maui. Then, too, more visitors sought pleasures in

Upcountry spaces. As the decade opened, Upcountry residents revisited planning and adopted a new community plan to guide the growth of their region through 2010. Even as they debated this plan, they considered two major developments, one which became known as the Barto development for Makawao and another known as the Kulamalu project for Lower Kula–Upper Pukalani. Consideration of the developments threw into high relief ideas about what Upcountry Maui should become.

Adopted in 1996, the Makawao-Pukalani-Kula Community Plan extended ideas put forward in earlier Upcountry plans. Like them, the new scheme had as its fundamental goal the preservation of "the rural and serene environment which defines Upcountry Maui's character." Dick Mayer, who lived in Kula and who served as vice-chair of the plan's citizens' advisory committee, later explained what he thought lay at the heart of the planning. "The Upcountry," he observed, "has a much bigger reservoir of people who do not want development." He thought that "most of the people up here want to keep this as a bedroom area where they can raise kids and keep it local." Above all, he believed, "they don't want Kiheization" of Upcountry Maui, by which he meant runaway urban sprawl. Even so, the 1996 plan recognized the desirability of some kinds of economic growth. The plan forecast an Upcountry population of 24,000 by 2010, an increase of about 5,000 from 1990, which would, the plan predicted, translate "into approximately 1,600 to 2,000 additional housing units."[54]

The question, once again, became how to accommodate growth to a desire to maintain a rural feel in the region. The 1996 plan sought to "preserve and enhance the 'country' atmosphere in all communities by maintaining the small-scale, unique and independent character of each of the three sub-regions." "'Country' atmosphere," the plan continued, is "defined by building style, a low density of residences, ranches, open spaces, greenways, plantings and cultivated lands." In bold bullet points the plan declared its intention to "support the long-term viability of agriculture, discourage 'urban sprawl,' discourage heavy industrial activities, discourage large scale hotels . . . protect the region's open space character, [and] maintain a separation of character between the Upcountry and the Kihei-Makena regions."[55] Nonetheless, the plan allowed considerable rezoning of agricultural land as residential: 460 acres in Kula, 300 acres near Hāli'imaile (a small town just down Haleakalā from Makawao), 160 acres in Pukalani, and 50 acres in Makawao.

Upcountry Maui was home to specialized agriculture, as shown in the painting "Copp Road Cabbage Harvest" by Maggie T. Sutrov. (Courtesy of Maggie T. Sutrov)

Following the plan's recommendations, the Maui County Planning Commission had recommended rezoning 2,000 parcels of Upcountry land by 1998.[56]

A signal that Upcountry Maui was not immune to development was a plan to build a commercial-residential complex in the heart of Makawao. In 1993 the California developer Jerrel Barto proposed to build on the eleven-acre Crook Estate in the center of the town. To be constructed by his son, Eric Barto, the project envisioned a 121,500-square-foot commercial center containing a supermarket along with a host of apartments just off the town's main street. Some residents favored this plan. The head of the Makawao Improvement Committee observed that Makawao had become a "very dysfunctional town," lacking shops and commercial establishments serving residents. Noting that the Crook Estate was "a natural place for a town center," he praised the Bartos for "proposing to develop it with integrity." Many residents, however, opposed the plan. Some viewed the Bartos as arrogant outsiders attempting to impose their views on Makawaoans. Others believed that such a large-scale development would dramatically alter their town in unwanted ways. They pointed out that it would triple the amount of its commercial space and feared that the resulting traffic congestion would end any sense of rural tranquillity. "It will Kihei the town," claimed the president of Maui Tomorrow, who had his real estate office in Makawao. By this statement he meant that he feared Makawao would be overdeveloped.[57]

Faced with mounting opposition, the Bartos scaled back their plans. By early 1996, after negotiating with the merchants composing the Makawao Main Street Association, the Bartos thought they had a plan that would satisfy all interested groups. It included 40,000 square feet of retail space along the main streets, Baldwin and Makawao Avenues — a major reduction from the 121,500 square feet originally planned — a public park about three acres in size, residential townhouses, and a pedestrian mall. To meet concerns about traffic congestion, the revised plan contained no traffic signals or left-turn lanes.[58] Even so, the scheme continued to generate opposition from merchants and residents who believed that it would cause traffic snarls and alter the character of their town too much. Opponents felt that little in the way of compromise should be allowed. As Mayer recalled, the Barto project was "controversial, that was war." By late 1997 the Bartos had abandoned their plans.[59]

More attuned to the desires of local residents than the Bartos, the Maui developer Everett Dowling succeeded in winning approval for his Upcountry plans, called the Kulamalu project. Prior to being purchased by Dowling's organization, the Kulamalu project initially called for the construction of 1,300 houses on 7,500-square-foot lots. The project would be located just opposite Kula 200, an upscale residential area off the Kula Highway in the Lower Kula–Upper Pukalani area.[60]

When he sought approval from county authorities for needed alterations to the Kulamalu scheme in the fall of 1997, Dowling refined the plans. Altogether, Dowling participated in fifty-three public meetings at which Upcountry residents discussed his plans. At the first dozen or so meetings, Dowling later recalled, he and his associates "just listened"; then they "went back to the drawing board and revised the plans." Responding to residents' requests, he cut back the housing plans to just 324 single-family residences, far fewer than the 1,300 in the prior owner's approved project, and included building a shopping center and a new Kamehameha School. To be set back at least one hundred feet from the Kula Highway to maintain a greenbelt along the road, the development was designed not to obstruct the views of Kula's 200 residents. A twenty-acre commercial village, Dowling said, might include a gas station, drugstore, movie theater, professional offices, and supermarket. He received permission for the commercial center in return for reducing the number of houses. This center would, he assured area residents, "create a pedestrian-friendly neighborhood" similar to those found in Makawao, Pā'ia, and Ha'ikū. "It's not a shopping center," he asserted, "it's more of a country town."[61] The development would also include a fifteen-acre park, five acres set aside for community purposes (churches, day care centers, and the like), a five-acre Hawaiian cultural learning center, and the Kamehameha School. Still another five acres would have fifty units of multifamily housing for the elderly.

Despite Dowling's efforts at compromise, controversy engulfed his proposed development, for even in revised form it raised tough questions about water usage, automobile traffic, and business development. Most fundamentally, it again called into question what type of region Upcountry Maui was to be: an independent, semirural area or a sprawling suburb of Wailuku and Kahului.

To the Kula Community Association, Dowling stressed that his project would benefit established residents in important ways. Dowling said that he would drill a well in Ha'ikū, at the cost of $2 million, to produce 1.5 million gallons of water per day. Water from that well would stay in Ha'ikū, and the well itself would be given free to the county. In return, Ha'ikū water would flow to the Kulamalu area. In a deal struck with the County Water Board, Dowling's project would receive up to 55 percent of that water. The remaining 45 percent would be available to other residents or would-be residents in the Kula-Pukalani region. At the time about 480 people were waiting for water hookups. The region was water poor, and Dowling hoped that bringing in water would win local support for his plans. Dowling also emphasized that his scaled-back residential plans would generate less traffic than had been originally anticipated and that his business center would supply badly needed services for area residents. As Dowling hoped, the Kula Community Association endorsed his plans, with three stipulations: that he consult with the community on the types of businesses recruited for his business center, that he prohibit 'ohana (family) home lots of less than one acre in size, and that he carefully consider the area's tight water situation.[62]

It soon became apparent, nonetheless, that other Upcountry residents harbored reservations about Kulamalu. Particularly irksome was the water arrangement. At a public hearing held a few weeks after the endorsement by the Kula Community Association, many residents of nearby Makawao, joined together in the Makawao Main Street Association, voiced opposition. It seemed to them that Dowling was gaining access to water unfairly.

At a time when they were being asked to conserve water and were having great difficulty in obtaining new water hookups, some Makawaoans believed that Dowling should not be granted water rights, even though the well he was drilling would be deeded over to the county and even though nearly half of the well's water would flow to residents outside of Dowling's development. "It seems that whether or not you get a water meter depends on who you are," exclaimed the chair of the Main Street Association. "Who are we as taxpayers?" she asked. "What are we? Chopped liver?"[63]

Passed on to the Maui County Council's Land Use Committee, the Kulamalu proposal generated continued controversy, with opposition focusing on the project's water provisions. The water agreement "verges on corruption," asserted Jeffrey Parker, the activist Upcountry orchid farmer. "It sells the future of Maui residents down the tubes." Others objected to the traffic that would result from development, to which Dowling replied that additional lanes would be added to the Kula Highway to accommodate more cars before houses were built. Some also feared that the possible construction of large stores, a supermarket and a Longs Drug Store, in the shopping center had "the potential to bury every small business Upcountry." Proponents of the project emphasized the construction and service jobs it would create and the services it would make available. Approved unanimously, the Kulamalu project went to the full county council for consideration.[64]

Hearings before the council were spirited. People revisited the water issue, with opponents lambasting the agreement worked out with the water board as unethical. Supporters argued, to the contrary, that Dowling would be providing a public service at no cost to taxpayers. Other aspects of the Kulamalu project won widespread praise: the provisions for the Hawaiian cultural center, the park, and the housing for the elderly. Council member Charmaine Tavares observed further that Dowling had reduced the number of houses in his project from the 1,300 approved earlier to just over 300. This number was, however, still too large for some opponents. Claiming that Dowling's plans would result in a density of 5.5 homes per acre, one Kula resident objected that such a high density "just ain't Upcountry no matter how you sing it."[65] In the end, economic arguments in favor of the project won the day. Jimmy Rust, the labor leader who headed the Pueo Coalition, argued forcefully that the Kulamalu development would provide sorely needed construction jobs. By a vote of six to one, the county council gave final approval to the project in late 1997. Writing to the *Maui News* on the same day that the council gave the go-ahead, one Pukalani resident provided a bitter postscript: "Up County was meant to be quiet and pastoral but, gee, that's just not profitable. How sad."[66]

Continuing Debates

As the 1990s came to a close, residents could boast of many examples of co-operation, while also lamenting continuing forms of conflict, in the development of South Maui and Upcountry Maui.[67] The 1998 community plan for South Maui garnered considerable support and won approval from the county council. Development would continue, but in a more controlled manner than in the 1970s and 1980s. Still, troubling issues remained. Māʻalaea's future development, strongly favored by its local community association, was vehemently opposed by environmental groups, which vowed to fight the expansion of the harbor and the construction of new housing in the area tooth and nail. Similarly, debates about Upcountry Maui raged in the late 1990s. One swirled around the issue of whether to connect the region to South Maui with a new road. The only direct route had been closed in the 1970s. A new road was expected to bring in a fair amount of tourist traffic. Glancing down the slopes of Haleakalā at what they viewed as runaway growth in Kīhei, members of the Kula Community Association were vociferous in trying to ensure that the Upcountry terminus would not be in their locale. The association endorsed a "no build" option, as did the 1996 Upcountry community plan. Yet many Upcountry residents worked in South Maui and desired an easier route to get there. As this debate suggested, in Upcountry Maui, as in other parts of the county, shadings of opinion existed on almost every developmental or environmental issue. There were signs that cooperation and compromise were possible. Even those most adamantly opposed to the new connector came to accept its building as probable. Observing that it was likely that a new highway would be constructed, the Kula Community Association wanted its terminus to be in Hāliʻimaile, "the least offensive option available."[68]

CONCLUSION: LEAVING MAUI

Maui's experiences show how closely related economic, environmental, and political issues are in the modern world. It is impossible to separate those issues, for to do so would be to do injustice to them. Nor have the specific topics dealt with in this study — land use, water rights, transportation, and electrical power matters — existed in a vacuum. Rather, the development of each issue has been related to that of the others. What transpired, for example, in the evolution of land use matters had a direct bearing on issues surrounding the controversy over whether or not to expand the Kahului Airport. This study demonstrates, once again, just how complex modern society and decision making have become. While Maui's residents sometimes viewed decisions taken in one area as discrete, those decisions often affected choices in other areas as well.

Developments on Maui resonated with similar economic and environmental developments around the globe. Efforts to diversify the economies of the islands composing Micronesia in the 1960s and 1970s proved only partly successful. Attempts to develop specialty agriculture and marine resources there largely failed. Developing tourism met with some success, but that success raised the hackles of residents on islands such as Yap who came to oppose the changes that tourism brought to their lifestyles. Similarly, efforts to replace flagging plantation agriculture — copra, sugar cane, and pineapple — with tourism on other Pacific islands raised as many questions as they answered. On Western Samoa, for example, the growth of tourism meant the commodification of native cultures, as it did in many areas. The spread of tourism also brought dramatic cultural changes to parts of Southeast Asia in the 1980s and 1990s, including significant alterations in relations among different ethnic groups within nations such as Indonesia. Rarely did indigenous peoples benefit much from tourism. Typically, most of the profits went to outsiders, while residents suffered from rising costs of living and often had to endure wrenching cultural changes. In the Caribbean the story was frequently similar, with the replacement of one monoculture (sugar cane), by another (tourism), bringing few benefits to most residents.[1]

Opposition to the changes caused by tourism was common. Writing in 1988 about Antigua, a small island in the British West Indies, Jamaica Kincaid stated bluntly, "A tourist is an ugly human being . . . a stupid thing, a piece of rubbish pausing here and there to gaze at this and taste that, and it will never occur to you that the people who inhabit the place in which you have paused can not stand you."[2] Similarly, Haunani-Kay Trask, the Native Hawaiian rights activist on O'ahu, observed that Hawai'i had become a "tinsel paradise for six and a half million tourists a year and a living nightmare for our impoverished, marginalized Native people." The experience of the Hawaiian Islands, she thought, offered a lesson for South Pacific Islanders. "The overpowering impact of mass tourism on island cultures" could, Trask believed, best be examined in Hawai'i, "where the multibillion dollar industry has resulted in [the] grotesque commercialization of Hawaiian culture . . . the creation of a racially stratified, poorly paid servant class of industry workers . . . and increasing dependence on multinational investments."[3]

Yet if tourism developments on Hawai'i resembled those in many parts of the globe, perhaps nowhere were they more similar than to developments in the American West. Scholars have long debated to what degree Hawaiian history should be considered a part of American history. In an important recent essay the historian John S. Whitehead has reviewed the places of Hawai'i and Alaska in the history of the Trans-Mississippi West. He finds that there were very close connections between Hawai'i, Alaska, and much of the Far West in the nineteenth century. However, those connections, he writes, became more attenuated in the twentieth century, especially as the Pacific Coast developed into an urban-industrial society. Looking specifically at the Hawaiian Islands, Whitehead concludes that conceptions of the islands as different — ideas held by both many residents and visitors — have been important in producing "a unique sense of place."[4] There are many lenses through which it is possible to view the history of the Hawaiian Islands and Maui, but it does seem to me — despite the existence of differences highlighted by scholars like Whitehead — that one fruitful way is to look at Maui's development against the backdrop of the history of America, especially the West.

Many of the same issues that have dominated debates on Maui were important in the Trans-Mississippi West's evolution. Strong similarities existed in types of economic development, above all in the dependence on monocultural economies (especially before World War II) but also in land use and water rights issues, and infrastructural developments in transportation and electric power. Of course, in taking this approach one must keep Hawai'i's history as an independent kingdom and republic in mind. Hawaiian history is not simply an extension of western American history. Hawaiian culture has often mediated in the evolution of economic and environmental matters on Maui and continues to influence decisions down to the present day.

As tourism replaced agriculture as Hawai'i's leading industry, most aspects of the state's economy were affected. This was certainly true on Maui. The county's economy remained imbalanced, perpetuating what critics decried as a "plantation" economy. The need to create well-paying, meaningful jobs was, Dick Mayer believed, still Maui's number-one concern in the late 1990s, "not to get rich, but to create jobs so that the children can stay nearby." While the situation was, he thought, better than it had been when Maui was dependent on plantation agriculture, there remained plenty of room for improvement. For the most part, tourism created service-sector jobs. Contrary to popular opinion, these jobs on average were more highly paid than jobs on the mainland, especially when tips were included in the calculation. In 1992 the average wage in Maui County was $22,784 and the average family income amounted to $42,784. Three years later Maui boasted an average annual pay per employee of $25,293, an amount higher than the $21,117 for all of the United States in 1996. In 1990 Hawai'i ranked tenth among the states in per capita income and had a lower proportion of its workers holding second jobs, just 5.2 percent, than was the case on the mainland, 6.2 percent.[5]

Still, statistics on income tell only part of the story. For many on Maui and throughout the Hawaiian Islands these relatively high incomes were inadequate, for the cost of living was much greater than that on the mainland. Food, gasoline, and housing were more expensive. In 1998, for example, the average selling price of a single-family house on Maui was $244,000. Taxes also were higher. State and local taxes left those living in the Hawaiian Islands among the most highly taxed people in the nation, with, ironically, many of the tax revenues going to pay for infrastructure improvements needed to support tourism. One respected source estimated that the average local and state tax burden was about 31 percent higher in Hawai'i than the average for the United States as a whole. Overall, in the early 1990s the cost of living in Hawai'i was about 36 percent higher than on the mainland, making average real wages lower for Hawai'i's residents than those for people on the mainland. (By 2000 the cost difference had narrowed a bit, to just 27 percent.) As critics had long maintained, tourism had not brought a high level of economic prosperity to all, or even most, on Maui.[6]

The slump in tourism that continued into the mid-1990s made a difficult situation worse. In 1996 business failures in the Hawaiian Islands climbed 47 percent, compared with 1 percent in all of the United States. In 1997 bankruptcy filings in Hawai'i rose an additional 44 percent, and in 1998 they climbed another 33 percent to top 5,000, a record number. In 1996–97 Hawai'i posted a net loss of 4,000 people, as residents left the islands for more promising opportunities elsewhere. Unemployment on Maui reached 7.5 percent by the summer of 1997; in early 1999 it still hovered around 6 percent, a rate considerably higher than the 4.4 percent for the United States as a whole.[7]

In 1997 Gov. Benjamin Cayetano appointed a twenty-six-member Economic Revitalization Task Force to look into ways to boost Hawai'i's slumping economy.[8] After months of discussion, the state legislature passed a package of bills embodying many of the task force's recommendations. These included cuts in the state budget, especially in funding for social welfare, health, and higher education. Some state agencies deemed unnecessary were abolished, resulting in the elimination of about 550 state jobs. The measures also included lowering the corporate and personal income taxes. The transient accommodation tax (the bed tax) was raised, with the increased revenues going to fund a renewed marketing effort by the state for its visitor industry. Governor Cayetano also spoke of developing a high-technology park near Honolulu and made some efforts to aid small-business development. Just how effective any of the measures were or would be in stimulating economic growth was a matter of considerable debate as the 1990s came to a close. While the magazine *Maui Business* gushed that "all of Hawaii owes a debt of gratitude to everyone involved" in Governor Cayetano's economic task force, many residents were less sanguine. Even some who had been intimately engaged in work with the governor doubted that their efforts would have much of an impact.[9]

James Apana, Maui's newly elected mayor, talked in early 1999 in similar terms, discussing the need to attract high-technology businesses to his island, the desirability of keeping tourism healthy, and a need to help market agricultural products. Tourism, he believed, would continue to be "a big part" of Maui's economy, but it would not be, he hoped, the entire picture. "Many of the jobs on Maui," he asserted, "are separate from tourism." A member of the mayor's Office of Economic Development added that while he believed that "tourism will remain large and important, a significant sector of the economy, especially if you define tourism as attracting business conferences, and things like that, what people are calling techno-tourism, econ-tourism," he did not think it would "become an even greater part" of the economy than it already was.[10]

Apana sought to lend substance to his words by convening a Mayor's Economic Summit in late 1999. Those invited to attend were supposed to represent economic "stakeholders" in Maui's future; the invitation list was compiled by Jeanne Skog, president of the Maui Economic Development Board (MEDB), and Lynne Woods, president of the Maui Chamber of Commerce. Noticeably absent were environmentalists and community activists. Nor were all segments of Maui's business community well represented; few from the retailing sector, for example, were invited. The summit endorsed forty-two recommendations, with six leading the rest: developing and distributing water resources (the number-one priority), attracting media and filmmakers to Maui, fostering high-technology businesses, promoting educational improvements for workforce development, uncovering and preserving a Native Hawaiian site in Lahaina, and lengthening the runway at the Kahului Airport. To many left outside the conference, the meeting seemed to be a throwback to the closed decision-making processes of earlier times. The summit was "the kind of exercise that creates distrust and oppositional attitudes," observed Dana Naone Hall.[11]

Mayor Apana took other steps to try to diversify Maui's economy. He traveled to Japan and California's Silicon Valley to drum up business for his county, with some promising results. Micro Gaia agreed to put up a micro-algae plant in the Maui Research and Technology Park (MRTP), at a cost of $10–$20 million. The firm expected to employ ten people initially and about one hundred within a few years. Another new venture, Trex Enterprises, looked especially promising. Apana also spurred efforts to revitalize downtown Wailuku. Working with state officials, he sought to improve the quality of secondary education on Maui, especially in high-technology fields.[12]

Nonetheless, in the late 1990s the Hawaiian Islands, including Maui, seemed to remain captives to their past. Despite continuing efforts at economic diversification, emphasis remained focused, for the most part, on tourism. In 1999 Maui was voted the "best island in the world" by the readers of *Condé Nast Traveler* for the sixth year in a row. Successful examples of economic diversification were rare. Nor, it seemed, was an end in sight. There were, the *Maui News* headlined on its editorial page on January 1, 1999, "no quick or easy fixes for Hawaii." In fact, a report issued in the summer of 1999 by the World Travel and Tourism Council predicted that the "long-term dominance of tourism in Hawaii" would "only increase during the next decade." As the *Maui News* commented, "While that may be good news for the visitor industry, those projections may be bad news overall for a state whose leaders have been preaching the importance of diversifying the economy and reducing dependence on tourism."[13]

Despite a considerable revival in tourism in 1999–2000, especially on Maui, long-term answers to basic questions about economic development continued to elude those living in the Hawaiian Islands. If tourism, high-technology businesses, and specialty agriculture were not the keys to economic growth, what were? Of course, it made sense to pursue all of these avenues. Those on Hawai'i could hope for the recovery of the Japanese economy and with that revival more Japanese tourists visiting their state. On average, tourists from Japan spent about three times as much per day as other tourists, making their return greatly desired. Still, more was needed. Perhaps most promising were efforts to develop industries and businesses related to tourism: sporting events, conventions, and the health industry, among others. Under way on Maui in the 1990s, such efforts might well bear fruit in the future.[14]

Even so, Maui's long-term economic future remained uncertain. With tax revenues down, county council members had to pare their county's budget in 1999. As scholars such as Hal K. Rothman have shown, tourism has not been the economic salvation many communities in the western states have hoped that it would. Rather, tourism has often been, to return to Rothman's accurate phrase, "a devil's bargain," raising as many questions for host communities as it has answered. By the 1980s and 1990s even officials in Southern California, an area long wedded to tourism, were questioning the value of the visitor industry. In 1995 a report by the San Diego Association of Governments criticized the visitor industry for creating mainly service-sector jobs with wages 40 percent lower on average than entry-level jobs in manufacturing. So it has been on Maui. As we have seen, the development of tourism on Maui has challenged the county's residents to continually rethink what they have wanted their lifestyles to be. Considerations of trade-offs between maintaining established ways of life and embracing new, often undesired, lifestyles associated with the spread of tourism permeated many of the issues dealt with in this work.[15]

The controversies on Maui showed that more stood between its residents than economic matters. Economic issues merged with social and cultural concerns. Differing views about Native Hawaiian issues and what the physical environment of their island should be divided people. At root lay competing visions about the quality of life on Maui and the roles different types of economic growth might play in creating those types of life.

Considerations of Native Hawaiian rights were entwined with many of the economic and environmental issues on Maui. Land use, water rights, transportation, and electrical power matters were all connected to Native Hawaiian rights issues. In some senses, these connections resembled those between Native American rights and similar issues on the mainland. Just as Native Americans had become a minority group in what had once been their homeland, so, too, had Native Hawaiians become a minority in what had once been their land. Just as Native Americans had been dispossessed, so, too, had Native Hawaiians lost most of their lands. Yet these similarities can be pushed too far. Native Hawaiians remained a much larger part of the population of the Hawaiian Islands in the 1990s than were Native Americans on the mainland, even in the West. Moreover, Native Hawaiians had never been isolated from the rest of society by their placement on reservations the way many Native Americans had been. The concerns of Native Hawaiians influenced the resolution of many economic and environmental issues on Maui to a greater extent than did those of Native Americans on the mainland.[16]

There was a growing appreciation of Native Hawaiian culture on Maui as the 1990s came to a close. To be sure, the visitor industry still sometimes packaged and commodified Hawaiian culture for tourists, as activists like Trask were quick to point out. Yet, at the same time, many of those in Maui's visitor industry demonstrated an awareness of the importance of Native Hawaiian culture as a shaping force in their island's past and present. In part, this awareness came from the efforts of Native Hawaiians, people like Charley Keau and Dana Naone Hall, to show others that their culture was alive and relevant in the present day. Thus, those pioneering in homesteading at Kahikinui talked of establishing a small museum to show visitors what Native Hawaiian culture had meant to Maui in the past and what it remained in the present. Similarly, those restoring a major *heiau* in the Hanā area — an altar built for Pi'ilani, the chief who probably united Maui as one kingdom in the 1500s — planned to put up a display to educate visitors about the importance of this Hawaiian site. Preservation and commodification of culture sometimes went together. In 1999 the architect August Percha carefully redesigned part of Maui's largest shopping mall to resemble a Hawaiian plantation town. He called his efforts "part model railroad at three-quarter scale, part Disneyland."[17]

Efforts to protect native plant and animal species from attack and replacement by alien species were, in part, an extension of the concern for Hawaiian culture. Because of its long isolation from the rest of the world, Hawai'i possesses one of the largest sets of endemic species — that is, flora and fauna found nowhere else. Yet this topic is complex. Efforts to protect species endemic to Hawai'i have also been part of an attempt to preserve biodiversity around the globe. Far from unique to Maui or the Hawaiian Islands, these efforts have represented attempts to stem the tide of "ecological imperialism" so eloquently described by Alfred Crosby and other scholars. A particularly telling example described by Crosby involved the impacts of settlers moving from Europe to the Madiera, Canary, and Azores Islands during the 1400s and 1500s. The changes they brought to the plants and animals of those island groups resemble the alterations brought by westerners to the Hawaiian Islands several hundred years later. As in Hawai'i, a sugar cane monoculture replaced a diversified indigenous plant life on many of the islands, with introduced plants and animals crowding out indigenous ones. Then, too, European settlers pushed aside or killed aboriginal peoples on the Canary Islands, with survivors forced into a commercial economy. Equally marked changes took place with the movement of Europeans into other parts of the globe, as plants and animals from Euro-Asia often encroached on native species.[18]

As transportation advances shrank the world, alien species became pests around the globe. A glance at the United States reveals the enormous extent of the problems. Purple loosestrife, a plant from Europe, has clogged wetlands in the American Midwest; *Arundo donax,* a giant cane from Spain, has crowded out cottonwoods in California; and knapweed has covered five million acres in Montana. Invasive plants caused about $123 billion in damages annually in the United States by the 1990s. Nor were alien plants the only culprits. Two mites arriving from Europe in the 1980s threatened to destroy America's population of honeybees, insects needed to pollinate crops.[19] As

has often been the case, economic and environmental matters have inter-
mingled. Efforts to ward off invasive plants and animals have been partially
economically motivated — as in the work on Maui to protect diversified
agriculture from unwanted invaders, especially brown tree snakes and insects.

Developments on Maui, including efforts to protect endemic species, demonstrate well the growing complexity of environmentalism in the United States.
As on the mainland, environmentalism on Maui broadened in scope from the
1960s to embrace an ever widening range of issues and groups. Nor was this
phenomenon limited to the United States. In a detailed look at the development of environmentalism, especially efforts to abate the emission of sulfur
dioxide from industrial plants, in Japan's Oita prefecture during the 1960s and
1970s, the sociologist Jeffrey Broadbent has stressed the importance of local
groups coming together through various networks to bring about change. "For-
mal and informal social institutions" at the regional level were more significant,
he has found, than national campaigns or movements.[20] In the European Community, and even in Great Britain, environmentalism came to resemble more
closely that in the United States during the 1970s and 1980s. As in the United
States, there was a growing involvement of citizen groups and an increasing
reliance on laws to enforce compliance with environmental standards by businesses.[21] However, environmentalism on Maui also retained some unique char-
acteristics. The history of the Hawaiian Islands as an independent kingdom and
republic, along with the continuing concerns of Native Hawaiians, dictated that
events in Maui County would have a life of their own.

As the United States developed what scholars have called a "consumer
amenity" society during the 1960s and later, a growing number of Americans
embraced environmentalism as part of their lifestyles. It was no longer sufficient for them to possess more and better material goods — televisions instead
of radios, or color televisions rather than simply black-and-white televisions.
Rather, a clean environment that could be used (or "consumed") for leisure-
time activities came to be seen as a birthright, leading to the passage of many
clean air and water laws in the 1960s and 1970s. Building on, but then going
far beyond, the conservation movement of the early and mid-twentieth century, environmentalism resulted from underlying changes in American
society and, in turn, created additional alterations.[22]

The historian Samuel P. Hays, a leading scholar in writing about environmental politics, has cogently explained that change. In his seminal works Hays

has stressed that "environmental differed markedly from conservation affairs." The conservation movement of the early twentieth century aimed at the efficient use of natural resources and "was an effort on the part of leaders in science, technology, and government." It was a top-down movement run by experts. The environmental movement, on the other hand, has been "far more widespread and popular, involving public values that stressed the quality of the human environment," Hays has concluded. Environmentalism has been, especially from the 1960s, Hays has argued, a much more broadly based movement. Its goals have differed from those of the earlier conservation campaign. "Conservation was an aspect of the history of production that stressed efficiency," Hays has shown, "whereas environmentalism was a part of the history of consumption that stressed new aspects of the American standard of living."[23]

From the late 1970s environmentalism broadened still more to include new, often urban concerns. Sometimes called an "environmental justice movement," this brand of environmentalism, as the historian Martin Melosi has explained, "found its strength especially among low-income people of color who faced serious environmental threats from hazardous wastes and other toxic materials."[24] Often existing in an uneasy relationship with the consumer-oriented environmentalism described by Hays, the environmental justice movement grew in importance throughout the 1980s and 1990s. More than other types of environmentalism, it attacked avowedly racial matters, such as the siting of toxic dumps in neighborhoods in which people of color lived.

On Maui, too, the environmental movement came over time to include a broader spectrum of people, although environmental justice concerns did not play much of a role in developments on the island. Environmentalism was mainly a grassroots movement on Maui. National bodies, such as the Sierra Club and the Audubon Society, were less important than "home-grown" organizations such as Life of the Land and Maui Tomorrow. Environmentalism on Maui was in this sense a movement from the "bottom up," with few ties to earlier conservation movements. Not mainly concerned with applying efficiency, science, and technology to the conservation of natural resources, environmental groups like Maui Tomorrow aimed more at preserving nature in as pristine a state as possible. While calling for "sustainable" growth, many members of Maui Tomorrow, their actions suggested, favored no growth.

While the leading environmental body on Maui, Maui Tomorrow was far from the only such group, and the development of other groups showed just how complex environmentalism had become. Native Hawaiians were not prominent in Maui Tomorrow — most of whose leaders and members were well-educated, relatively affluent Caucasians, many originally from the mainland — but Native Hawaiians were important in other groups. As the Native Hawaiian Renaissance became wrapped up in concerns for land use and water rights issues, Native Hawaiians — led by Dana Naone Hall, Charles Maxwell, and others — put forward their own versions of environmentalism. Hearkening back to Hawai'i's past as a kingdom, these versions emphasized the sacredness of the land, the 'āina, and stressed the importance of place.

Although various proponents of environmentalism on Maui differed in their origins and sometimes in their goals, they often agreed on methods. Reflecting the organizational thrust of modern American life, they worked through groups. While often informal in culture and organization, these bodies represented the desires of their members in a variety of ways. Their officers testified at public hearings, made presentations to community planning groups, published newsletters, and maintained Web sites on the Internet. Above all, they used legal challenges to delay and modify construction projects, forcing developers to mitigate substantially the impacts of their projects. Yet if groups were important, so were individuals. Maui and the Hawaiian Islands were small in size and population when compared to mainland America. Even as groups developed, Maui remained a place of face-to-face contacts. Even as people disagreed, often strongly so, they could remain on speaking terms. To a large extent, Maui remained a place where the personal touch was important. Friends and family ties counted for a lot.

The controversies over the Kahului Airport, land and water usage, electrical power generation, and community development on Maui are revealing. Most importantly, they highlight the nature of Maui's economy and varying visions different groups had for its development. Some continued to opt for an economy basically dependent on one industry. They saw economic growth on Maui, like that in the American West before World War II, as best coming from monocultural developments. Others, however, favored efforts to build a more diversified economic base for their island, even if doing so might mean slower growth, and decried an overdependence on tourism.

An emerging developmental matter on Maui in 1999–2000 illustrated the continuing strengths of the two viewpoints. At issue was a request by Alexander and Baldwin to build housing subdivisions on both sides of the Hanā Road near Spreckelsville. The proposed project included a thirty-lot subdivision near the ocean, a 400-lot subdivision just uphill from the ocean, and a nine-hole extension of the Maui Country Club's golf course. Testimony before the State Land Use Commission and the Maui County Council was largely negative, focusing on the loss of agricultural lands and open spaces and the strains the subdivisions would place on Maui's infrastructure and water supplies. Opponents also lamented the loss of a quiet way of life they thought the construction would cause for residents living in that part of Maui. Native Hawaiians testified, in addition, that they had a right to the land and that the land should be returned to them, not developed. Those speaking in favor of the subdivisions argued that they would provide jobs and houses badly needed by Maui's residents. In a divided vote the Land Use Commission approved rezoning needed for the subdivisions, whereupon the matter went to the Maui County Council for deliberation. In early 2000 council members turned down Alexander and Baldwin's proposal to put up homes on the ocean side of the road, just in back of Baldwin Beach, but had not yet taken definitive action on the larger development intended for the other side of the highway.[25]

If the issues dealt with in this study revealed significant differences separating residents of Maui, the topics also laid bare a fair amount of common ground. Compromises often seemed possible. Mitigation measures were agreed on for a number of developments. Especially at the community level, in Upcountry Maui and in even in South Maui, residents seemed able to hammer their differences into workable compromises. People reached those compromises through actions in the political arena, and politics in the Hawaiian Islands, including Maui, became increasingly open after World War II. Especially in the 1990s, politicians on Maui came to consider the environmental impacts of development measures very closely. Development would continue, but limits would be placed on it. If the past is any guide to the future, Maui's residents would succeed in working out a compromise for the emotionally charged Spreckelsville development.

NOTES

INTRODUCTION

1. Rita Ariyoshi, *Maui on My Mind* (Honolulu: Mutual Publishing, 1985), is a beautiful photographic portrait of Maui.

2. Hal K. Rothman, *Devil's Bargains: Tourism in the Twentieth-Century American West* (Lawrence: University Press of Kansas, 1998), 10. A good place to start in understanding tourism in the American West is Earl Pomeroy, *In Search of the Golden West: The Tourist in Western America* (New York: Knopf, 1957). The November 1996 issue of the *Pacific Historical Review* is devoted to the history of western tourism. See, especially, David Farber and Beth Bailey, "The Fighting Man as Tourist: The Politics of Tourist Culture in Hawai'i During World War II," *Pacific Historical Review* 65 (November 1996): 641–60. See also Thomas Cox, "Before the Casino: James G. Scrugham, State Parks, and Nevada's Quest for Tourism," *Western Historical Quarterly* 24 (August 1993): 333–50; and Susan G. Davis, "Landscapes of the Imagination: Tourism in Southern California," *Pacific Historical Review* 68 (May 1999): 173–91. For a solid introduction to the history of tourism on mainland America, especially during the 1920s and 1930s, see John A. Jakle, *The Tourist: Travel in Twentieth-Century North America* (Lincoln: University of Nebraska Press, 1985); chap. 11 looks at the development of tourism in the Trans-Mississippi West.

3. Seen by the author, 1 July 1999.

4. Roderick Nash, *Wilderness and the American Mind* (New Haven: Yale University Press, 1967), remains an excellent overview of changing American attitudes toward the wilderness; for a different approach and conclusions, see Richard Judd, *Common Lands, Common People: The Origins of Conservation in Northern New England* (Cambridge, Mass.: Harvard University Press, 1997). Samuel P. Hays, *Conservation and the Gospel of Efficiency* (New York: Atheneum, 1969); and Samuel P. Hays, *Beauty, Health, and Permanence: Environmental Politics in the United States, 1955–1985* (Cambridge: Cambridge University Press, 1987), are solid introductions to environmental politics in the United States. See also Samuel P. Hays, ed., *Explorations in Environmental History: Essays by Samuel P. Hays* (Pittsburgh: University of Pittsburgh Press, 1998). Hal K. Rothman, *The Greening of a Nation: Environmentalism in the United States since 1945* (New York: Harcourt Brace and Company, 1998), offers a succinct introduction to the development of environmentalism in America, emphasizing connections between social changes and changes in attitudes during the 1950s and 1960s.

5. For a valuable look at such questions, see Terence Kehoe, *Cleaning Up the Great Lakes: From Cooperation to Confrontation* (Dekalb: Northern Illinois University Press, 1997). For introductions to topics comprising the field of environmental history, see Char Miller and Hal K. Rothman, eds., *Out of the Woods: Essays in Environmental History* (Pittsburgh: University of Pittsburgh Press, 1997); and Emily W. B. Russell, *People and the Land through Time: Linking Ecology and History* (New Haven: Yale University Press, 1997).

6. David Vogel, "The 'New' Social Regulation in Historical and Comparative Perspective," in *Regulation in Perspective: Historical Essays*, ed. Thomas McCraw (Cambridge

Mass.: Harvard University Press, 1981), was one of the first scholars to deal with this development. For a more complete examination of Vogel's ideas, see David Vogel, *National Styles of Regulation: Environmental Policy in Great Britain and the United States* (Ithaca: Cornell University Press, 1986). Vogel has cogently argued that when compared to environmentalism in other nations, especially Great Britain, that in the United States was shaped more by the impacts of grassroots citizens groups, especially during the 1970s. For a recent look at the importance of grassroots groups in American environmentalism, see Thomas Wellock, "Stick It in L.A.! Community Control and Nuclear Power in California's Central Valley," *Journal of American History* 84 (December 1997): 942–78; and Thomas Wellock, *Critical Masses: Opposition to Nuclear Power in California, 1958–1978* (Madison: University of Wisconsin Press, 1998).

7. Articles and essays written by the historian John Whitehead are especially valuable on the complex relationships between the development of Hawai'i and the Trans-Mississippi West. See especially John Whitehead, "Noncontiguous Wests: Alaska and Hawai'i," in *Many Wests: Place, Culture, and Regional Identity*, ed. David M. Wrobel and Michael C. Steiner, (Lawrence: University Press of Kansas, 1997), 315–41.

8. Gavan Daws, *Shoal of Time: A History of the Hawaiian Islands* (Honolulu: University of Hawai'i Press, 1968); and Lawrence Fuchs, *Hawaii Pono: A Social History* (New York: Harcourt Brace Jovanovich, 1961), are standard histories.

9. For applications of world systems theory to Hawaiian history, see Noel Kent, *Hawaii: Islands under the Influence*, 2d ed. (Honolulu: University of Hawai'i Press, 1993); Elizabeth Buck, *Paradise Remade: the Politics of Culture and History in Hawaii* (Philadelphia: Temple University Press, 1993); and Ira Rohter, *A Green Hawai'i* (Honolulu: Nā Kane O Malo Press, 1992). From World War II, the Trans-Mississippi West has developed a more diversified, independent economy; see Gerald Nash, *The American West Transformed: The Impact of the Second World War* (Bloomington: University of Indiana Press, 1985); and Gerald Nash, *World War II and the West: Reshaping the Economy* (Lincoln: University of Nebraska Press, 1990).

10. Dean MacCannell, *The Tourist: A New Theory of the Leisure Class* (New York: Schoken Books, 1976), 3. See also Valene Smith, ed., *Hosts and Guests: The Anthropology of Tourism*, 2d ed. (Philadelphia: University of Pennsylvania Press, 1989).

11. One example is Colin Hall, *Tourism and Politics: Policy, Power, and Place* (New York: Wiley, 1994).

12. For one effort see Paul Smith, ed., *The History of Tourism: Thomas Cook and the Origins of Leisure Travel*, 4 vols. (London: Routledge/Thoemmes Press, 1998).

13. Particularly valuable are Colin Hall, *Tourism in the Pacific Rim* (Melbourne: Wiley, 1994); David Hanlon, *Remaking Micronesia: Discourses over Development in a Pacific Territory, 1944–1982* (Honolulu: University of Hawai'i Press, 1998), especially chaps. 5–7; Martin Oppermann, ed., *Pacific Rim Tourism* (Wallingford, Oxon: CAB International, 1997); and Michel Picard and Robert Wood, eds., *Tourism, Ethnicity, and the State in Asian and Pacific Societies* (Honolulu: University of Hawai'i Press, 1997). Essays by Jon Samy, Ronald May, and Herbert Hiller in Richard Brislin, ed., *Culture and Learning: Concepts, Applications, and Research* (Honolulu: East-West Center, University of Hawai'i Press, 1977), remain useful. The essays comprising K. R. Howe, Robert C. Kiste, and Brij V. Lal, eds., *Tides of History: The Pacific Islands in the Twen-*

tieth Century (Honolulu: University of Hawai'i Press, 1994), offer a solid introduction to the history of the islands of the Pacific.

14. For seminal works on how different groups have affected their environments at the local level in America, see William Cronon, *Changes in the Land: Indians, Colonists, and the Ecology of New England* (New York: Hill and Wang, 1983); and Richard White, *Land Use, Environment, and Social Change: The Shaping of Island County, Washington* (Seattle: University of Washington Press, 1980).

1. MAUI'S ECONOMIC DEVELOPMENT

1. James "Kimo" Apana, interview by author, Wailuku, 29 June 1999.
2. Thomas Hitch, *Islands in Transition* (Honolulu: First Hawaiian Bank, 1992), chaps. 1, 2; and Kent, *Hawaii*, chaps. 1, 2. For more detail see Arrell Gibson with John Whitehead, *Yankees in Paradise: The Pacific Basin Frontier* (Albuquerque: University of New Mexico Press, 1993); and Theodore Morgan, *Hawaii: A Century of Economic Change, 1778–1876* (Cambridge, Mass.: Harvard University Press, 1948). For events on Maui, see Gail Bartholomew, *Maui Remembers: A Local History* (Honolulu: Mutual Publishing, 1994), 11, 115; and Cummins Speakman Jr., *Mowee* (Salem: Peabody Museum of Salem, 1978), 98.
3. Carol A. MacLennan, "Hawai'i Turns to Sugar: The Rise of Plantation Centers, 1860–1880," *Hawaiian Journal of History* 31 (1997): 97. See also Carol A. MacLennan, "Foundations of Sugar's Power: Early Maui Plantations, 1840–1860," *Hawaiian Journal of History* 29 (1995): 33–56. For sketches of the development of the sugar cane and pineapple industries on Maui see also Bartholomew, *Maui Remembers*, 42–43, 70.
4. Melody Kapilialoha MacKenzie, ed., *Native Hawaiian Rights Handbook* (Honolulu: Office of Hawaiian Affairs, 1991), 4. For more detail, see Patrick Kirch, *Feathered Gods and Fishhooks: An Introduction to Hawaiian Archaeology and Prehistory* (Honolulu: University of Hawai'i Press, 1985), especially chaps. 1, 4, 7, 11, 12. For a look at Maui before contact with the West, see Elspeth P. Sterling, *Sites of Maui* (Honolulu: Bishop Museum Press, 1998). A pioneering archaeologist on O'ahu and Maui, Sterling died in 1972, with her work on Maui published twenty-six years later. For a biographic sketch of Sterling, see *Maui News*, 27 June 1999.
5. MacKenzie, *Native Hawaiian Rights*, chaps. 1, 2. For more detail on the results of the Great Mahele, see Jocelyn Linnekin, "Statistical Analysis of the Great Mahele, Some Preliminary Findings," *Journal of Pacific History* 22 (January 1987): 15–33.
6. Linda Parker, *Native American Estate: The Struggle over Indian and Hawaiian Lands* (Honolulu: University of Hawai'i Press, 1989), especially chaps. 2, 5.
7. Hitch, *Islands in Transition*, chap. 3; Kent, *Hawaii*, chaps. 3–5; and Ronald Takaki, *Pau Hana: Plantation Life and Labor in Hawaii, 1835–1920* (Honolulu: University of Hawai'i Press, 1983). More was involved in the revolution of 1893 than simple economics. In part, it resulted from a struggle between Queen Lili'uokalani and several groups for control over the Hawaiian Islands.
8. Kent, *Hawaii*, 58, 89. See also Theon Wright, *Disenchanted Isles: The Story of the Second Revolution in Hawaii* (New York: Dial Press, 1972). Pineapple acreage in the Hawaiian Islands rose from 5,000 in 1910 to 65,000 in 1930.
9. George Cooper and Gavan Daws, introduction to *Land and Power in Hawaii* (Honolulu: Benchmark Books, 1985).

10. Patricia Nelson Limerick, *The Legacy of Conquest: The Unbroken Past of the American West* (New York: W. W. Norton, 1987), surveys the history of the West from a "new" perspective, paying attention to economic exploitation and environmental damage. On the new western history, see also William Cronon, George Miles, and Jay Gitlin, eds., *Under an Open Sky* (New York: Norton Publishing, 1992); and Patricia Nelson Limerick, Clyde A. Milner II, and Charles E. Rankin, eds., *Trails: Toward a New Western History* (Lawrence: University Press of Kansas, 1991). William G. Robbins, *Colony and Empire: The Capitalist Transformation of the American West* (Lawrence: University Press of Kansas, 1994), offers a probing look at the development of the Trans-Mississippi West since the mid-nineteenth century, focusing on the impact of capitalism on the region. On capitalism, broadly conceived, as a tool through which one can best understand developments in the American West, see also William G. Robbins, "In Pursuit of Historical Explanation: Capitalism as a Conceptual Tool for Knowing the American West," *Western Historical Quarterly* 30 (autumn 1999): 277–93.

11. Robert L. Kelley, "The Mining Debris Controversy in the Sacramento Valley," *Pacific Historical Review* 25 (November 1956): 331–46, looks at damage to farming in California caused by hydraulic mining. Nannie Alderson, *A Bride Goes West* (Lincoln: University of Nebraska Press, 1969), provides a firsthand account of damage to the cattle industry in Montana in the mid-1880s. Gilbert Fite, "Daydreams and Nightmares: The Late Nineteenth Century Agricultural Frontiers," *Agricultural History* 40 (October 1966): 285–93, is a classic account of the problems of farming on the Great Plains; see also Jonathan Raban, *Bad Land: An American Romance* (New York: Pantheon Books, 1997). For an introduction to the history of the Alaskan salmon industry, see Richard Cooley, *Politics and Conservation: The Decline of the Alaskan Salmon* (New York: Harper Row, 1963). On the Alaskan king crab industry, see Mansel Blackford, *Pioneering a Modern Small Business: Wakefield Seafoods and the Alaskan Frontier* (Greenwich, Conn.: JAI Press, 1979).

12. Cesar Ayala, *American Sugar Kingdom: The Plantation Economy of the Spanish Caribbean, 1898–1934* (Chapel Hill: University of North Carolina Press, 1999), 1; Hanlon, *Remaking Micronesia;* and Howe, Kiste, and Lal, eds., *The Tides of History.*

13. Jacob Adler, *Claus Spreckels: The Sugar King in Hawaii* (Honolulu: Mutual Publishing, 1966); Arthur Dean, *Alexander and Baldwin, Ltd. and the Predecessor Partnerships* (Honolulu: Alexander and Baldwin, 1950); Edwin Hoyt, *Davies: The Inside Story of a British American Family in the Pacific and Its Business Enterprises* (Honolulu: Topgallant Publishing, 1983); Frederick Simpich Jr., *Dynasty in the Pacific* (New York: McGraw-Hill, 1974); Scott Stone, *The Story of C. Brewer and Company, Ltd.* (Aiea, Hawai'i: Island Heritage Publishing, 1991); Frank Taylor, *From Land and Sea: The Story of Castle and Cooke* (San Francisco: Chronicle Books, 1976); and William Worden, *Cargoes: Matson's First Century in the Pacific* (Honolulu: University of Hawai'i Press, 1981). Claus Spreckels's importance on Maui was short-lived, from the mid-1870s to the mid-1880s. Spreckels sold his Hawaiian Commercial and Sugar Company on Maui to Alexander and Baldwin in 1898. On the Big Five, see also John Whitehead, "Western Progressives, Old South Planters, or Colonial Oppressors: The Enigma of Hawai'i's 'Big Five,' 1898–1940," *Western Historical Quarterly* 30 (autumn 1999): 295–326.

14. Bartholomew, *Maui Remembers,* 70; Hitch, *Islands in Transition,* 186–93; Kent, *Hawaii,*

chap. 8.; and Edward Beechert, *Working in Hawaii: A Labor History* (Honolulu: University of Hawai'i Press, 1985), chaps. 13–15.

15. Takaki, *Pau Hana*, 28. On the decline in the Native Hawaiian population, see David Stannard, *Before the Horror: The Population of Hawaii on the Eve of Western Contact* (Honolulu: Social Science Research Institute of the University of Hawai'i, 1989); and O. A. Bushnell, *The Gifts of Civilization: Germs and Genocide in Hawai'i* (Honolulu: University of Hawai'i Press, 1993). Estimates of the number of inhabitants of Hawai'i at the time of contact in 1778 vary tremendously. For a valuable discussion, see Tom Dye, "Population Trends in Hawai'i before 1778," *Hawaiian Journal of History* 28 (1994): 1–20. Using archaeological evidence for trends in agriculture, deforestation, and *heiau* (religious altar) construction, Dye estimates that the Hawaiian population reached a high of 140,000–200,000 around A.D. 1450, before declining to 110,000–150,000 in 1778. While containing many different population groups by the twentieth century, the Hawaiian Islands did not become one big happy family of races. See Johnathan Okamura, "Why There Are No Asian Americans in Hawai'i: The Continuing Significance of Local Identity," *Social Process in Hawai'i* 35 (1994): 161–78.

16. *Haleakala Times,* 21 July–3 August 1999; *Maui County Data Book, 1996–97* (Honolulu: Small Business Development Network, 1997), 81–82; and *Maui News,* 27 June 1995, 23 and 29 June 1998, 7 July 1999, and 30 and 31 August 1999. For more detail, see Decision Analysts Hawaii, *Hawaii's Sugar Industry and Sugarcane Lands: Outlook, Issues, and Options* (Honolulu: State of Hawaii, Department of Business and Economic Development. 1989), ES-14.

17. Seiji Naya, "An Economic Perspective of Tourism Issues and Policies in Hawaii" (paper presented to the Hawaiian House of Representatives, 22 February 1996, Wailuku Library). For more detail on the development of tourism in Hawai'i, see Bryan Farrell, *Hawaii: The Legend That Sells* (Honolulu: University of Hawai'i Press, 1982); Noel Kent, "The End of American Abundance: Whither Hawai'i?" *Social Process in Hawai'i* 35 (1994): 179–95; and James Mak and Marcia Sakai, "Tourism in Hawai'i: Economic Issues for the 1990s and Beyond," in *Politics and Public Policy in Hawai'i,* ed. Zachary Smith and Richard Pratt (Albany: State University of New York Press, 1992), 185–200. Henry Kaiser illustrated how a visitor industry might be developed. Coming to Hawaii in retirement, Kaiser constructed major hotels on O'ahu. See Mark Foster, *Henry J. Kaiser* (Austin: University of Texas Press, 1989), chap. 15.

18. Elmer Cravalho, interview by author, Kahului, 28 February 2000. Also, see Economic Research Center, "An Economic Study of the County of Maui, 1965–67," vol. 2 (Honolulu: University of Hawai'i, 1965), 27–35 (a typescript copy of this four-volume report is available in the Maui Community College library); and "Master Plan for Maui, 1959" (Honolulu: R.M.T. Will Corporation and Community Planning, Inc., 1959), 20 (a typescript copy of this report may be found in the Kahului Public Library Reference Room).

19. "Master Plan for Maui, 1959," 4, 8; *Maui News,* 13 January 1960; and Antonio V. Ramil, *Kalai'aina: County of Maui* (Wailuku: Anvil-Maui Press, 1984), 84, 176–78, 192–93, 208. Hawai'i thus established a territorywide planning office two years before the State of California, one of the leaders in planning on the mainland, established its better-known state planning agency in 1959. See Stephanie Pincetl, *Transforming California:*

A Political History of Land Use and Development (Baltimore: Johns Hopkins University Press, 1999), 140–42.

20. "Economic Study of Maui," vol. 2, 22–35.

21. Ibid.

22. "Economic Study of Maui," vol. 1 (1967), 12–14; and Farrell, *Hawaii*, 88–98. See also Bryan Farrell, "The Tourist Ghettos of Hawaii," in *Themes on Pacific Lands,* ed. M. C. R. Edgell and Bryan Farrell (Victoria, B.C.: Western Geographical Series, University of Victoria, 1974), 181–209.

23. Donald Malcolm, "Recollections, Getting Started on Maui" (typescript memoir), 2.

24. Farrell, *Hawaii*, 99–112; and Donald Malcolm, interview by author, Kapalua, 21 February 2000.

25. See, for example, Maui Economic Development Board, *Maui's Economic Future: Proceedings of the Kapalua Symposium,* December 9–11, 1981.

26. Bartholomew, *Maui Remembers,* 84–85; *Maui County Data Book,* 157; Farrell, *Hawaii,* 33; *Hawaii Business and Industry* 14 (August 1968), 42; Hitch, *Islands in Transition,* 238; *Honolulu Star-Bulletin and Advertiser,* 24 June 1984; *Maui News,* 26 March 1973; and *Time,* 26 March 1979.

27. Bartholomew, *Maui Remembers,* 132. For a description of the ponds and their bird life after World War II, see Will Kyselka and Ray Lanterman, *Maui: How It Came to Be* (Honolulu: University of Hawai'i Press, 1980), 78–79. For a more general discussion of the roles fish ponds played in Hawaiian life before contact, see Kirch, *Feathered Gods,* 3, 130, 211–13, 305. Maui possessed 16 of the 449 fish ponds known to have been constructed in the Hawaiian Islands before 1830.

28. Alexander and Baldwin, *Ampersand* 19, special anniversary edition (30 June 1985): 38–43; and Ramil, *Kalai'aina,* 112, 121–23, 144–45.

29. First Hawaiian Bank, *Maui County in 1981* (pamphlet in Wailuku Public Library).

30. Cravalho, interview, *Hawaii Business and Industry* 14 (August 1968): 17–20; and Speakman, *Mowee,* 191.

31. Speakman, *Mowee,* 194–95.

32. Maui County Council meeting, 5 January 1979.

33. *General Plan for the County of Maui, 24 June 1980,* 1–4. For public hearings and discussions on this plan, see Maui County Council meetings, 6 November 1979 and 15 February 1980. In 1975 the Hawaii legislature had passed a law requiring the development of a "State Policy Plan" for economic development. Counties were, in turn, to establish plans to guide their development, hence the county plan of 1980. For an interesting comparison of statewide planning in the 1970s see Pincetl, *Transforming California,* 140–42, 156, 234.

34. Malcolm, interview; MEDB *Maui's Economic Future, 1981,* 1; and MEDB, *Partners in Planning, 1988,* 237.

35. In the late 1970s and early 1980s conferences dealing with many of the same issues for all of the Hawaiian Islands were held on O'ahu. See Wright, *Disenchanted Isles,* chap. 22.

36. Maui County Council meetings, 2 October 1981 and 6 August 1982; MEDB, *Maui's Economic Future, 1981,* 1–9; and *Maui News,* 10, 11, 14 December 1981.

37. MEDB, "Mission Statement" (pamphlet, available at the MEDB in Kīhei); *Maui News,* 26 June 1985; and State of Hawaii, Department of Planning and Economic Develop-

ment, "Hawaii High Technology Development Plan, September 1, 1981" (Honolulu: State of Hawaii, 1981), 1. See also Robert Johnson, interview by author, Kīhei, 6 July 1998; Lyons Michael II, interview by author, Kahului, 16 June 1999; Malcolm, telephone conversation, 31 May 1999; and Jeanne Unemori Skog, interview by author, Kīhei, 23 June 1999. In the 1980s the state government also set up the Hawaii Information Network Corporation, the Office of Space Industry, the Hawaii Innovation Development Program, the Hawaii Strategic Development Corporation, and the Research and Development Industry Promotion Program to attract high-technology businesses. See Paul Herbig and Hugh Kramer, "The Potential for High Tech in Hawai'i," *Social Process in Hawai'i* 35 (1994): 58.

38. Malcolm, interview.
39. Lyons, interview; Malcolm, interview and telephone conversation; and Malcolm, "Recollections." For a biographical sketch of Malcolm, see MEDB, *Partners in Planning, 1988,* 250–51.
40. MEDB, *Maui's Economic Future, 1981,* inside cover; and MEDB, *MEDB in 1993,* 1.
41. Malcolm, interview; MEDB, *Maui's Economic Future: Activities in Site Selection, October 1983;* MEDB, "Timeline" (typescript available at MEDB headquarters); and *Maui News,* 26 June 1985.
42. Malcolm, interview; and Skog, interview.
43. Johnson, interview; Malcolm, interview; Lyons, interview; and MEDB, "Timeline."
44. Linda Lingle to Donald Malcolm, 16 March 1993; Malcolm interview and telephone conversation; MEDB, *MEDB in 1993,* 1–2; and Skog, interview. The MEDB's role in sponsoring conferences changed over time. In 1984 the MEDB set up the Maui Pacific Institute to hold the meetings; in 1987 the institute was spun off as the Kapalua Pacific Center; and in 1993 this body became the Maui Pacific Center.
45. Johnson, interview; Malcolm, interview; and Skog, interview.
46. Ibid.; *Maui News,* 6 May 1998 and 17 February 2000; and *Wall Street Journal,* 13 January 2000.
47. Thomas Bean and Jan Zulich, "Education in Hawai'i: Balancing Equity and Progress," in Smith and Pratt, *Politics and Public Policy,* 215–28.
48. Maui County Council meetings, 10 June 1976 and 15 April 1983; *Honolulu Star-Bulletin and Advertiser,* 5 October 1975, and *Maui News,* 12 July 1998. The MEDB held a major conference on Maui's higher education needs in 1985; see MEDB, *Maui's Economic Future: The Business/Academic Partnership, May 2–3, 1985.*
49. Robbie Guard, interview by author, Wailuku, 13 July 1998; *Maui News,* 29 December 1997 and 2 October 1998; Mayor's Four-Year College Task Force, *Final Report, 1994, viii;* and University of Phoenix, *Hawai'i Campus* (1999 brochure).
50. Founded as a land grant university in 1907, the University of Hawai'i had (and has) its main campus in Honolulu. Limited in the scope of its offerings for decades, the university expanded dramatically during the 1960s. However, expansion ground to a halt in the 1970s; in fact, between 1972 and 1980 the university's budget, when adjusted for inflation, fell by more than 10 percent. Expansion renewed during the 1980s, only to slow again during the 1990s. State funding for the University of Hawai'i system was cut every year between 1994 and 2000, for a total decrease of 13 percent. See Sumner La Croix, "The University of Hawai'i," in *The Price of Paradise: Lucky We Live Hawaii?,* vol. 1, ed. Randall W. Roth (Honolulu: Mutual Publishing, 1992), 219–23.

On internal problems at the University of Hawai'I, see David Yount, *Who Runs the University? The Politics of Higher Education in Hawaii* (Honolulu: University of Hawai'i Press, 1996). For a refutation of Yount's criticisms of university governance, see the review of his book by Dan Boylan, a professor of history at the University of Hawai'i, in *Hawaiian Journal of History* 31 (1997): 238–39.

51. Maui Research and Technology Park, "MRTP Tenants, 1998," <www.mrtp.com/tenants.html> (3 March 1998); see also *High Tech Maui* (a quarterly newletter put out by the Maui Research and Technology Center), First Quarter 1997 <www.mrtc. org/htm/NewsLetters/1/page 2.html> (14 September 2000).

52. Herbig and Kramer, "Potential for High Tech in Hawai'i," 56–70; and *Forbes*, 31 May 1999, 220–33.

53. Stuart Leslie and Robert Kargon, "Selling Silicon Valley: Frederick Terman's Model for Regional Advantage," *Business History Review* 70 (winter 1996): 435–72; and Annalee Saxenian, *Regional Advantage: Culture and Competition in Silicon Valley and Route 128* (Cambridge, Mass.: Harvard University Press, 1994). See also Sheridan Tatsuno, *The Technopolis Strategy: Japan, High Technology, and the Control of the Twenty-first Century* (New York: Prentice Hall, 1986).

54. Lyons, interview; Malcolm, telephone conversation; and Donald Malcolm, "Tapping Hawaii's Unrecognized Technological Resources" (paper prepared for Gov. Benjamin Cayetano's Economic Revitalization Task Force, October 1997), 1. For another positive assessment of a high-technology future for Maui, see Apana, interview. Apana hoped that high-technology ventures would become "a big part" of Maui's economy. "Once we get high-tech up and running," he thought, "Maui will be known not only as a place to vacation, but actually to do business." In 1999 and 2000 Apana traveled to Silicon Valley to try to attract firms to Maui.

55. MEDB, *MEDB in 1993*, Chart 1. Federal government support was crucial for high-technology developments throughout the Hawaiian Islands. In 1993–97, for example, the federal government spent about $822 million on high-technology projects in the state of Hawai'i. See Malcolm, "Tapping Hawaii's Unrecognized Technological Resources," table.

56. *Aloha from Maui* (undated pamphlet in the clipping file at the Maui Community College library).

57. "Economic Study of Maui," vol. 3, 1; and MEDB, *Maui's Economic Future, 1981*, 97–104.

58. Maui County Council meetings, 20 August 1979 and 18 May 1984; *Maui County Data Book*, 87; and *Honolulu Star-Bulletin and Advertiser*, 10 January 1971.

59. Agriculture file of newspaper clippings, Wailuku Public Library. See also *Maui News*, 26 July 1998; and "Agriculture," <www.hshawaii.com/databook/maui/ag.html> (11 March 1998).

60. Maui County Council meeting, 6 June 1969.

61. Ibid., 17 February 1978.

62. Ibid., 1 December 1979, 15 February 1980, and 16 December 1982; Farrell, *Hawaii*, 178; First Hawaiian Bank, *Maui County in 1981*; and *Maui News*, 21 July 1998 and 13 January 1999.

63. *Data Book*, 80–86; and "Economic Study of Maui County," vol. 3, table 7; and *Maui's Economic Future, 1981*, 89.

64. Farrell, *Hawaii*, 17, 170–78; and MEDB, *Maui's Economic Future, 1981*, 90.

65. Harry Eagar, interview by author, Wailea, 1 July 1998. See also Mark Sheehan, interview by author, Makawao, 30 July 1998. The illicit crop of marijuana, known on Maui as "Maui Wowee," might provide a partial answer to the problems of growers. Some have estimated the value of its production as being as great as that of sugar cane by the 1970s.

66. Rohter, *A Green Hawai'i*, 66–67, 338. See also "Economic Study of Maui," vol. 3, 16, 43.

67. Guard, interview; and *Maui News*, 5 January 1999 and 3 January 2000.

68. *Maui County Data Book*, 148–58.

69. On Japanese investments in Hawai'i, see Farrell, *Hawaii*, 330–32; and Marion Kelly, "Foreign Investment in Hawai'i," Karl Kim, "The Political Economy of Foreign Investment in Hawai'i," and Okamura, "Why There Are No Asian Americans in Hawai'i," in *Social Process in Hawai'i* 35 (1994): 15–56, 165–66. On early reactions to Japanese investments, see *Maui News*, 25 May 1977.

70. *Maui County Data Book*, 148, 157; and *Maui News*, 23 June, 8 July, 17 and 26 August, and 16, 17, 20 November 1998.

71. *Maui County Data Book*, 150–51; Guard, interview; and Marsha Wienert, interview by author, Kahului, 24 July 1998.

72. "Economic Study of Maui," vol. 2, xxi.

73. *Maui News*, 27 April 1997, 28 January, 31 August, 2 October, 1998, and 4, 22 January 1999; and Terryl Vencl, interview by author, Kahului, 15 July 1998.

74. *Maui County Data Book*, 162; *Maui News*, 3 August 1984 and 10 October 1996; and Karen Horton, "A Farm for All Seasons," *Spirit of Aloha* (March-April 1985): 21.

75. Eagar interview; and Wienert, interview. A poll taken in the fall of 1999 by the Maui Visitors Bureau showed that tourists on Maui came from a broad range of ages and engaged in a wide variety of activities. See *Maui News*, 17 September 1999. On the possibility of a multipurpose facilty, see SMS Research, "A Multipurpose Facility for the Island of Maui: A Market Feasibility Study" (June 1994).

76. Hawaii Tourist Authority, "Competitive Strategic Assessment of Hawaii Tourism: Executive Summary" (29 June 1999), 5; and HTA, "Hawaii Tourism Product Assessment," vol. 1 (30 June 1999). For newspaper commentary on Maui about the work of the HTA, see *Maui News*, 1, 13 July 1999.

77. Jackie Carlin, letter to the editor, *Maui News*, 15 June 1999.

78. Eagar, interview; Guard, interview; Vencl, interview; and Weinert, interview.

79. Maui County Council meetings, 4 May 1973, 4 August 1978. For an example of how Hawaiian culture has been commodified for the tourist trade, see T. D. Webb, "Missionaries, Polynesians, and Tourists: Mormonism and Tourism in Lā'ie, Hawai'i," *Social Process in Hawai'i* 35 (1994): 195–212.

80. Wienert, interview. The issue of Hawaiian crafts was complex. Without sales to resorts and tourists, many of the crafts might not survive. As one writer observed in 1997, "The demand for Hawaiian handicrafts is on the upswing, which is great news for people who want to develop native crafts as a cottage industry." She warned, however, that "it is very important that a high level of quality be maintained and that traditional HAWAIIAN techniques be used if the item is to be marketed as truly Hawaiian." See Leilehua Yuen, "Native Hawaiian Crafts Culturally Appropriate Commerce," *Maui Business* 2 (April 1997): 26–27.

81. *Maui News,* 29 October 1998; and Dorothy Pyle, interview by author, Kahului, 8 July 1999.
82. "Economic Study of Maui," vol. 2, *xiv, xxii.*
83. County of Maui, "General Plan for the County of Maui, 1990," *ii,* 1–8.
84. *Maui Talks,* (pamphlet, summer 1999), 8.

2. PEOPLE, GROUPS, AND MOVEMENTS

1. On the importance of organizational activity in modern America, see Louis Galambos, "The Emerging Organizational Synthesis in Modern American History," *Business History Review* 44 (autumn 1970): 279–90; and Louis Galambos, "Technology, Political Economy, and Professionalization: Central Themes of the Organizational Synthesis," *Business History Review* 57 (winter 1983): 472–93. For a dissenting point of view, see Brian Balogh, "Reorganizing the Organizational Synthesis: Federal-Professional Relations in Modern America," *Studies in American Political Development* 5 (spring 1991): 119–72.
2. Harold Livesay, "Entrepreneurial Dominance in Businesses Large and Small, Past and Present," *Business History Review* 63 (spring 1989): 1–21.
3. Information about the Maui Chamber of Commerce may be found at <www.mauichamber.com>.
4. Vencl, interview.
5. Wienert, interview.
6. Gail Bartholomew, "Maui: Amid Great Growth, A Persistent Past," *Spririt of Aloha* 50 (August 1986): 14; Farrell, *Hawaii,* 274; and MEDB, *Partners in Planning, December 14, 15, 16, 1988,* 85.
7. Maui County Council meetings, 25 February 1980, 1 October 1982, 6 January and 3 February 1984.
8. *Maui News,* 18 June 1998; and Wienert, interview.
9. *Maui News,* 10 June 1998; and Wienert, interview.
10. Vencl, interview.
11. Ibid.
12. Guard, interview; and Office of the Mayor, County of Maui, "Budget Proposal, Fiscal Year 1997."
13. Vencl, interview; and Wienert, interview.
14. *Maui News,* 14 June 1992. For discussions of Colin Cameron's leadership, see Lyons, interview; Malcolm, interview; and Skog, interview.
15. Maui Land and Pineapple, *Annual Report, 1998,* 16. When Cameron died in 1992, his sister, Mary Cameron Sanford, took over the reins at Maui Land and Pineapple and basically extended the policies begun by her brother.
16. This biographical sketch is based on my interview with Lyons 16 June 1999; all quotations are from that interview.
17. This biographical sketch is based mainly on my interview with Dowling 30 June 1999; all quotations are from that interview. See also *Maui News,* 7 August 1998.
18. Not all on Maui shared this point of view. For a dissenting opinion, see Diane Logsdon, Pukalani, letter to the editor, *Maui News,* 14 August 1998.
19. Speakman, *Mowee,* 192–93.
20. Rothman, *The Greening of a Nation,* xi.

21. *Maui News,* 26 March 1973, and date unclear, 1974; Dick Mayer interview by author, Kula, 6 July 1999; and Robert Wenkman, *Maui: The Last Hawaiian Place* (New York: Seabury Press, 1970), 79–91. Even so, the State of Hawai'i lagged behind other states in funding environmental improvements. In 1986 Hawai'i spent $19 per capita for environmental activities, considerably less than the fifty-state average of $37. See Richard Tobin and Dean Higuchi, "Environmental Quality in America's Tropical Paradise," in Smith and Pratt, *Politics and Public Policy,* 126.

22. The Web site for the Maui Group of the Hawaiian Chapter of the Sierra Club is <www.mauimapp.com/community/sierra.htm>. See also Lucienne de Naie, interview by author, Kahului, 14 July 1999.

23. Madelyn "Benni" D'Enbeau, interview by author, Wailuku, 25 June 1999.

24. Ibid.

25. Ibid.; and Mayer, interview, 6 July 1999. See also Cooper and Daws, *Land and Power in Hawaii.*

26. Farrell, "Tourist Ghettos of Hawaii," 202.

27. Celeste King, interview by author, Kahului, 13 July 1998. King, an environmentalist in her own right, was the mother of Madelyn D' Enbeau and the mother-in-law of Anthony Hodges.

28. D'Enbeau, interview.

29. Ibid.; King, interview; and Ramil, *Kalai'aina,* 238.

30. Maui County Council meeting, 27 September 1973; D'Enbeau, interview; and King, interview.

31. Mark Sheehan, interview. In 1998 Anthony Rankin was vice-president of Maui Tomorrow and King was one of its directors. The name Maui Tomorrow may have been inspired by the name of a similar organization, California Tomorrow, formed in 1962. Other community-based environmental groups of the time had names such as Maine's Future, Vermont Tomorrow, and Delaware's Future. See Hays, *Beauty, Health, and Permanence,* 389; and Pincetl, *Transforming California,* 152–54, 161–62.

32. D'Enbeau, interview; and King, interview.

33. Sheehan, interview.

34. Ibid; and Mayer, interview, 6 July 1999.

35. Sheehan, interview.

36. Ibid.; and Maui Tomorrow, "Mission and Purpose," at <www.maui-tomorrow.org./purpose.html> (30 March 1998).

37. Mayer, interview, 6 July 1999.

38. This biographical sketch is based on my interview with Mayer 6 July 1999. Unless otherwise noted, all quotations are from that interview.

39. *Maui News,* 20 March 1971.

40. *Lahaina Sun,* 20 September 1972.

41. Mayer, interview, 6 July 1999.

42. This biographical sketch is based mainly on my interview with Isaac Hall, Wailuku, 1 July 1999; all quotations are from that interview.

43. This biographical sketch is based on my interview with Sally Raisbeck, Kahului, 14 July 1998; all quotations are from that interview.

44. Dana Naone Hall, ed., *Mālama: Hawaiian Land and Water,* special issue of *Bamboo Ridge: The Hawaiian Writers' Quarterly* 29 (winter 1985): 3. An early sign of change

on Maui occurred in 1973 with the formation of the group Na Mele O Maui. As the body's president later explained in a public letter to Maui's residents, Na Mele O Maui had as its goal "to preserve the cultural identity of Hawai'i by teaching its language, music and dance to our children." Working with the Hawaiian State Department of Education, Na Mele O Maui taught Maui's schoolchildren Native Hawaiian songs, chants, and culture. Each fall Na Mele O Maui held countywide competitions for elementary and middle-school children; in 1998, 1,100 students competed. Proceeds from the competition went into scholarships for college students interested in studying Native Hawaiian culture. See *Maui News,* 3 December 1998.

45. Haunani-Kay Trask, "The Birth of the Modern Hawaiian Movement: Kalama Valley, O'ahu," *Hawaiian Journal of History* 21 (1987): 126–53; and Haunani-Kay Trask, "Kupa'a'aina: Native Hawaiian Nationalism in Hawai'i," in Smith and Pratt, *Politics and Public Policy,* 243–60. For a full elaboration of Trask's ideas, see Haunani-Kay Trask, *From a Native Daughter: Colonialism and Sovereignty in Hawai'i* (Honolulu: University of Hawai'i Press, 1999). See also Robert H. Mast and Anne B. Mast, eds., *Autobiography of Protest in Hawai'i* (Honolulu: University of Hawai'i Press, 1996), 403. Wright, *The Disenchanted Isles,* 258, looks at early problems with the Bishop Estate.

46. Trask, "Kalama Valley," 126–27. For a valuable comparison, see Linda Parker, *Native American Estate: The Struggle over Indian and Hawaiian Lands* (Honolulu: University of Hawai'i Press, 1989). For a listing of Native Hawaiian actions, island by island, see Luciano Minerbi, "Native Hawaiian Struggles and Events: A Partial List, 1973–1993," *Social Process in Hawaii* 35 (1994): 1–14.

47. County of Maui, "Kaho'olawe Community Plan, 1995," 5–6, presents a good description of the island.

48. Stanton Enomoto, "Kaho'olawe Clean-up" (presentation at the Bailey House on Maui, 18 June 1999). Enmoto was remediation project coordinator for the Kaho'olawe Island Reserve Commission. See also *Kaho'olawe: Nā Leo o Kanaloa* (Honolulu: 'Ai Pohaku Press, 1995), unpaged chronology (Kanaloa is the traditional name for Kaho'olawe). Pauline King, "A Local History of Kaho'olawe Island: Tradition, Development, and World War" (typescript, 1993, Maui Community College Library), covers the history of Kaho'olawe from the 1770s through the 1940s). See, finally, Kirch, *Feathered Gods,* 153–54; and Robert C. Schmitt and Carol L. Silva, "Population Trends on Kaho'olawe," *Hawaiian Journal of History* 18 (1984): 39–46.

49. *Kaho'olawe.*

50. Maui County Council meetings, 3 October 1969, 16 January 1970, 10 February and 19 March 1971, and 7 September 1973.

51. Francis Norris, "Kaho'olawe: Island of Opportunity" (master's thesis, University of Hawai'i, 1992), 92. See also Myra Tuggle, "The Protect Kaho'olawe 'Ohana: Cultural Revitalization in Contemporary Hawaiian Movement" (master's thesis, University of Hawai'i, 1982), especially chap. 3. Particularly important in leading the opposition to the bombing of Kaho'olawe was Emmett Aluli, a founding member of both Hui Alaloa and the Protect Kaho'olawe 'Ohana. In the mid-1980s Dana Naone Hall wrote of Aluli that "he lives on Moloka'i, the only island along with Ni'ihau where the population is overwhelmingly Hawaiian. He is a doctor experienced in the practice of both Western and Hawaiian medicine. . . . A dedicated advocate and practitioner

of Hawaiian ways, he is an almost tireless traveler among his home islands, as well as other islands of the Pacific." See Hall, *Mālama*, 151.

52. Maui County Council meetings, 17 January 1976, 4 February 1977, 5 May 1978, and 5 March, 2 April, 8 April, and 21 May 1982; *Kaho'olawe*, chronology; and Teresa Donham, "Kaho'olawe Clean-up" (presentation at the Bailey House on Maui, 18 June 1999). Donham was an archaeologist working as a Preservation Navy Technical Representative. See also Ramil, *Kalai'aina*, 246–47. For a detailed description of the archaeological sites, see Kirch, *Feathered Gods*, 144–54.

53. Keoni Fairbanks, "Kaho'olawe Restoration Report," 14 July 1997, <www.hookele.com/mt/forum/messages/33.html> (22 April 1998); County of Maui, "Kaho'olawe Community Plan, 1995," 12, 18; *Maui News*, 20 June and 4 December 1997, and 30 January, 27 February, and 20 March 1998; "Memorandum of Understanding Between the United States Department of the Navy and the State of Hawai'i Concerning the Island of Kaho'olawe, May 6, 1994," printed in English and in Hawaiian; and "Restoring Kaho'olawe," *Honolulu Star Bulletin*, 20 August 1996.

54. *Maui News*, 30 January, 9 July, 10, 21 October and 16 November 1998.

55. Hanlon, *Remaking Micronesia*, 210–13.

56. Maui County Council meeting, 27 November, 1984. On the Seibu businesses, see Thomas Havens, *Architects of Affluence: The Tsutsumi Family and the Seibu-Saison Enterprises in Twentieth-Century Japan* (Cambridge, Mass.: Harvard University Press, 1994).

57. Dana Naone Hall, interview by author, Wailuku, 14 July 1999. See also Hall, *Mālama*, 3, 32–33.

58. Dana Naone Hall, interview, 14 July 1999.

59. Maui County Council meetings, 3 March 1978, 15 February 1980, 2 April, 15 May, 17 July, and 6 November 1981, 18 March, 4 April, and 5 August 1983, and 2 March and 15 May 1984; and *Maui News*, 9 December 1981.

60. Isaac Hall, interview.

61. Ibid.; Dana Naone Hall, interview, 14 July 1999; and *Maui News*, 30 July 1987.

62. Isaac and Dana Naone Hall interviews.

63. Mahealani Kamau'u and H. K. Bruss Keppeler, "Sovereignty," in Roth, *The Price of Paradise*, 295. For more detail, see MacKenzie, *Native Hawaiian Rights Handbook*, chap. 4; Mast and Mast, *Autobiography of Protest*, pt. 5; and Trask, *From a Native Daughter*, 37–38, 70–71, 74–79.

64. Maui County Council meeting, 6 May 1983; *Maui News*, 5 January 1997 and 21 August 1998; and *Honolulu Star-Bulletin*, 10 April, 11 September, and 25 November 1996.

65. MacKenzie, *Native Hawaiian Rights Handbook*, chap. 12.

66. *Maui News*, 1, 12 December 1997, and 2 March, 13 April, 18 November, and 7 December, 1998. Native Hawaiians reinstated *makahiki* ceremonies on Kaho'olawe in 1982.

67. Ibid., 30 March 1998.

68. M. J. Harden, ed., *Voices of Wisdom: Hawaiian Elders Speak* (Kula, Maui: Aka Press, 1999), 85–91; Charles Keau, untitled presentation at the Bailey House on Maui, 7 July, 1999; and Pyle, interview.

69. Speakman, *Mowee*, 158–59.

70. Keau, presentation.

71. Hall, *Mālama*, 33.

72. Dana Naone Hall, interview, 1 July 1999.

73. Ibid.

74. Ibid.

75. Hall, *Mālama,* 7, 32–33.

76. Dana Naone Hall, interview, July 14, 1999.

77. Ibid.

78. *Maui News,* 12 December 1998, and 4 January, 16 April, and 13 June, 1999.

79. Ibid., 7 December 1998 and 4 January, 1999.

80. René Sylva, "Native Plants," in Hall, *Mālama,* 77. For an overview of the issue of alien plants and animals in the Hawaiian Islands see George W. Cox, *Alien Species in North America and Hawaii: Impacts on Natural Ecosystems* (Washington, D.C.: Island Press, 1999), chap. 13.

81. Dana Naone Hall and Victoria Keith, "Back to the Roots" (video available at the Maui Community College Library).

82. Sherwin Carlquist, preface, *Hawaii: A Natural History* (Lāwa'i, Hawaii: Pacific Tropical Botanical Garden, 1980); and Tobin and Higuchi, "Environmental Quality," 124.

83. Bartholomew, *Maui Remembers,* 163; and Maui County Council meeting, 18 June 1971.

84. Carlquist, *Hawaii,* chap. 3; Cox, *Alien Species,* 176–77; Kirch, *Feathered Gods,* 22–29, 65, 216–17, 290–93; and Kenneth M. Nagata, "Early Plant Introductions in Hawai'i," *Hawaiian Journal of History* 19 (1985): 35–61.

85. Cox, *Alien Species,* 177; and Nagata, "Early Plant Introductions."

86. Sean McKeown, "Brown Tree Snakes — Their Damage to Guam and Keeping Them out of Hawaii," *Reptiles* 6 (May 1998): 58. See also *Haleakala Times,* 21 April–4 May, 1999; *Maui News,* 26, 27, 28, 30 June and 7 September, 1998; and Oliver Sachs, *The Island of the Colorblind* (New York: Alfred Knopf, 1996), 153–54, 236.

87. Rocky Barker, "Mending Fences: Lessons in Island Biodiversity Protection from Hawai'i," East-West Center Working Papers, Environmental Series 45 (September 1995), 2–3; Cox, *Alien Species,* 173–75; René Sylva, "Saving Endangered Species of Hawai'i," *Journal* (a publication of the Bailey House Museum on Maui), (fall 1999): 3; and Tobin and Higuchi, "Environmental Quality," 124–25. For a look at similar problems in California, see Pincetl, *Transforming California,* 270–71, 279–80.

88. State of Hawaii, *Session Laws of Hawaii, 1997,* 479. See also *Maui News,* 5 February, 19 March, 20 July, and 22 September 1999.

3. LAND USE ISSUES

1. Speakman, *Mowee,* 162.

2. David L. Callies, *Regulating Paradise: Land Use Controls in Hawaii* (Honolulu: University of Hawai'i Press, 1984), 1.

3. Ramil, *Kalai'aina,* 18. See also Antonio Ramil, interview by author, Kahului, 24 June 1999.

4. For details on political change in the Hawaiian Islands, see Wright, *The Disenchanted Isles,* especially chaps. 9–17.

5. Skog, interview.

6. *Maui News,* 8 November, 1944; and Ramil, *Kalai'aina,* 23, 36, 44, 80–81, 84, 98, 106–7.

7. Cooper and Daws, *Land and Power in Hawaii*, chap. 1; and Farrell, *Hawaii*, 67, 112.

8. Callies, *Regulating Paradise*, 1–3, 6–7; and David Callies, "Dealing with Scarcity: Land Use and Planning," in Smith and Pratt, *Politics and Public Policy*, 131.

9. Ramil, *Kalai'aina*, 190–91.

10. Ibid., 38, 46, 49, 139.

11. Ibid., 188, 192, 210; *Kihei Times*, 23 December 1998–12 January, 1999; and "Master Plan for Maui, 1959," 64–65.

12. The State Land Use Commission classified 52 percent of the state's land as agricultural, 45 percent as conservation (mainly mountains and forest), about 3 percent as urban, and less than 1 percent as rural (a low-density residential classification calling for half-acre lots). Not much had changed by 1995. In that year 48 percent of the state's land was designated as conservation, with another 47 percent classified as agricultural. Only 4.5 percent was classified as urban, with the remainder, again less than 1 percent, designated as rural. See Farrell, *Hawaii*, 120–25; and Peter Garrod and Bruce Plasch, "Agricultural Lands," in Roth, *The Price of Paradise*, 138–44.

13. *Maui County Data Book*, 51.

14. Callies, *Regulating Paradise*, 12–20. For explanations of how planning worked on Maui, see Dick Mayer, interview by author, Kula, 30 June 1998; and Hannibal Tavares, "Welcome," in MEDB, *Partners in Planning, 1988*, 6–7.

15. Cooper and Daws, *Land and Power in Hawaii*, 86–87; Rohter, *A Green Hawai'i*, chap. 1; and Wright, *Disenchanted Isles*, 338.

16. On Maui the average price of a single-family home rose from $12,000 in 1960 to $32,000 in 1970 and $285,000 in 1992. Bartholomew, *Maui Remembers*, 154; Cooper and Daws, *Land and Power in Hawaii*, 87; and Kent Keith, "Land Regulation," in Roth, ed., *The Price of Paradise*, 1993, 133–37.

17. Cooper and Daws, *Land and Power in Hawaii*, chap. 2; and Ramil, *Kalai'aina*, 92.

18. Eagar, interview.

19. Apana, interview; and Ramil, interview.

20. Cravalho, interview.

21. Ibid.

22. Ramil, *Kalai'aina*, 117, 124–26, 163–73; and Speakman, *Mowee*, 177–79.

23. Cravalho, interview.

24. Ibid.

25. Farrell, "Tourist Ghettos of Hawaii," 201–2; *Hawaii Business and Industry* 14 (August 1968): 15; Ramil, *Kalai'aina*, 232, 235; and Ramil, interview.

26. Apana, interview; Cravalho, interview; and Ramil, interview.

27. Maui County Council meetings, 3 September and 19 November 1976.

28. Ibid., 5 September 1969; and Callies, *Regulating Paradise*, 43.

29. Maui County Council meeting, 15 February, 1974.

30. Ibid., 18 December 1970 and 6 March and 5 April 1974.

31. Ibid. On the creation of project districts in Hawai'i, see Callies, *Regulating Paradise*, 43; and MEDB, *Partners in Planning*, 54. Special districts had been used in some parts of the United States from the early 1900s. On their use in California for urban infrastructural improvements, see Pincetl, *Transforming California*, 63–64, 125.

32. Maui County Council meeting, 6 March 1974.

33. Ibid., 29 September 1977.

34. Ibid., 2 December 1977.

35. Ibid., 5 January 1979.

36. Apana, interview; *Maui News*, 21 April 1996 and 13 January 1999; MEDB, *Partners in Planning*, 5, 253–54; and Ramil, interview.

37. Ibid.

38. Maui County, "General Plan, 1980," 1.

39. Wright, *Disenchanted Isles*, chap. 22.

40. Maui County, "General Plan, 1980," 2.

41. Ibid., 4; Eagar, interview; and Alice Lee, interview by author, Wailuku, 15 July 1998.

42. Maui County, "General Plan, 1980," 3–5; see also Maui County Council meetings, 6 January 1978, November 6 1979, 6 March 1980, 4 January 1982, and 16 September 1983.

43. Maui County Council meeting, 16 September 1983.

44. Ibid., 6 March and 3 April 1981, and 2 March 1984.

45. MEDB, *Partners in Planning*, 238.

46. Maui County, "General Plan of the County of Maui, 1990," 2–3.

47. Maui County Council meeting, 20 February 1981. In lieu of providing land for parks developers could make cash payments to the county. On subdivisions in the Hawaiian Islands, see Callies, *Regulating Paradise*, chap. 4.

48. Callies, *Regulating Paradise*, 25; and State of Hawaii, *Session Laws of Hawaii*, 1989, 5–6.

49. *Maui News*, 4 June 1997. On the meaning of the classification "interim," see Callies, *Regulating Paradise*, 44.

50. *Maui News*, 23 June 1997 and 4 January 1999.

51. Pincetl, *Transforming California*, 147–52.

52. Maui County Council meetings, 1 May 1969 and 19 July 1974.

53. Ibid., 16 January 1981.

54. Ibid., 3 September 1982.

55. Ibid., 1 June 1984.

56. Ibid., 30 October 1997 and 13 January 1998; and Maui County, "General Plan, 1990," 2.

57. Maui County Council Land Use Committee, "Hearing Notification, Agricultural Land Subdivision Moratorium, January 26, 1998"; and Maui Tomorrow to County Council, 15 January 1998, <www.hookele.com/mt/forum/messages/179.html> (6 February 1998). See also *Maui News*, 28 January and 22 April 1998.

58. Maui County Council meeting, 18 May 1998.

59. Ibid., 2 October, 11, 23 November, and 17, 21 December 1998; *Kihei Times*, 23 December 1998–12 January 1999; and Lee, interview. See also Lucienne de Naie, open letter, 15 December 1998, and Anthony Rankin to Maui County Council, 15 December 1998, <www.hookele.com/mt/forum/messages/179.html> (6 February 1998).

60. Ibid.

61. Lucienne de Naie, "Maui Takes a Stand on Sprawl — A Local Story, December 20, 1998," <www.hookele.com/mt/forum/messages/179.html> (6 February 1998).

62. *Maui News*, 21 December 1998 and 5 January, 1999. See also Hays, *Beauty, Health, and Permanence*, 294.

63. Callies, "Dealing with Scarcity," 135–36; and Maui County Council meeting, 6 April 1984.

64. Hays, *Beauty, Health, and Permanence*, 454; and Pincetl, *Transforming California*, 229–30.

65. Author's observations at a meeting among members of Maui Tomorrow, the Trust for Public Land, and Mayor James Apana on open-space issues, 22 June 1999; *Maui News*, 18 December 1998, 28 September 1999 and 15 February 2000; Maui Tomorrow, "Community Lands and Open Space Acquisition Fund of 'Land Bank'" (23 January 1998) <www.hookele.com/mt/forum/messages/179.html> (6 February 1998); and *South Maui Times*, 25 February 1998.

66. *Maui News*, 30 October 1998.

67. MacKenzie, *Native Hawaiian Rights Handbook*, 15–16. For a detailed look at how some Native Hawaiians viewed the loss of their lands, see Native Hawaiians Study Commission, *Report on the Culture, Needs, and Concerns of Native Hawaiians*, vol. 2 (report prepared for Congress, 23 June 1983), especially Part 1. The federal government took a substantial block of land for its own use. By 1959 this land totaled 287,000 acres — with the federal government leasing another 117,000 acres and controlling an additional 28,000 acres.

68. MacKenzie, *Native Hawaiian Rights Handbook*, 45. There were loopholes, which the plantations exploited to secure large landholdings. Still, the law was an annoyance. Paul Gates, *History of Public Land Law Development* (Washington, D.C.: U.S. Government Printing Office, 1968), is a classic work on federal land policies.

69. Davianna Pōmaika'i McGregor, "'Āina Ho'opulapula: Hawaiian Homesteading," *Hawaiian Journal of History* 24 (1990): 1–38. See also *Report on the Culture*, vol. 2, chap. 6.

70. McGregor, "'Āina," 30–31. At the insistence of the Big Five companies, the 1921 act was a temporary five-year measure, but it was made permanent in 1926.

71. Department of Hawaiian Home Lands, "Overview of Activities," (1999), 4–7.

72. McGregor, "'Āina," 37–38.

73. *Maui News*, 1 October 1999; DHHL "Overview," 8–9; and State of Hawaii, *Session Laws of Hawaii, 1995*, 696–703.

74. H. K. Bruss Keppeler, "Native Hawaiian Claims," in Roth, *The Price of Paradise*, 195–204; MacKenzie, *Native Hawaiian Rights Handbook*, chap. 2.; and *Maui News*, 16 July and 21 August 1998.

75. DHHL, *Report on the Culture*, 148. Chap. 8 presents a statistical profile of Native Hawaiians compared with other residents of the Hawaiian Islands.

76. Maui County Council meetings, 20 February 1970, and 19 July 1974.

77. Ibid., 15 June 1973; and Ramil, *Kalai'aina*, 212.

78. DHHL, *Annual Report, FY 1997–98*, 7, 10; "Draft Environmental Assessment, Waiehu Kou, Phase 2" (prepared by Townscape Inc., January 1998); and *Maui News*, 19 July, 10, 14 September, 28 October, and 2 November 1998, and 7 July 1999.

79. *Maui News*, 10 September 1992, and 19 January, 19 June, and 7 August 1998.

80. I am indebted to Maggie Sutrov of Kula, Maui, for sharing her research on Kahikinui with me, including her paper "Standing Together at Kahikinui." On Native Hawaiian homesteads more generally, see "Can Native Hawaiians Make a Living on Homesteads?" *Honolulu Star-Bulletin*, 6 December 1997.

81. Kirch, *Feathered Gods*, 137–38, 304; and Sterling, *Sites of Maui*, 192–213, describe Kahikinui in precontact times. On the hearings, see *Maui News*, 10 September and 28 October 1992.

82. *Ka Nūhou* (newsletter of the DHHL) 21 (September 1995): 4–5.
83. *Maui News,* 30 September 1997 and 1 January 1998.
84. Ibid.
85. Based on a daylong visit by the author to Kahikinui for the lease-giving ceremony and discussion by the author with Mo Moler and others at the ceremony, 19 July 1998. See also *Maui News,* 16, 22 June 1999.
86. Farrell, *Hawaii,* 122–23; and *Maui News,* 23, 25, 27 March 1998.
87. Ibid. On the efforts of Native Hawaiians to regain their fishing rights more generally, see Parker, *Native American Estate,* 168–70.
88. *Environment Hawaii* 9 (February 1999): 6–7.
89. *Maui News,* 16 December 1998 and 3 March, and 27 June 1999.
90. *Honolulu Advertiser,* 8 October 1988; MacKenzie, *Native Hawaiian Rights Handbook,* 253–55; Malcolm, interview; and *Maui News,* 27 February 2000.
91. *Maui News,* 12 December 1997, and 2 March and 13 April 1998.
92. *Columbus Dispatch,* 22 November and 20 December 1998, and 11 April 1999; and *Wall Street Journal,* 8 October 1998. On the work of the Nature Conservancy and similar groups, see Hays, *Beauty, Health, and Permanence,* 108, 513; and Pincetl, *Transforming California,* 241.
93. Mansel G. Blackford, *The Lost Dream: Businessmen and City Planning on the Pacific Coast, 1890–1920* (Columbus: Ohio State University Press, 1993), examines planning efforts, mainly abortive, in Seattle, Portland, Oakland, San Francisco, and Los Angeles. One exception was Salt Lake City, planned as a "temple city" by the Mormon church. For a pioneering work on western urban development, see Gunther Barth, *Instant Cities: Urbanization and the Rise of San Francisco and Denver* (New York: Oxford University Press, 1975).

4. WATER CONTROVERSIES

1. Maui County Planning Department, "Water Use and Development Plan, Executive Summary," March 21, 1990, 9; and "An Economic Study of Maui," vol. 1, 18.
2. David Craddick, director, Department of Water Supply, County of Maui, personal communication, 4 March 1999.
3. Board of Water Supply, County of Maui, *Annual Report for Fiscal Year 1996,* 20.
4. Jim Hernandez, "Water: Protecting the Source of All Life," *Maui* 6 (January/February 1991): 17–22. On water in the Hawaiian Islands, see James Moncur, "Water Policy," in Roth, *The Price of Paradise,* 175–81.
5. Classic works on the Trans-Mississippi West as an arid region include Walter Prescott Webb, *The Great Plains* (New York: Ginn and Company, 1931); and Wallace Stegner, *Beyond the Hundredth Meridian* (New York: Houghton Mifflin, 1962).
6. Donald Pisani is the scholar who has been most important recently in exploring the history of land and water policies in the West. See Donald Pisani, *To Reclaim a Divided West: Water, Law, and Public Policy, 1848–1902* (Albuquerque: University of New Mexico Press, 1992); and Donald Pisani, *Water, Land, and Law in the West: The Limits of Public Policy, 1850–1920* (Lawrence: University Press of Kansas, 1996). Also valuable are Robert Dunbar, *Forging New Rights in Western Waters* (Lincoln: University

of Nebraska Press, 1983); and Donald Worster, *Rivers of Empire: Water, Aridity, and the Growth of the American West* (New York: Pantheon, 1985).

7. Pisani, *To Reclaim a Divided West*, 39–46. For more detail, see Jose Rivera, *Acequia Culture: Water, Land and Community in the Southwest* (Albuquerque: University of New Mexico Press, 1998).

8. James Willard Hurst, *Law and the Conditions of Freedom in the Nineteenth-Century United States* (Madison: University of Wisconsin Press, 1967).

9. There were exceptions. In 1886 Wyoming adopted a water code that in theory gave ownership of all water to the state. No other western state went that far in the nineteenth century. See Pisani, *To Reclaim a Divided West*, chap. 3.

10. Kirch, *Feathered Gods*, 220; and MacKenzie, *Native Hawaiian Rights Handbook*, 149–52. See also Carol Wilcox, *Sugar Water: Hawaii's Plantation Ditches* (Honolulu: University of Hawai'i Press, 1996), chap. 2.

11. Wilcox, *Sugar Water*, 1.

12. Adler, *Claus Spreckels*, chaps. 3 and 4. The lease given Spreckels even stipulated that if Alexander and Baldwin did not complete the construction of their ditch within two years, their water rights would revert to the king, who could then reissue them to Spreckels.

13. Wilcox, *Sugar Water*, chap. 2, 121.

14. MacKenzie, *Native Hawaiian Rights Handbook*, 152.

15. Ibid.; and Adler, *Claus Spreckels*, 48.

16. Arthur Dean, *Alexander and Baldwin*, 16–19. For a recent retelling see *Maui News*, 14 February 2000.

17. Ibid.; and Speakman, *Mowee*, 122–23.

18. Wilcox, *Sugar Water*, chaps. 3, 8. See also *Maui News*, 30 July 1995 and 7 November 1996.

19. David Craddick, interviews by author, Wailuku, 2 July 1998, and 13 July 1999; Kyselka and Lanterman, *Maui*, 80–82; and Wilcox, *Sugar Water*, 121.

20. Wilcox, *Sugar Water*, chaps. 1, 3, 8.

21. Ramil, *Kalai'aina*, 116, 126–27.

22. Ibid., 181, 231; and "Charter, County of Maui, 1993."

23. "Economic Study of Maui," vol. 1, 18–19; and "Master Plan for Maui," 40.

24. Tobin and Higuchi, "Environmental Quality in America's Tropical Paradise," 115.

25. Maui County Council meetings, 7 July 1972, 7 September 1973, 7 November 1975, 16 January 1976, and 5 August 1977.

26. On the Kula rule, see Craddick, interview, 13 July 1999; *Maui News*, 7 September 1977 and 3 September 1999; and "Rule Regulating for an Interim Period the Issuance of Water Meters and the Approval of Subdivision Applications from the Upper Kula Waterline and the Lower Kula Waterline, 1977," with later amendments, at the Board of Water Supply headquarters in Wailuku.

27. Maui County Council meetings, 1 June and 20 November 1970, 21 September and 5 October 1973, and 6, 19 August and 3 September 1976.

28. Ibid., 11 July 1973 and 7 November 1975.

29. Ibid., 16 September 1977.

30. Ibid., 7 September 1979 and 21 January 1983.

31. Pisani, *To Reclaim a Divided West*, 167.
32. MacKenzie, *Native Hawaiian Rights Handbook*, 158–65, offers an especially valuable analysis of the *McBryde* decision. See also Linda Parker, *Native American Estate*, 171–72.
33. Wilcox, *Sugar Water*, 36–38.
34. Ibid.; and Maui County Council meeting, 6 November 1979.
35. Ibid.; and *Maui News*, 10 September 1989.
36. The 1987 water law also set up a Review Commission on the State Water Code to take a close look at the working of the law five years after its passage. After holding fifty-two meetings and numerous public hearings, the commission made recommendations in late 1994. Two reached the farthest. The commission urged that the state government take over the management of all water supplies throughout the islands, not just those designated as being overused. The commission also urged that Native Hawaiian water rights be given greater consideration. The recommendations remained under consideration in 2000. See Review Commission on the State Water Code, "Final Report to the Hawai'i State Legislature, December 28, 1994."
37. Craddick, interviews; and Maui County Council, Planning, Land Use, and Economic Development Committee, minutes of meeting, 21 October 1985.
38. "Central Maui Source Development Agreement, July 28, 1975," in the Maui Board of Water Supply office. The shares of the companies in the development expense and in the resulting water were to be: Wailea Development, 7/19; Seibu, 4/19; Hawaiiana, 4/19; C. Brewer, 4/19; and Alexander and Baldwin, 4/19.
39. Ibid. See also Craddick, interviews; Craddick, personal communication; and Cravalho, interview. This was an efficient system. Since the wellheads were located at an altitude of 500 feet, any location below about 400 feet in elevation could be served with water delivered by gravity feed.
40. Craddick, interview, 2 July 1998.
41. Board of Water Supply, "Report, 1996," 6; Maui County Council meetings, 21 January 1977 and 24 August 1981; and *Maui News*, 10 September 1989. The problem of depleting aquifers was common in the West. For a look at an aquifer underlying large parts of the southern Great Plains, see Donald Green, *Land of Underground Rain: Irrigation on the High Texas Plains, 1910–1970* (Austin: University of Texas Press, 1973); and John Opie, *Ogallala: Water for a Dry Land* (Lincoln: University of Nebraska Press, 1993).
42. *Maui News*, 28 July and 14 November 1997. At about the same time, a similar controversy arose on how best to use water from the aquifer underlying the island of Lāna'i, part of Maui County. The Lanai Company wanted to take 650,000 gallons per day from the aquifer to irrigate a golf course. Residents, joined together as Lanaians for Sensible Growth, successfully opposed that effort.
43. Ibid., 26 August and 12 September 1997. See also Board of Water Supply, "Report, 1996," 14.
44. *Maui News*, 3 September 1997.
45. Ibid., 29 July and 17 October 1997.
46. Ibid., 4 September 1997.
47. Ibid., 12 September 1997.

48. Ibid., 17 October 1997.
49. Ibid., 15 September and 17 October 1997; and Maui Tomorrow, 9 October 1997, <www.maui-tomorrow.org>.
50. Vencl, interview. See also Craddick, interview, 2 July 1998, and Eagar, interview.
51. *Maui News,* 23 October and 13 November 1997.
52. Craddick, personal communication; and *Maui News,* 29 November 1999 and 18 February 2000.
53. Sheehan, interview; and Sierra Club, Maui Group, "Newsletters," February–March and April 1998, <www.mauimapp.com/community/sierra.htm#kahului> (17 March 1998).
54. Maui County Council meetings, 25 August 1979, 9 June 1980, and 14 March 1983; Cravalho, interview; Maui County Department of Water Supply, "Annual Report, 1979–80," 6; *Maui News,* 30 June 1995, 7 November 1996, 17 September 1997, and 3 September 1999; and Mayer, interview, 6 July 1999.
55. Ibid.
56. MEDB, Maui's *Economic Future, 1981,* 134.
57. *Maui News,* 23 October 1996. See also Maui County Department of Water Supply, *A Decade of Accomplishments to Improve Your Water on Maui* (undated); and U.S. Department of Agriculture, "Draft Watershed Plan — Environmental Impact Statement, Upcountry Maui Watershed, December, 1995."
58. *Haleakala Times,* 18 February 1998; and *Maui News,* 11, 13 February 1998.
59. *Maui News,* 13, 23, 27 February 1998.
60. Ibid., 11, 13, 19 March 1998.
61. The *Maui News* carried stories about Upcountry water shortages almost daily throughout June and July 1999. For the responses of residents, see letters to the editor, *Maui News,* 27, 29 June and 9 July 1999.
62. The *Maui News* continued to cover the story of Upcountry water problems almost daily. See especially *Maui News,* 15, 16, 18, 20, 30 July, 17 August, 10, 24 September, 18, 20, 29 October, and 26 November 1999, and 25 February, 10, 16, 21 March, and 3 April, 2000. See also Department of Water Supply, "News," 7 December 1999, <www.ccmaui.com/~h2oeng/res9818.html> (7 December 1999).
63. Author's observations at a meeting of the Kula Community Association with David Craddick, 24 February 2000; and Kula Community Association, "Policy and Position Statements on Water," 3 February 2000.
64. Craddick, interview, 2 July 1998; Eagar, interview; and Sheehan, interview. See also *Maui News,* 3, 4 August 1998, 21, 30 July and 24 September, 1999, and 14, 28 January 2000.
65. *Maui News,* 24 March and 14 April 2000.
66. Ibid.
67. State of Hawaii, *Session Laws of Hawaii, 1990,* 435–37.
68. "East Maui Watershed Partnership: Management and Research," <ice.ucdavis.edu/~robyn/mauimgt.html> (3 November 1998); and the author's tours of the watershed with members of the Nature Conservancy in September 1997. See also *Maui News,* 30 July 1995, 7 November 1996; Sheehan, interview; and Trust for Public Land, "East Maui Resource Inventory," February 1998.
69. Robert Holt, "The Maui Forest Trouble: Reassessment of an Historic Forest Dieback" (master's thesis, University of Hawai'i, 1988), 30, 143.

70. *Maui News,* 24, 26 November 1999 and 13, 18 February 2000.
71. Ibid., 11, 12, 23 November 1998 and 18 March 1999.
72. *New York Times,* 14 June 1998. For a much less optimistic view, see Marc Reisner, *Cadillac Desert: The American West and Its Disappearing Water* (New York: Viking, 1986). In the late 1990s Reisner became an advocate of the privatization of water policies. See *Wall Street Journal,* 23 March 1999.

5. THE QUESTION OF ELECTRIC POWER

1. State of Hawaii, Department of Business, Economic Development, and Tourism, Energy Division, *Hawaii Energy Strategy, October 1995* (Honolulu: State of Hawaii, 1995), chap. 4, 1.
2. I am indebted to K. T. Cannon-Eger for sharing with me her ongoing research on the history of the Maui Electric Company. A commissioned history, her work will be published as *Sweetness and Light: An Authorized History of the Maui Electric Company* by Maui Electric. Cannon-Eger provided me with draft chapters for the years before World War II and with copies of her notes for the chapters that will be written for later years. I also thank the Maui Electric Company for permission to use information from Cannon-Eger's work in my writing. For sketches of Maui Electric's history, see Harry Eagar, "The Power of Maui for 75 Years," *Maui News,* 21 April 1996; and Sara Lenzer, *Maui Electric Company: 75 Years of Service* (undated).
3. Lenzer, *Maui Electric Company,* 1. Bagasse is the residue of sugar cane or sugar beets after the juice has been extracted. After drying, bagasse can be burned as a fuel.
4. Ibid.; Cannon-Eger, *Sweetness and Light,* 2–3, 14–16; *Maui News,* 21 April 1996; and Speakman, *Mowee,* 124–25.
5. Cannon-Eger, *Sweetness and Light,* 20–21, 24, 29, 39, 44, 46, 51, 53–54.
6. Ibid., 51, 54, 76, 82–84, 89, 102; and Lenzer, *Maui Electric Company,* 1.
7. A standard work on the development of electrical energy is Thomas Hughes, *Networks of Power: Electrification in Western Society, 1880–1930* (Baltimore: Johns Hopkins University Press, 1983). See also David Nye, *Consuming Power: A Social History of American Energies* (Cambridge, Mass.: MIT Press, 1998). For an excellent case study of the development of one electric utility in the late nineteenth and early twentieth centuries, see David B. Sicilia, "Selling Power: The Rise of Modern Marketing and Public Relations at Boston Edison" (doctoral dissertation, Brandeis University, 1991).
8. Cannon-Eger, *Sweetness and Light,* 101, 108, 117.
9. Ibid., 31, 40–41, 49, 56–57; Lenzer, *Maui Electric Company,* 2; and *Maui News,* 12 April 1996.
10. Cannon-Eger, *Sweetness and Light,* 61, 72, 79–80.
11. Ibid., 87–88, 106, 108–9, 115, 122, 129–31, 135–36, 141, 146; Lenzer, *Maui Electric Company,* 2–3; and *Maui News,* 21 April 1996.
12. Cannon-Eger, notes on the 1940s, 11, 13, 20–22, notes on the 1950s, 5, 10, and notes on the 1960s, 4, 17; and Lenzer, *Maui Electric Company,* 4–5.
13. Cannon-Eger, notes on the 1940s, 1, 7, 9, 20, notes on the 1950s, 16, and notes on the 1960s, 9, 13–14; Maui Electric Company, *Annual Report,* 1967; and *Maui News,* 21 April 1996.
14. Cannon-Eger, notes on the 1980s, 2–4. Hit with similar complaints, some mainland

utilities burned low-sulfur fuels during the day and cheaper, high-sulfur fuels at night when no one could see the smoke.

15. Hawaiian Electric Company, *Annual Reports,* 1970–1985.

16. Ibid., 1976, 17, 22; and Maui County Council Meetings, 4 January 1974, 18 February 1977, 3 August 1979, and 5 June 1981. See also C. Dudley Pratt Jr., "The Need for a Reliable Supply of Energy," in MEDB, *Proceedings of the Kapalua Symposium of December 9–11, 1981,* 121–28 (Pratt was president of Hawaiian Electric and chairman of the board of MECO); and Arden C. Henderson, "Energy and Water Resources," in MEDB, *Maui's Economic Future, October 1983,* 37–41 (Henderson was president of MECO). See also Mayor's Energy Advisory Committee, County of Maui, "Report," 15 December 1980; and *Maui News,* 15 July 1975 and 23 January 1981. For an introduction to the story of national energy conservation efforts, see Samuel P. Hays, "From Conservation to Environment: Environmental Politics in the United States Since World War II," in Miller and Rothman, *Out of the Woods,* 101–26. For a valuable analysis of how California responded to the energy crises of the 1970s, see Pincetl, *Transforming California,* 196–98.

17. Cannon-Eger, notes on the 1970s, 6, notes on the 1980s, 5–6, and notes on the 1990s, 7–9; and Maui County Council meetings, 5 April 1974 and 21 August 1978.

18. *Maui News,* 10 May 1976; and Mayer, interview.

19. Cannon-Eger, notes on the 1970s, 1–3, 6–7, 10, 18, and notes on the 1980s, 5–6, 9–10, 16; Hawaiian Electric, *Annual Report,* 1980, 4; and Lenzer, *Maui Electric Company,* 5. Maui always remained the center of MECO's activities, but the utility also reached out to the other islands composing Maui County. Hawaiian Electric had long considered buying Molokai Electric, and in 1989 MECO purchased the firm. MECO bought power generation facilities on Lāna'i from Castle and Cooke in 1988. See Cannon-Eger, notes on the 1940s, 2, notes on the 1970s, 8, and notes on the 1980s, 17–18, 20, 23.

20. Hays, *Beauty, Health, and Permanence,* 227–45; Richard Vietor, *Energy Policy in America since 1945* (Cambridge: Cambridge University Press, 1984), part 3; and Richard Vietor, *Contrived Competition: Regulation and Deregulation in America* (Cambridge, Mass.: Harvard University Press, 1994), chap. 3.

21. Hawaiian Electric, *Annual Report,* 1976, 19. See also William Bonnet, interview by author, Kahului, 2 July 1999; and Maui County Council meeting, 25 February 1980.

22. The electric utilities were not alone in their concerns. Beginning in 1989 HPOWER, a City and County of Honolulu project, operated a trash-burning power plant on O'ahu, which generated enough energy to power 50,000 homes and reduced the volume of solid waste going to the island's landfills by 90 percent. Cities in other regions also experimented with trash-burning power plants. Columbus, Ohio, operated one for a decade, before closing it as uneconomical. See Tobin and Higuchi, "Environmental Quality in America's Tropical Paradise," in Smith and Pratt, *Politics and Public Policy,* 21.

23. Maui County Council meetings, 18 January 1974 and 2 November 1984; and Hawaiian Electric, *Annual Reports,* 1976, 19, 1979, 17, 1980, 14–16, 1981, 12, and 1985, 14–15. For an examination of the ups and downs in using windpower to generate electricity in America, see Robert Righter, *Wind Energy in America: A History* (Norman: Uni-

versity of Oklahoma Press, 1996). On a recent revival in some parts of the United States, see James Chiles, "A Second Wind," *Smithsonian* 30 (March 2000): 50–58.

24. Maui County Council meeting, 18 January 1974; and *Maui Sun*, 4 September 1974.

25. For the national clean air story during the 1970s, see Hays, *Beauty, Health and Permanence*, 73–76, 121–23, 159–62; and Richard Vietor, "The Evolution of Public Environmental Policy: The Case of 'No Significant Deterioration,'" in Miller and Rothman, *Out of the Woods*, 127–43.

26. Cannon-Eger, notes on the 1980s, 2–4, 8, 10; Hawaiian Electric, *Annual Report*, 1978, 3; *Maui News*, 17 February 1982; and Pratt, "Need for a Reliable Supply," 122.

27. Cannon-Eger, notes on the 1990s, 6.

28. David Frankel to Wilfred Nagamine, 4 April 1998 at <www.hookele.com/mt/forum/messages/232.html> (10 April 1998); and Sierra Club, "Maui Electric Violates Clean Air Laws, April 2, 1998," <www.hookele.com/mt/forum/messages/229.html> (16 April 1998).

29. On geothermal possibilities on Maui, see State of Hawaii, Department of Planning and Economic Development, *Geothermal Power Development in Hawaii, June 1982*, vol. 1 (Honolulu: State of Hawaii, 1982), 16, 19–20, 43; and Hawaiian Electric Company, *Annual Reports*, 1982, 15, 1985, 8–9. In 1982 state government investigators also suggested that La Perouse Bay might be a suitable location for a spa whose waters could be heated by geothermal sources.

30. Department of Geography, University of Hawai'i, *Atlas of Hawaii* (Honolulu: University of Hawai'i Press, 1983), 34–44. I presented a paper on the history of geothermal energy in Hawai'i as "Tourism, the Environment, and Public Policy Making: The Case of Maui in the 1980s and 1990s," at the Policy History Conference, Clayton, Missouri, 27–30 May 1999.

31. State of Hawaii, *Geothermal Power Development*, vol. 1, 1–5; Hawaiian Electric Company, *Annual Reports*, 1976, 19, 1978, 15, 1979, 17–18, 1980, 16, 1981, 13–14, 1982, 15, and 1985, 8–9; Hawaiian Electric Company, "Hawaii Deep Water Cable Program" (report prepared for the U.S. Department of Energy, 1990) 1–3; and State of Hawaii, Department of Business and Economic Development, *Environmental Review: 500 MW Geothermal Development, March 1989* (Honolulu: State of Hawaii, 1989), chap. 1, 1–3.

32. Bonnet, interview, 2 July 1999; and State of Hawaii, *Environmental Review*, chap. 1, 1.

33. Bonnet, interview, 25 June 1998; Joan Conrow, "Geothermal: Pele's Last Stand," *Honolulu* 24 (June 1990): 50–86; and State of Hawaii, *Environmental Review*, chap. 1, 7.

34. Hawaiian Electric Company, "Hawaii Deep Water Cable Progam," 1. See also State of Hawaii, *Geothermal Power Development*, vol. 1, 63; and Hawaiian Electric Company, *Annual Report*, 1985, 10.

35. Conrow, "Geothermal," 59, 78; and Parker, *Native American Estate*. See also State of Hawaii, *Environmental Review*, chap. 1, 16–17.

36. Conrow, "Geothermal," 56–57.

37. State of Hawaii, *Environmental Review*, chap. 1, 21. For additional details on Native Hawaiian opposition, see Minerbi, "Native Hawaiian Struggles," 2–3, 8.

38. Conrow, "Geothermal," 82.

39. William Bonnet, interview, 25 June 1998. The story was a bit more complicated. Federal funding had supported putting in the 3-megawatt generator and was involved in the Deep Water Cable program. The State of Hawai'i had also applied for federal

funds to do exploratory drilling on the Big Island. However, the Sierra Club brought suit in the federal court system alleging that these three projects were really not separate projects, but simply different phases in the construction of the 500-megawatt power generating system. The Sierra Club argued that no further work should be allowed until an acceptable federal environmental impact statement had been prepared. When the court ruled in favor of the Sierra Club, interest in the project on the part of Hawaiian Electric waned. As Bonnet later explained, "The interest of the utility and the consortia with which it was negotiating became non-existent under this business risk environment." Bonnet, personal communication, 22 February 1999.

40. *Hawaii Energy Strategy*, chap. 1, 1.
41. Richard Rocheleau and Heidi Wild, "Energy Sources," in Roth, *The Price of Paradise*, 264–71.
42. *Hawaii Energy Strategy*, chap. 1, 1.
43. Ibid., chap. 2, 3–4.
44. Ibid., chap. 1, 7, and chap. 2, 5. See also Bonnet, interviews. The integrated resource planning (IRP) advisory board's recommendations were not binding on MECO; however, documentation of the board's meetings and MECO's responses to its suggestions were forwarded to the state's Pubic Utilities Commission (PUC), along with the IRP, and thus could influence the PUC's decisions with regard to MECO.
45. For a discussion of IRP and energy issues throughout the United States in the 1990s see U.S. Congress Office of Technology Assessment, *Energy Efficiency: Challenges and Opportunities for Electric Utilities* (Washington, D.C.: U.S. Government Printing Office, 1993), especially chap. 2.
46. Mā'alaea Community Association, "Press Release," 1995; and *Maui News*, 27 March 1998.
47. Bonnet, communication to MECO customers, 4 February 1998; and *Maui News*, 27 February 1998. The nineteen production units either online or planned for the Mā'alaea plant produced most of MECO's power. By early 1997 only about thirty-eight megawatts were generated by the Kahului plant. See MECO, "Environmental Assessment: Proposed Waena Power Generating Station, February 1997," especially 13. MECO remained a wholly owned subsidiary of Hawaiian Electric. In 1997 Hawaiian Electric provided 95 percent of the electricity consumed by the state of Hawai'i's 1.2 million residents. See Hawaiian Electric's home page on the Internet, <www.heco.com>.
48. Bonnet, interview, 2 July 1999; State of Hawaii, Department of Business, Economic Development, and Tourism, "Hawaii Renewable Energy Data Report — 1995," table 16, <www.hawaii.gov/dbedt/ert/hirenw> (12 March 1998); and Zond Pacific, "Draft, Kaheawa Pastures 20 MW Windfarm, Maui, Hawaii, Environmental Impact Statement, May 26, 1999."
49. Bonnet, interview, 25 June 1998; and MECO, "Environmental Assessment," 13.
50. Ibid.; and Bonnet, personal communication.
51. Bonnet, interviews; and Bonnet's résumé.
52. Ibid.
53. Ibid.
54. Bonnet, interview, 25 June 1998; David DeLeon, interview by author, Wailuku, 17 July 1998; Mayer, interview, 30 June 1998; and Sheehan, interview.

55. Ibid.; and *Pacific Business News,* 10 November 1997.

56. MECO, "Environmental Assessment," 10–14.

57. *Pacific Business News,* 10 November 1997. MECO considered building a pipeline to transport the oil but rejected that option as more expensive than truck transportation.

58. De Naie, interview; and MECO, *Final Environmental Impact Statement: Waena Generating Station, November 1997,* appendix.

59. Ibid., chap. 3, 41.

60. Sierra Club, Hawaiian Chapter, Maui Group, "Newsletter," February-March 1998, <www.mauimapp.com> (17 March 1998).

61. "MECO Generating Station LUC Hearing," <www.maui-tomorrow.org>.

62. Richard Heede to State Land Use Commission, 24 February 1998, <www.maui-tomorrow.org>. See also Rocky Mountain Institute, *Newletter,* Spring 1996 and Summer 1996, <www.maui-tomorrow.org>.

63. *Maui News,* 27 February 1998.

64. Ibid., 9, 24 April 1998.

65. Ibid., 27 February and 24 April 1998; and Bonnet, interview, 25 June 1998.

66. Ibid.

67. *Maui News,* 27 February and 27 April 1998; and postings by Celeste King and Dick Mayer, <www.maui-tomorrow.org>.

68. *Maui News,* 27 February 1998; and "Reply to MECO's Plans," 28 February 1998, <www.maui-tomorrow.org>.

69. *Maui News,* 27 February and 24 March 1998.

70. State Land Use Commission, "Docket No. A97-722, Petitioner, Maui Electric Company," 22 June 1998.

71. Casey Jarmen, "Statement on Docket No. A97-722," 18 June 1998, <www.maui-tomorrow.org>.

72. "Maui Tomorrow Challenges MECO's Powerplant Proposal," March 1998, <www.maui-tomorrow.org>.

73. Sierra Club, Maui Group, "MECO Testimony for Planning Commission," 10 March 1998, <www.hookele.com/mt/forum/messages/212.html> (17 March 1998).

74. *Maui News,* 24 March 1998; and *Consumer Lines,* April 1998.

75. Sierra Club, "MECO Testimony."

76. Michael Potts to Maui County Planning Commission, 5 March 1998, <www.hookele.com>.

77. Ibid.; Bonnet interview, 25 June 1998; and Sierra Club, "MECO Testimony."

78. *Maui News,* 13 March 1998.

79. Ibid., 4, 11 September 1998; and MECO, *MECO General Information, 1998,* 5. See also *Maui News,* 13 July 1998; and *Consumer Lines,* July 1998.

80. Maui Tomorrow and Maui Group of the Sierra Club, "Press Release," 28 September 1998, <www.maui-tomorrow.org>.

81. *Maui News,* 12, 18 November 1998. The law was the Public Utility Regulatory Policies Act of 1978. See OTA, *Energy Efficiency,* 41–42.

82. *Maui News,* 16 December 1998 and 20 January 1999.

83. Bonnet, interview, 2 July 1999; *Maui News,* 1 September and 2 November 1999; and Maui Tomorrow, "MECO's Waena Power Plant — Council hearing TODAY 8/16,"

and postings on the work of the Alternative Energy Committee, by Sean Lester, a committee member, 30 September and 31 October 1999, <www.maui-tomorrow.org>.

84. *Maui News,* 30 November 1999 and 3, 24 January 2000; and Maui Tomorrow posting, 3 January 1999, <www.maui-tomorrow.org>.

85. *Honolulu Star-Bulletin,* 11 January 2000; *Maui News,* 25 January 2000; and Maui Tomorrow posting, 19 January 2000, <www.maui-tomorrow.org>.

86. *Maui News,* 21 March 2000; and 9 and 14 July 2000.

87. Investigations into creating an interconnected electrical grid for the Hawaiian Islands were conducted at various times. The last major such examination, conducted in the early 1990s, estimated that it would cost at least $100 million to do so. As Bonnet observed in 1999, "Conceptually the idea of interlocking the islands is a wonderful idea," but the cost was simply too great. Bonnet, interview, 2 July 1999.

6. THE CONTROVERSY OVER THE KAHULUI AIRPORT

1. Oscar Winther, *The Transportation Frontier: Trans-Mississippi West, 1865–1890* (New York: Holt, Rinehart and Winston, 1964), remains the best introduction to the history of western transportation. I presented preliminary findings on the Kahului Airport controversy as a paper at the forty-fourth annual meeting of the Business History Conference, held at College Park, Maryland, 13–15 March 1998. That paper was published as "Business, Government, and the Environment: Maui in the 1980s and 1990s," in *Business and Economic History* 27 (fall 1998): 207–212.

2. Bartholomew, *Maui Remembers,* 79–80. For more detail on the history of the Kahului Railroad, see *Maui News,* 30 August and 6 September 1998.

3. Douglas Karsner, "Aviation and Airports: The Impact on the Economic and Geographic Structure of American Cities, 1940s-1980s," *Journal of Urban History* 23 (May 1997): 406–36, offers a valuable analysis.

4. *Maui News,* 16 April 1930.

5. Ibid., 12, 19 October 1929, 12 May 1937, and 25 February and 15 April 1939; and Ramil, *Kalai'aina,* 26, 47.

6. Ibid.

7. Bartholomew, *Maui Remembers,* 84, 113, 141, 165.

8. *Maui News,* 24 May and 11, 25 June 1947; and Ramil, *Kalai'aina,* 45, 145.

9. Gail Ainsworth, telephone interview by author, 15 April 1998.

10. Donald D. Johnson, *The City and County of Honolulu: A Government Chronicle* (Honolulu: University of Hawai'i Press, 1991), 369–70.

11. Maui County Council meetings, 11 November 1969 and 21 June 1974. In 1977 council members could agree that enlargements were needed for the airport's terminal buildings, which, they thought, had become an "eyesore"; they petitioned the state government to make alterations. See Maui County Council meetings, 4 February and 18 March 1977. On Cravalho's stance, see *Hawaii Business and Industry* 14 (August 1968): 20, 41.

12. Maui County Council meetings, 5 September 1969, 1 June and 27 July 1979, 20 February and 4 September 1981, and 4 February, 4 March, 4 April, and 5 November 1983; DeLeon, interview; and *Maui News,* 11 December 1981.

13. *General Plan for the County of Maui,* 1979, 1–4.

14. U.S. Department of Transportation, Federal Aviation Administration (FAA), and Hawaii Department of Transportation (HDOT), Airports Division, *Draft Environmental Impact Statement: Kahului Airport Improvements, Kahului, Maui, Hawaii, March, 1996*, vol. 1, chap. 3, 38.
15. Bill Wood, "Airport Expansion," in Roth, *The Price of Paradise*, 227–33.
16. *Maui News*, 23, 25, 28 August 1992.
17. Ibid.; and *Maui Inc.* (July 1992): 40.
18. *Maui News*, 25 August 1992.
19. Ibid., 8 October 1992; and MEDB, *Summary/Conclusions Concerning the Kahului Airport Runway* (July 1992), 8.
20. *Maui News*, 23, 25, 28 August and 8 October 1992.
21. Sierra Club, Hawai'i Chapter, "Alien Plant Control Policy" (9 March 1986), <www.hi.sierraclub.org/info/policy/alienplant.html> (17 March 1998).
22. Maui County Council meetings, 20 May and 20 June 1983; and *Maui News*, 25 August 1992.
23. Ibid. On the real and symbolic value of SPAM, see Paul Theroux, *The Happy Isles of Oceania: Paddling the Pacific* (New York: Ballantine Books, 1993). It will be recalled that those trying to preserve Makena Beach chose State Park at Makena as the name of their group, with the acronym SPAM. In the late 1990s the Maui County Fair held an annual cooking contest for the best dishes made of SPAM. See *Maui News*, 15 October 1999.
24. HDOT, *Kahului Airport Master Plan, June 1993* (Honolulu: State of Hawaii, 1993).
25. Ibid., chap. 2, 38.
26. Ibid., chap. 3.
27. HDOT, Airports Division, *Annual Report*, 1993, 1–2, <www.state.hi.us/dot/93air.htm> (11 March 1998).
28. HDOT, *Airport Master Plan, 1993*, chap. 6.
29. Ibid., chap. 8.
30. FAA and HDOT, *Draft EIS, 1996*, vol. 1, 5–10, 23, 38; and DeLeon, interview. Slightly revised assumptions underlay work on the new environmental impact statement. The continuing recession and slump in tourism led the federal and state agencies to accept a new estimate of just under 8 million people — 2 million on nonstop overseas flights (including 511,000 international passengers) and 5.4 million on interisland flights — as the number most likely to pass through the Kahului Airport by 2010. In light of this lower estimate, officials delayed recommended dates for airport changes: the lengthening of runway 2-20 by 2002 (rather than 1996) and the construction of the second parallel runway by 2016 (instead of 2010). Still, the basic premise remained unchanged. "Tourism," the investigators agreed, would continue as "the primary industry on Maui."
31. FAA and HDOT, *Draft EIS, 1996*, vol. 2.
32. Ibid.
33. Ibid.
34. Ibid.
35. Ibid; and *Haleakala Times*, 6 December–19 December, 1995.
36. FAA and HDOT, *Draft EIS, 1996*, vol. 2.
37. Ibid.
38. Ibid.

39. Ibid.; and *Maui News*, 22 January, 13 February, and 9 March 1998.
40. FAA and HDOT, *Draft EIS, 1996*, vol. 2.
41. Ibid.; Mayer, interview, 30 June 1998; *Maui News*, 16 April 1999; and Pyle, interview.
42. FAA and HDOT, *Draft EIS, 1996*, vol. 2.
43. Ibid., vol. 1, chap. 3, 81–101.
44. Ibid., 98–101.
45. McKeown, "Brown Tree Snakes," 71.
46. *Maui News*, 19 April 1996 and 13 October 1997. See also the statement of Dana Naone Hall in "FAA May Imperil Hawaiian Species," 30 July 1996, <www.npca.org/np96-07/ja9609ne.html> (11 March 1998); and *Pacific Business News*, June 2, 1997. For more detail on the testimony, see FAA and HDOT, *Final Environmental Impact Statement, Kahului Airport Improvements* (September 1997).
47. *Maui News*, 11, 14 September 1997.
48. Ibid., 15 October 1997; and *Honolulu Star-Bulletin*, 1 December 1997.
49. *Maui News*, 31 August and 31 September 1998; and Vencl, interview.
50. "Airport Maui," television presentation on Maui's Akaku Community Channel, 13 June 1999; author's observations on State Land Use Commission, hearings, 24, 25 June and 9 July 1999; *Haleakala Times*, 7–20 July 1999; and *Maui News*, 15 January, 19, 24, 26 February, 19 March, 2, 23, 26 April, 7, 10 May, 4, 25, 27 June, 5, 8, 16 July, 6, 27, 30 August, 3, 24 September, 22, 29 October and 4 November 1999.
51. Raisbeck, interview.
52. *Maui News*, 21 June 1999.
53. Lee, interview. See also Apana, interview. Gauging public opinion on airport matters was difficult. No comprehensive poll was ever taken on airport expansion, and no public referendum was ever held on the matter.
54. *Maui News*, 31 January, 13 February, and 24 March, 2000.

7. TWO COMMUNITIES

1. Bartholomew, *Maui Remembers*, 141–42; Cooper and Daws, *Land and Power in Hawaii*, 280; and *Maui News*, 4 July 1999.
2. Maui County Council meeting, 16 July 1976; Courtney Farrell, "The Honorable Mayor of Kihei," *Spirit of Aloha* (November/December 1980): 20–22; and *Maui News*, 22 March 1988.
3. Farrell, "The Honorable Mayor," 20.
4. Maui County Council meetings, 18 July and 19 December, 1969. "Questionnaire Results," in "Kihei Civic Development Plan," 1971 (appendix).
5. "Kihei Civic Development Plan," 1971. It was called a 701 plan, because the financing for its development came from Section 701 of the Housing Act passed by Congress in 1954.
6. Ibid.
7. Ibid.
8. Maui County Council meeting, 2 December 1975.
9. For examples of the ease with which developers obtained variances, see Maui County Council meetings, 16 February and 10 December 1979.
10. Cooper and Daws, *Land and Power*, chap. 9. See also Speakman, *Mowee*, 188–89; Maui County Council meetings, 19 September and 23 October 1980, 1 May 1981, and 6 April 1984. See also King, interview.

11. For Alexander and Baldwin's initial plans for Wailea, see Alexander and Baldwin, *Annual Report, 1968: Land Development.* On the progress of developments at Wailea, see Maui County Council meetings, 15 October 1971, 19 July 1974, and 15 February 1980. Alexander and Baldwin, *Ampersand* 19, special anniversary edition (30 June 1985): 44–46; *Maui Today* (June 1981): 5; and Mary Lou Whitman, interview by author, Wailea, 22 July 1998, provide overviews of what Wailea had become by the mid-1980s. For a retrospective look at Wailea's development, see *Maui News,* 2 February 1997.

12. Ibid.

13. Maui County Council meetings, 24 August 1970 and 20 March and 2 June 1972.

14. Ibid., 4 August 1972 and 19 April 1973. See also Farrell, *Hawaii,* 75–76; *Honolulu Star-Bulletin,* 26 March 1973; and *Maui News,* 25 January 1973.

15. Maui County Council meetings, 17 May and 19 October 1979, 7, 21 March, and 16 May 1980, and 2 April 1981.

16. Farrell, *Hawaii,* 158; Mayer, interview, 30 June 1998; and Sheehan, interview.

17. "Kihei-Makena Community Plan, 1981," 5.

18. Ibid., 9–14.

19. *Maui News,* 7 December 1981.

20. "Proposed Revisions to the Kihei-Makena Community Plan, 1984," Ordinance no. 1490, Maui County Council Bill 95, 1984.

21. Maui County Council meetings, 2 October and 21 December 1984.

22. "Kihei-Makena Community Plan, 1985." See also MEDB, *Partners in Planning, 1988,* 55.

23. DeLeon, interview; and *Honolulu Star-Bulletin,* 14 March 1996.

24. *South Maui Times,* 6 December 1989.

25. *Honolulu Star-Bulletin,* 20 March 1996.

26. Maui Tomorrow, "Kihei-Wailea-Makena Community Plan Update," 14 July 1997, <www.maui-tomorrow.org/southmaui-plan.html> (11 March 1998).

27. "Kihei-Makena Community Plan, 1998," 16–17.

28. *Maui News,* 17 September and 13 November, 1997.

29. Ibid., 14 January, 23, 25 March, 19 July, and 8 August 1998.

30. Ibid., 8 July 1997 and 27 July 1998.

31. Ibid., 17 September 1997 and 20 April 1998.

32. Author's observations at a Maui County Council meeting, 13 July 1999; *Kihei Times,* 9–22 June, 1999; and *Maui News,* 3, 25 June, 14, 18 July, 6 August, and 8, 15, 18, 22, 31 December, 1999, and 16, 17, 18, 22 February and 18 May 2000.

33. *Maui News,* 13 June and 14 July 1997; *South Maui News,* 13 July 1997; *South Maui Times,* 19 August 1992 and 12 June 1997; *South Maui Weekly,* 24–30 June 1999; and "What Is the Focus of the South Maui Heritage Corridor?" <www.mrtc.org/~makai/focus.htm> (11 March 1998).

34. *Maui News,* 21 October 1996, 12, 14, November and 16, 18 December, 1997, 2 June 1999, and 20 February 2000. David Craddick, director of Maui's Department of Water Supply, warned those who wanted to further develop Mākena that water might not be available in the future. See Craddick to Milton Arakawa, 9 April 1998, letter attached to Munekiyo, Arakawa and Hiraga Inc., "Draft Environmental Assessment: Makena Resort Roadway and Utility Infrastructure Improvements," June 1998.

35. *Maui News,* 14 May and 18, 21 June, 1998.

36. Maui County Council meetings, 28 February 1969, 1 May 1970, 3 September 1976, and 17 November 1978; *Draft Supplement II Environmental Impact Statement for Ma'alaea Harbor for Light Draft Vessels, Maui, Hawaii, May 1998* (Honolulu: U.S. Army Engineer District, 1998), chap. 1, 1; and Mayer, interview, 6 July 1999.

37. *Draft Supplement II EIS for Maalaea,* chap. 1, 2.

38. Ibid., for pages of testimony for and against the harbor improvements. See also *Maui News,* 21 June 1998.

39. De Naie, interview.

40. *Maui News,* 22 May and 24 June 1998; and *Haleakala Times,* 15 July–4 August 1998.

41. *Maui News,* 5, 25 September 1997; *Draft Supplement II EIS for Maalaea,* chap. 5, 77; and Sierra Club, Maui Group, "Malama Maalaea," <www.mauimapp.com/community/sierraecoissues.html> (24 March 1998).

42. *Maui News,* 6, 23 March and 4, 18 June 1998. See also Lee, interview; and Eagar, interview.

43. *Maui News,* 27 March, 10 April, 14 August, and 8 September, 1998, and 6 May 1999.

44. Bartholomew, *Maui Remembers,* 115–16, 120–23; Kirch, *Feathered Gods,* 31; "Maui's Uncommon Upcountry," *Spirit of Aloha* (January 1993): 45–48; and Speakman, *Mowee,* 140–43.

45. Maui County Council meetings, 19 March 1970, 16 February 1973, 18 January 1974, 21 October 1975, and 18 March 1977; and Ramil, *Kalai'aina,* 143.

46. Maui County Council meeting, 1 August 1974.

47. Ibid.

48. Ibid.

49. "Proposed Makawao-Pukalani-Kula General Plan, 1976," reprinted in Maui County Council meeting minutes, 10 March 1976; and "Makawao-Pukalani-Kula Community Plan, 1981." Like the 1971 South Maui plan, this was a 710 plan. See also Maui County Council meeting, 6 July 1973.

50. Maui County Council meetings, 5 September 1975 and 10 March and 6 August 1976; and *Maui News,* 17 September 1976.

51. "Makawao-Pukalani-Kula Community Plan, 1996," 10.

52. Maui County Council meetings, 3 February, 19 May, and 17 June 1978.

53. Ibid., 6 April and 7 May 1984.

54. "Makawao-Pukalani-Kula Community Plan, 1996," 11, 15; and Mayer, interview, 30 June 1998.

55. "Makawao-Pukalani-Kula Community Plan, 1996," 18–19.

56. *Haleakala Times,* 7–20 February 1996; and *Maui News,* 30 January 1998.

57. *Haleakala Times,* 3–16 August 1994; and *Maui News,* 8 August 1993.

58. *Haleakala Times,* 7–20 February 1996.

59. *Maui News,* 30 January 1998; and Mayer, interview, 30 June 1998.

60. *Maui News,* 11 July and 5 September 1997; and *Pacific Business News,* 5 September 1997.

61. *Maui News,* 11 July, 1997; and Dowling, interview.

62. *Maui News,* 5 September 1997; and Mayer, interview, 30 June 1998.

63. *Maui News,* 7 October 1997.

64. Ibid., 4 November 1997.

65. Ibid., 2, 10 December 1997.

66. Ibid.; and Candace Barnhart, "Pastoral No More?" 10 December 1997 posting, <www.

hookele.com/mt/forum/messages/161.html> (23 December 1997). See *Maui News*, 13 August and 19 September 1999.

67. *Maui News*, 20 August 1999, reviewed pending developments in Kula, observing that "with the addition of some sizeable housing projects, commercial development, and possibly a new highway, this Upcountry community faces the potential for significant change in the coming years."

68. Kula Community Association, minutes of general meeting, 20 November 1997, and minutes of board meetings, 4 December 1997 and 5 March 1998, <www.kulamaui.com/board> (10 June 1998); *Maui News*, 15 May and 7 August, 1992, 5 May 1998, and 11 August, 17, 27 September, and 1, 14 October 1999; and HDOT, "Kihei-Upcountry Maui Highway Environmental Assessment, May 1995."

CONCLUSION

1. Hanlon, *Remaking Micronesia*, chap. 4; and Picard and Wood, *Tourism, Ethnicity, and the State*. A good place to start on tourism in the Caribbean is Herbert Hiller, "The Organization and Marketing of Tourism for Development: An Argument for the Necessity of Intervention in the Marketplace," in Brislin, *Culture and Learning*, 245–55. On tourism in the Florida Keys, see Frank Deford, "The Florida Keys: Paradise with Attitude," *National Geographic* (December 1999): 32–53.

2. Jamaica Kincaid, *A Small Place* (New York: Plume Books, 1988), 14, 17.

3. Trask, *From a Native Daughter*, 50, 89.

4. Whitehead, "Noncontiguous Wests," 335.

5. Farrell, *Hawaii*, chap. 11; Kent, *Hawaii*, chap. 10; Mayer, interview, 30 June 1998; and Bruce Plasch, "Tourism and Jobs," in Roth, *The Price of Paradise*, 109–14. See also *Maui News*, <www.mauinews.com>; and *Maui News*, 10, 23 October 1997. According to one credible estimate, 90 percent of the jobs on Maui were service-sector jobs by the summer of 1999; see *Maui Talks*, 8.

6. Ibid.; *Maui News*, 20 February 2000; and Luciano Minerbi, "Sustainability Versus Growth in Hawai'i," *Social Process in Hawaii* 35 (1994): 144–60. On housing prices, see *Maui Business* (May/June 1999): 14.

7. Examinations of Hawai'i's recent economic problems may be found in the *Honolulu Advertiser*, 1 February 1998; *Honolulu Star-Bulletin*, 22 July 1997 (which has a particularly valuable special section devoted to "Hawaii's Economic Crisis"), *New York Times*, 28 September 1997; and *USA Today*, 7 November 1997. For bankruptcy figures, see *Maui News*, 2 July, 2 October, and 20 November 1998. Employment figures for Maui are from "Labor Force, Annual Average, Followed by Monthly Series, Maui County," <www.state.hi.us/workforce/1fmc9097.text> (11 March 1998); and *Maui News*, 5 March 1999. Developments in Maui's economy may be followed in the *Maui News*, 14 November and 5, 12, December 1997, 9, 20 January, 30 April, 8, 19 May, 3, 24 June, 3, 20 July, and 13 August 1998, and 1 January, 11, 18, 24 June, 19 July, 27 August, and 10 September 1999. For interviews with political and business leaders about Maui's economic future, see *Maui Talks*, and *South Maui Weekly*, 1–7 July 1999.

8. "Recommendations of the Hawaii Economic Revitalization Task Force," reprinted verbatim in *Honolulu Star Bulletin*, 22 October 1997.

9. *Maui News*, 11 December 1997, 20–21 January, 6 February, 13 May, 12 July, and 16 October 1998, and 22 January, 12 February, 5 March, and 31 December 1999. See also

Maui Business 3 (March/April 1998): 20. For a negative assessment, see Lyons, interview. On the compromises involved in the legislation, see Raisbeck, interview. A major increase in Hawai'i's general excise tax was considered but not enacted.

10. Apana, interview; and Neil Luna, interview by author, Wailuku, 29 June 1999.

11. *Maui News*, 3, 8, 12 November 1999. See also Roz Baker (director of the Office of Economic Development), press release, 8 November 1999, <www.co.maui.hi.us/press/pressrb110899.txt> (7 December 1999).

12. *Maui News*, 31 March 2000.

13. Ibid., 1 January, 1, 18 February, 26 March, 25 June, 1, 9 November, and 15 December 1999, and 25 February and 14 March 2000.

14. David McClain, "Hawaii's Competitiveness," in Roth, *The Price of Paradise*, 7–13; Eagar, interview; and *Maui News*, 15 October and 10, 15, 24 December 1999, and 7 January, 20, 27 February, and 8 March 2000. By the winter and spring of 2000, hotel occupancy rates were high, and land sales were up, as new California money entered Maui.

15. Davis, "Landscapes of the Imagination," 190; and Rothman, *Devil's Bargains*, 10.

16. Since the 1950s Native Americans have won victories, often through legal actions, on a wide range of topics, including land ownership, water rights, and fishing rights. Good places to start in understanding the situations of Native Americans in the United States since World War II are Joane Nagel, *American Indian Ethnic Renewal: Red Power and the Resurgence of Identity and Culture* (New York: Oxford University Press, 1996); and Donald Parman, *Indians and the American West in the Twentieth Century* (Bloomington: Indiana University Press, 1994). On water rights, see Lloyd Burton, *American Indian Water Rights and the Limits of Law* (Lawrence: University Press of Kansas, 1991).

17. *Maui News*, 12 March and 22 October 1999.

18. Alfred W. Crosby, *Ecological Imperialism: The Biological Expansion of Europe, 900–1900* (Cambridge: Cambridge University Press, 1986), chap. 4. See also Alfred W. Crosby, *The Columbian Exchange: Biological and Cultural Consequences of 1492* (Westport, Conn.: Greenwood Press, 1972); and Jared Diamond, *Guns, Germs, and Steel: The Fates of Human Societies* (New York: W. W. Norton, 1998). On changes in the Pacific Basin, see Alfred W. Crosby, "Biotic Change and Nineteenth-Century New Zealand," and Thomas Dunlap, "Australian Nature, European Culture: Anglo Settlers in Australia," both in Miller and Rothman, *Out of the Woods: Essays in Environmental History;* and Barry Lopez, *About this Life* (New York: Alfred Knopf, 1998), chap. 3 (on the Galapagos Islands).

19. See *Columbus Dispatch*, 27 September 1998 and 2 August and 26 September 1999; Hays, *Beauty, Health, and Permanence*, 258; and David McCumber, *The Cowboy Way* (New York: Avon Books, 1999), 241–42.

20. Jeffrey Broadbent, *Environmental Politics in Japan: Networks of Power and Protest* (Cambridge: Cambridge University Press, 1998), 10.

21. Vogel, *National Styles of Regulation*.

22. Hays, *Beauty, Health, and Permanence;* and Vogel, "The 'New' Social Regulation." See also Vietor, "The Evolution of Public Environmental Policy," and Robert Gottlieb, "Reconstructing Environmentalism: Complex Movements, Diverse Roots," both in Miller and Rothman, *Out of the Woods*.

23. Hays, *Beauty, Health, and Permanence*, 13.
24. Martin V. Melosi, "Equity, Eco-racism, and Environmental History," in Miller and Rothman, *Out of the Woods*, 194–211, is a solid introduction to this topic.
25. See Apana, interview; author's observations at hearings before the State Land Use Commission, 25 June and 8 July 1999; Lucienne de Naie and Richard La Fond Jr. (both of the Sierra Club) to Mercer Vicens, vice president of A and B Properties, 25 June 1999; *Haleakala Times*, 21 July–3 August 1999; and *Maui News*, 19 March, 27 June, 15 October, 4, 16 November, and 3 December 1999, and 16 February and 7 April 2000.

Relatively few secondary works have been written about Maui's history, but I have found several to be of considerable value. Mona Nakayama and Marie Strazar, eds., with Dawn E. Duensing as the researcher, *Maui in History: A Guide to Resources* (Honolulu: State Foundation on Culture and the Arts, 1998), is an annotated guide to many secondary and some primary sources, useful especially for the years before statehood. Gail Bartholomew, *Maui Remembers: A Local History* (Honolulu: Mutual Publishing, 1994), captures Maui's past in a series of short essays, well illustrated with photographs. Cummins E. Speakman Jr., *Mowee: An Informal History of the Hawaiian Island* (Salem: Peabody Museum of Salem, 1978), is especially valuable for its descriptions of developments during the 1950s and 1960s, as viewed by a participant. Bryan Farrell, *Hawaii: The Legend that Sells* (Honolulu: University of Hawai'i Press, 1982), looks at the history of tourism in the Hawaiian Islands and contains important information on Maui's early resort developments. Antonio V. Ramil, *Kalai'aina: County of Maui* (Wailuku: Anvil-Maui Press, 1984), provides a look at political developments on Maui through the 1970s. Elspeth P. Sterling, *Sites of Maui* (Honolulu: Bishop Museum Press, 1998), is an archaeological survey of Maui.

I have consulted many primary sources. Among those most valuable have been the minutes of the meetings of the Maui County Council, located in the county clerk's office in Wailuku. These minutes usually include the verbatim discussions among the council members on issues, and they often reprint verbatim public hearings on issues. Community and countywide plans were also valuable sources for me. These may be found in the various public libraries and, sometimes, in the county clerk's office. I have also consulted reports in the various county offices, such as those in the water department. Environmental impact statements have been extremely valuable sources, for they reprint correspondence and testimony at public hearings verbatim, often running to hundreds of pages. The *Maui News* has been a useful source of information, for the newspaper covers developmental and environmental matters extensively. Recent issues may be examined at <www.mauinews.com>. I have also consulted other (weekly) newspapers published on Maui. Finally, I have had the pleasure of conducting oral history interviews with numerous people; their names are listed in my acknowledgments in the front matter of this work.

Of course, Maui's history has been part of the history of the Hawaiian Islands. Gavan Daws, *Shoal of Time: A History of the Hawaiian Islands* (Honolulu: University of Hawai'i Press, 1968), and Lawrence Fuchs, *Hawaii Pono: A Social History* (New York: Harcourt Brace Jovanovich, 1961), are standard accounts; both books conclude with Hawai'i's attainment of statehood in 1959. Noel Kent, *Hawaii: Islands under the Influence*, 2d ed. (Honolulu: University of Hawai'i Press, 1993), and Elizabeth Buck, *Paradise Remade: The Politics of Culture and History in Hawaii* (Philadelphia: Temple University Press, 1993), offer more recent interpretations. Theon Wright, *The Disenchanted Isles: The Story of the Second Revolution in Hawaii* (New York: Dial Press, 1972), describes the Democratic political revolution. Ronald Takaki, *Pau Hana: Plantation Life and Labor in Hawaii, 1835–1920* (Honolulu: University of Hawai'i Press, 1983), and Edward Bechert, *Working in Hawaii: A Labor History* (Honolulu: University of Hawai'i Press, 1985), are useful on labor matters. Essays by John Whitehead place Hawaiian history in the context of western American history. See especially his "Noncontiguous Wests: Alaska and Hawai'i," in *Many Wests: Place, Culture, and Regional Identity,* ed. David Wrobel and Michael Steiner (Lawrence: University Press of Kansas, 1997), 315–41, and his "Western Progressives, Old South Planters, or Colonial Oppressors: The Enigma of Hawai'i's 'Big Five,' 1898–1940," *Western Historical Quarterly* 30 (autumn 1999): 295–326.

On Hawai'i today, see the essays in Randall W. Roth, ed., *The Price of Paradise: Lucky We Live Hawaii?* two volumes (Honolulu: Mutual Publishing, 1992 and 1993). Also valuable are the many essays comprising *Social Process in Hawaii* 35 (1994), and Zachary Smith and Richard Pratt, eds., *Politics and Public Policy in Hawai'i* (Albany: State University of New York Press, 1992).

Hawai'i's economic development may be followed in works about the Big Five companies and their competitors: Jacob Adler, *Claus Spreckels: The Sugar King in Hawaii* (Honolulu: Mutual Publishing, 1966); Arthur Dean, *Alexander and Baldwin, Ltd. and the Predecessor Partnerships* (Honolulu: Alexander and Baldwin, 1950); Edwin Hoyt, *Davies: The Inside Story of a British American Family in the Pacific and Its Business Enterprises* (Honolulu: Topgallant Publishing, 1983); Frederick Simpich Jr., *Dynasty in the Pacific* (New York: McGraw-Hill, 1974); Scott Stone, *The Story of C. Brewer and Company, Ltd.*

(Aiea, Hawai'i: Island Heritage Publishing, 1991); Frank Taylor, *From Land and Sea: The Story of Castle and Cooke* (San Francisco: Chronicle Books, 1976); and William Worden, *Cargoes: Matson's First Century in the Pacific* (Honolulu: University of Hawai'i Press, 1981). George Cooper and Gavan Daws, *Land and Power in Hawaii* (Honolulu: Benchmark Books, 1985), and Thomas Hitch, *Islands in Transition* (Honolulu: First Hawaiian Bank, 1992), offer valuable insights into recent economic developments.

INDEX